Projects for Woodworkers
Volume I

Projects for Woodworkers
Volume I

The Editors of *The Woodworker's Journal*

Madrigal Publishing Company

We at Madrigal Publishing have tried to make this book as accurate and correct as possible. Plans, illustrations, photographs, and text have been carefully researched by our in-house staff. However, due to the variability of all local conditions, construction materials, personal skills, etc., Madrigal Publishing assumes no responsibility for any injuries suffered or damages or other losses incurred that result from material presented herein. All instructions and plans should be carefully studied and clearly understood before beginning any construction.

For the sake of clarity, it is sometimes necessary for a photo or illustration to show a power tool without the blade guard in place. However, in actual operation, always use blade guards (or other safety devices) on power tools that are equipped with them.

Printed in the United States of America.

Fourth Printing: March 1992

Library of Congress Cataloging-in-Publication Data:

Projects for Woodworkers.

    Includes index.
    1. Woodworking.   I. Woodworker's journal.
TT185.P76   1987   684'.08   87-15414
ISBN 0-9617098-1-2 (pbk.)

Madrigal Publishing Company
517 Litchfield Road
P.O. Box 1629
New Milford, CT 06776

Contents

(continued on next page)

Acknowledgment

The editors wish to thank the following individuals whose contributions and cooperation helped make this book possible:

Sam Allen, Moab, Utah for the Musical Jewelry Box, Message Cube, and Weather Station; Henry Diamond, Sherman, Connecticut for the Rocker Footrest; Thomas A. Gardner, Aurora, Colorado for the 19th Century Cherry Table, Miniature Empire Chest, and Sewing Cabinet with Tambour Doors; Harvey E. Helm, Fairfield, Connecticut for the Laminated Bookrack; Richard W. Koch, Pelham, New Hampshire for the Doll House Bed; Paul Levine, Sherman, Connecticut for the 18th Century Trestle Table, Cutting Boards, Contemporary Cabinet, Spoon Rack, Oak Writing Desk, and the Multipurpose Cabinet; Robert A. McCoy, Asheville, North Carolina for the Vanity and the 18th Century Tavern Table; Larry Miller, Belton, Missouri for the Quilt Rack; Ted J. Pagels, Wausau, Wisconsin for the Longhorn Steer; Victor F. Ptasznik, Grosse Pt. Farms, Michigan for the Bagel Slicer; Alan C. Sandler, Garnerville, New York for the Calculator Stand; Roger E. Schroeder, Amityville, New York for the Cabinetmaker's Workbench, 17th Century Mantle Clock, Black Forest Clock, Anchor Thermometer, Tile Clock, and the Wine Glass Holder; Raymond Schuessler, Venice, Florida for the Fireplace Bellows; Donald F. Stearns, Toledo, Ohio for the Bud Vase and Toy Truck; Richard Wonderlich, Mt. Pleasant, Iowa for the Old-Time Icebox.

Also our thanks to Cherry Tree Toys, Belmont, Ohio for the Toy Hippo and the Seal Push Toy; Joe Gluse, Prospect, Connecticut who did the technical art for the Hand Mirror, Cutting Boards, Tic-Tac-Toe, Vanity, Half-Round Table, 18th Century Sleigh Seat, Sewing Cabinet with Tambour Doors, Old-Time Icebox, and Weather Station; John Kane of Silver Sun Studios, New Milford, Connecticut for many of the project photographs.

Introduction

What is your woodworking pleasure? Do you seek a few hours of relaxation and confine your efforts to woodworking projects such as simple toys or small household items? Or are you motivated only by the challenge of intricate joinery and the advanced techniques needed to build major pieces of furniture?

Whatever your woodworking inclinations may be, the intent of this book is to help you satisfy your creative needs. It doesn't matter whether you are a novice with a limited collection of hand tools or a seasoned woodworker with a shop full of machinery. There should be more than enough interesting projects within these pages to keep you busy for some time.

If you prefer to design your own projects, there are plenty of ideas here that can be used as a starting point, a basis on which to exercise your creativity.

In our correspondence with hundreds of woodworkers, we've found that most like to add their own personal touches to published plans. All approaches are valid and good so long as you work safely, enjoy what you are doing and are pleased with the finished product.

This collection of project plans has been selected from past issues of *The Woodworker's Journal,* covering the period from September 1980 to December 1981. Although these back issues are now out-of-print, the plans themselves remain relatively timeless and are appropriate for today.

A few words of advice: approach each project, whether it be simple or complex, with the determination to build something of which you will be proud. *Don't hurry* . . . measure and cut with care. *Always* use safety devices such as protective goggles and blade guards when operating fast-moving machinery. Please note that, for the sake of clarity, it is sometimes necessary for us to show a machine in use with its guards removed.

When the joinery is done, sanding and the application of finish can either enhance or ruin your project, so allow plenty of time for this final step. Above all . . . enjoy yourself.

The Editors

Cabinetmaker's Workbench

by Roger E. Schroeder

This fine European-style workbench is made of maple throughout and is capable of holding a board 80 inches long between bench dogs. Well designed with plenty of drawer space, it can be made for under $400, a big savings when compared to similar imported benches.

Before the workbench is begun, I strongly advise buying the hardware. I know of at least one woodworker who found out too late that the plans he worked from didn't allow for a proper fit of available bench dogs. These, as well as a bench screw for the end vise, can be purchased from Woodcraft Supply Corp., 41 Atlantic Ave., Woburn, MA 01888. The Ulmia bench dogs are stock numbered 16A71 and the German bench screw is numbered 01H41. These can be ordered by phone at 1-800-225-1153 with a credit card. The front vise is a Sears model, catalog number 5195C.

The base should be made first. Cut parts A, B, and C to size. The top corners of the feet, parts B, can be rounded with a router, and a sanding drum on a drill press or radial arm saw will take out some of the underneath of parts B to allow the bench to rest on four points. The 2-inch long tenons of the legs were made with a dado blade attached to a radial arm saw. The mortises in the feet and cleats (C) should be carefully marked out with a pencil and done with

very sharp chisels. A router can also do the job. Parts A, B, and C can now be glued and clamped. For extra strength I used ¼-inch dowels to pin the tenons inside the mortises. This assures that there will be no separation over the years.

The stretchers (D) are now cut to size. Inch-long tenons are put on their ends as shown in the detail, and mortises are made in the legs. A very tight fit is not necessary since the legs and stretchers are held together with ½-inch by 5 inch carriage bolts. A 1½-inch diameter by 1⅜-inch deep hole on the inside of the stretchers will have to be made (see Fig. 1). This is where the nut is inserted. Since most spade bits have long points, I drilled part way into the stretcher with the bit and continued the hole with a ¼-inch router bit. Now assemble the legs and stretchers and start the hole for the bolt with a ½-inch drill bit. Remove the stretcher, clamp a doweling jig to the top of tenon where the hole was started and continue drilling until the 1½-inch hole is reached.

Before reassembling the base, the plywood shelf should be made since its dimensions will not allow it to be put into place after the stretchers are bolted to the legs. A ¾-inch box-end wrench will tighten the hex nuts.

The top can now be started. It comprises 9 pieces of 8/4 maple cut at least 2½ inches wide to allow for planing to a finish thickness of 2⅜", and glued face to face with splines of ¼-inch by 1-inch wide plywood.

I would inquire at local lumber yards or woodworking shops for the availability of a thickness planer. I found a lumber yard that had one and was charged two dollars for the milling of the glued-up top. This easily saved a day's labor. If this is done, the bench top pieces should be cut to 2¾ inches and the bench dog holes that hold the heads of the dogs will have to be made deeper.

Before gluing up, certain operations will have to be done on the front and rear pieces of the top. On the rear piece, cut a dado ⅜ by ⅜ inches to accept the tool trough bottom (Fig. 5). This can be done on a table saw. On the front piece, the channels for the bench dog can be made using a dado blade. The enlarged tops of the channels can be started with a dovetail or backsaw and finished with chisels.

To avoid having to cut out a rectangular piece for the end vise, I cut pieces 1, 2 and 3 to size and ripped a section out of piece 4 (Fig. 4). I made sure, when joining pieces 2, 3 and 4 that the plywood splines did not show at the tail vise end by using blind splines. The dadoes for the splines can be made on a table saw. Since pieces 1 and 2 cannot be joined with a spline, I used five ⅜-inch dowel pins spaced to avoid the bench dog holes.

The top, after being squared off, can be positioned on the base. I used pairs of ¾-inch dowels on the tops of the cleats and then 5-inch by ½-inch lag bolts for positioning and securing.

Referring to Fig. 7, cut part H to size with the appropriate notches and then part P. Align the two pieces where the hole will be drilled for the German bench screw. The holes should be slightly oversized so the screw threads will not bind. Clamp the two pieces together and use a spade bit to bore through them. Attach the bench screw nut to the inside of part H which can now be attached to the top with ½ x 4-inch lag bolts. Run the screw through part P and H and screw the collar to the outside of P.

Part S can be cut to size. This is a critical part that may need some trimming so that there is no binding on the underside of the top. Next comes the end screw top, part N (Fig. 4). The bench dog holes can be made later. Using countersunk 1¼-inch wood screws, part N can be joined to parts P and S. The tail vise side, part O (Fig. 1), also held with countersunk 1¼-inch wood screws, can be put on to give the vise rigidity.

Part V, the spacer block, shown in Figs. 6 and 8, will have to be made and secured to the underside of the bench with ⅜ x 3 inch lag bolts and washers.

The end vise guides, parts T and U, should be made and attached with ⅜ x 3 inch lag bolts. Slightly oversized holes for the lag bolts will help to align them should there be binding when the bench screw is turned. Binding may also occur where part N moves over part H and where part S contacts the bench.

N can now be removed and the bench dog holes set in with chisels. Once these are made, part W is made (Fig. 6). This gives the added thickness to part N to equal the thickness of the bench top. After N is reattached to parts P and H, part W is held underneath it and the outlines for the channels made. The channels can be done with a dado blade and chisels will set in the lip that holds the bench dog head. Part W can be attached to the underside of N with countersunk 2-inch wood screws and glue.

At this point remove the tail vise assembly, clamp and glue all pieces together, and cover all sountersunk screws with ½-inch wood plugs which are sanded flush.

Attach the other bench top end, part G, with ½-inch by 4 inch lag bolts. Part J (Fig. 6), the trough bottom, can be made and set into place in the dado made in piece 9. After this, part I is cut to size, also with a dado ⅜ inches deep and wide. This will be held to parts G and H with countersunk 1¼ wood screws which will be plugged with ½-inch wood

(continued on next page)

Leg and stretcher are clamped together and the bolt hole is drilled through the leg and just far enough into the stretcher tenon to locate center.

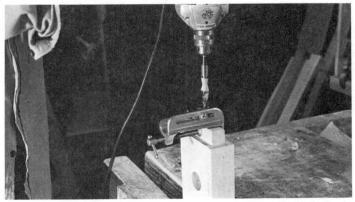

A doweling jig is used to continue drilling bolt hole in stretcher to intersect with the circular recess for the carriage bolt nut.

A dovetail saw is used to start the cut which will form the ledge of the bench dog hole. Waste is then removed with a chisel.

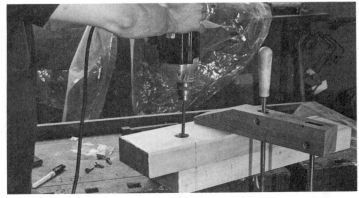

Parts P and H are clamped together and bored through for the tail vise screw.

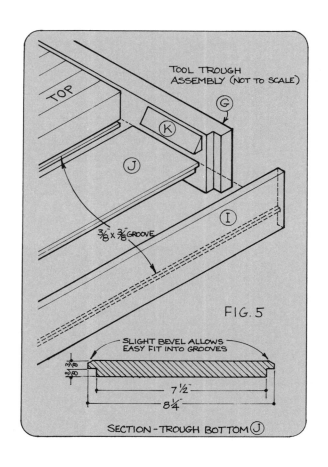

TOOL TROUGH
ASSEMBLY (NOT TO SCALE)

TOP

Ⓖ

Ⓚ

Ⓙ

Ⓘ

3/8 x 3/8 GROOVE

FIG. 5

SLIGHT BEVEL ALLOWS
EASY FIT INTO GROOVES

3/8
3/8

7 1/2"

8 1/4"

SECTION - TROUGH BOTTOM Ⓙ

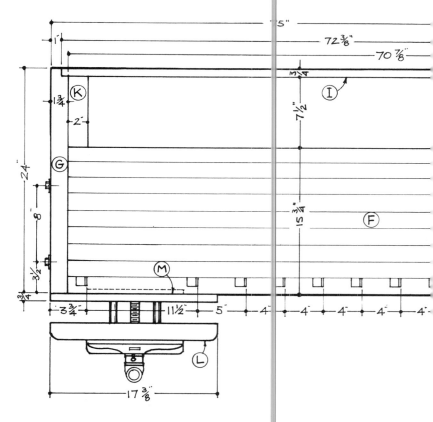

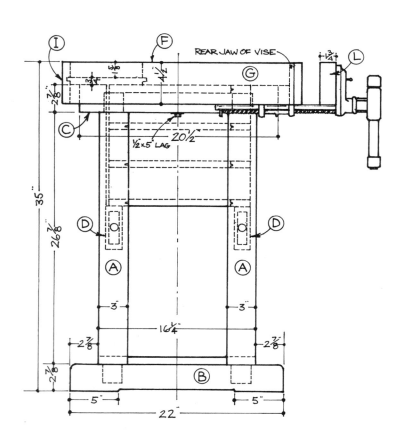

FIG. 2 LEFT END ELEVATION

REAR JAW OF VISE

Ⓘ   Ⓕ   Ⓖ   Ⓛ

1 3/4

4 1/2

Ⓒ

1/2 x 5 LAG

20 1/2

35"

26 7/8"

2 7/8"

Ⓓ   Ⓓ

Ⓐ   Ⓐ

3"   3"

16 1/4"

2 7/8"   2 7/8"

Ⓑ

5"   5"

22"

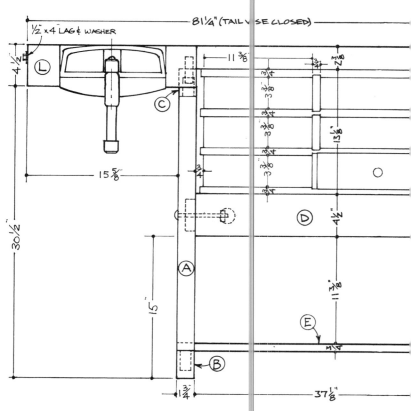

FIG. 1 FRONT ELEVATION

81 1/4" (TAIL VISE CLOSED)

1/2" x 4 LAG & WASHER

Ⓛ

4 1/2

Ⓒ

11 3/8

15 5/8

Ⓓ   4 1/2"

1 3/8"

Ⓐ

15"

11 3/8"

Ⓔ

1/4"

Ⓑ

1 3/4

37 1/8"

4

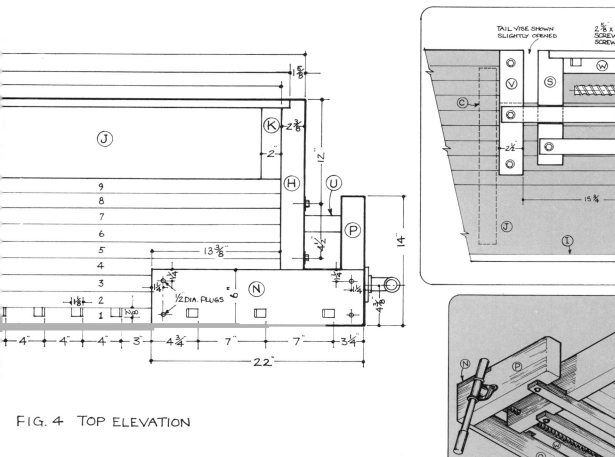

FIG. 4 TOP ELEVATION

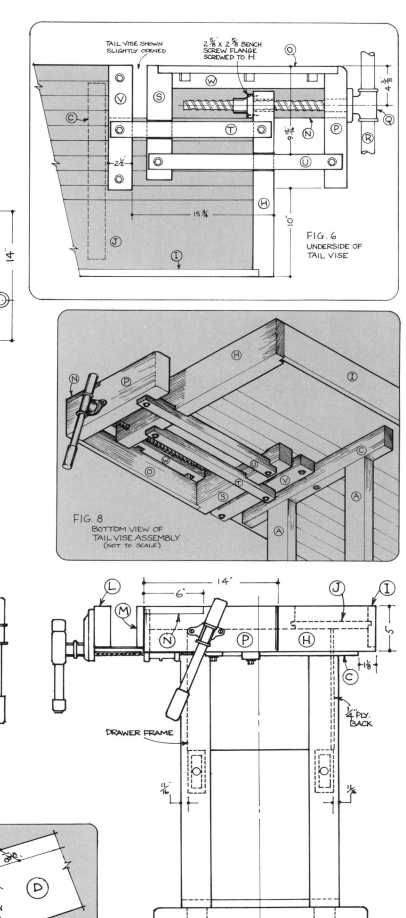

TAIL VISE SHOWN
SLIGHTLY OPENED

2⅝" x 2⅝" BENCH
SCREW FLANGE
SCREWED TO H

FIG. 6
UNDERSIDE OF
TAIL VISE

FIG. 8
BOTTOM VIEW OF
TAIL VISE ASSEMBLY
(NOT TO SCALE)

BENCH DOG
HOLE

¾" x 2½" DOWELS
HOLD TOP TO BASE

DRAWER
FRONTS
OVERLAP
FRAMES

¼" x #10 F.H. SCREWS
COUNTERBORED AND
PLUGGED

1½" DIA. X
1⅜" DEEP

½" x 5" CARRIAGE BOLT
W/WASHER & SQUARE NUT

½" DIA. PLUGS

DETAIL: UPPER AND
LOWER LEG TENON

DETAIL:
STRETCHER
TENONS

DRAWER FRAME

¼" PLY.
BACK

FIG. 3 RIGHT END ELEVATION

(continued on next page)

5

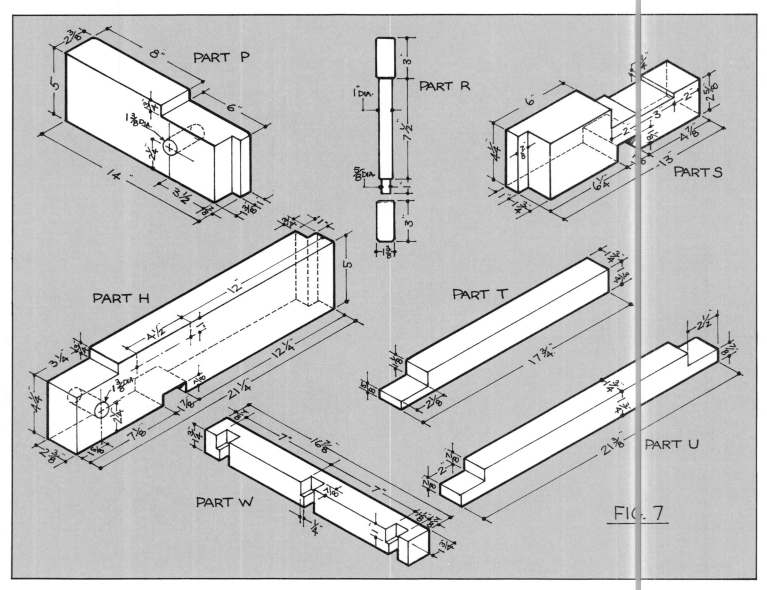

PART P

PART R

PART S

PART H

PART T

PART W

PART U

FIG. 7

dowels.

The front vise is mortised into the front of the bench top. This can be done with a router or chisels. Care should be used since the vise top is mortised only ⅜ inch from the bench top. Since use of the vise will tend to separate pieces 1 and 2 of the top over the years, I used 3-inch wood screws to hold the inside face of the Sears bench vise to the top edge. The inside face of the vise will be covered by a board, part M, and the outside face of the vise will have an 8/4 board, part L.

Next comes the chest of drawers. The frame and nine drawers can be made from common pine or scrap lumber and plywood. This chest is made of maple throughout with the exception of the drawer fronts, which are birch, and the chest sides, which are ¾-inch solid stock. The construction of the frame comprises two sides, front and rear rails, side and drawer divider rails, and drawer dividers. The front and rear rails have ¼-inch wide by ⅜-inch deep dadoes cut their entire lengths. All other rails have ¼-inch by ⅜-inch tenons.

Make the sides first from solid stock, making sure the grooves for the side rails are evenly spaced so that the drawers can be made of equal size. Cut all rails to size, taking care with the dadoes in the divider rails. The side and rails can be glued and clamped and the drawer dividers slipped in later.

The drawers for the chest are made to overlap the rails, though flush drawers can also be made to save time. I do find, however, that the overlapping drawers are less likely to stick in warm weather and especially if your bench will be in a basement. The sides and backs of the drawers are made

of ½-inch stock and the fronts are 1-inch stock while the drawer bottoms are ¼-inch plywood or masonite. This chest has a ¼-inch plywood back, though it's certainly an option.

Note that there are no screws, bolts or brackets that hold the chest to the bench. Yet a tight fit will assure the bench's rigidity over the years. One way to make a tight fit is to make the chest frame 1/16 inch longer than the stretchers. The bolts can then be loosened and retightened when the

A view of the front of the tail vise with side O & filler block W removed. Note bench screw flange secured to the inboard side of part H.

chest is set on the stretchers.

The final touches can now be done. The trough ends, parts K, are ripped at a 45 degree angle and cut to size. Blind nailing will hold them to the bench ends.

The bench screw handle comprises two pieces held together with a ⅝-inch mortise and tenon. This can be turned from a leftover scrap of 8/4 maple.

Don't forget to round off the outside edges of the tail vise and front vise with a ⅜-inch router bit.

At this point it's worthwhile to note that the top (F) is not glued to the base, thereby making it easier to disassemble and move. Part F simply fits on four dowels, two in each cleat (C), and is secured with one ½" x 5" lag screw at the center of each part C.

A belt sander and cabinet scraper will smooth the bench top. I would apply several coats of linseed oil. After this dries, apply several coats of tung oil and a coat of wax. A yearly coat of tung oil on the top of the bench will assure a smooth working surface.

Editor's Note: Several workbench parts are specified as ¾" thick. This is purchased as 1" nominal (4/4) stock that may actually measure between ¾" and 13/16" thickness. If the 1" nominal stock you purchase measures more than ¾", it will be necessary to revise all affected dimensions accordingly. The other alternative is to plane the stock down to ¾" thickness.

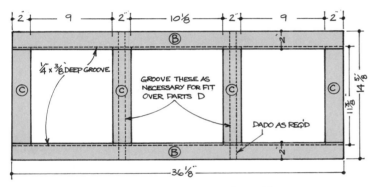

DRAWER FRAME LAYOUT - (4 REQ'D)

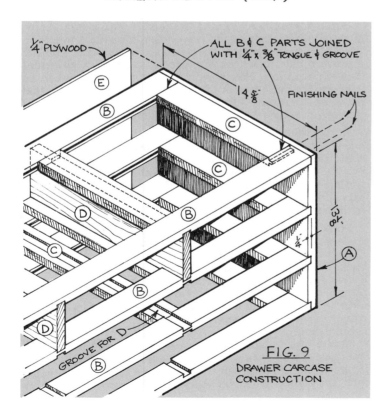

FIG. 9
DRAWER CARCASE
CONSTRUCTION

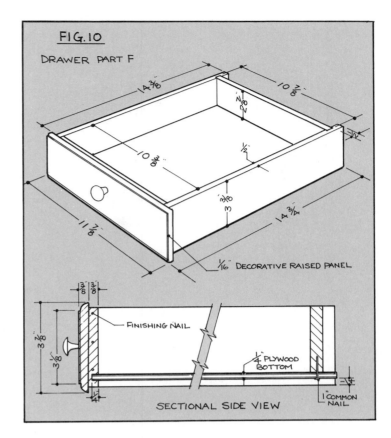

FIG. 10
DRAWER PART F

SECTIONAL SIDE VIEW

Bill of Materials (All Dims. Actual)			
Part	Description	Size	No. Req'd
A	Leg	1¾ x 3 x 30⅞ (Includes tenons)	4
B	Foot	1¾ x 2⅞ x 22	2
C	Cleat	1¾ x 2⅞ x 20½	2
D	Stretcher	1⅝ x 4½ x 39⅛ (Includes tenons)	2
E	Shelf	¾ x 16¼ x 40⅝	1
F	Top	2⅜ x 15¾ x 70⅞	1
G	Left End	1¾ x 4½ x 24	1
H	Right End	(See Detail)	1
I	Trough Back	¾ x 4½ x 72⅜	1
J	Trough Bottom	¾ x 8¼ x 70⅞	1
K	Trough Ends	1⅝ x 2 x 7½	2
L	Outside Vice Face	1¾ x 4½ x 17⅜	1
M	Inside Vice Face	¾ x 4½ x 17⅜	1
N	Tail Vise Top	¾ x 6 x 22	1
O	Tail Vise Side	⅞ x 4¼ x 20	1
P	Tail Vise Face	(See Detail)	1
Q	Bench Screw	Woodcraft 01H41-AW	1
R	Bench Screw Handle	(See Detail)	1
S	Tail Vise Back	(See Detail)	1
T	Tail Vise Support	(See Detail)	1
U	Tail Vise Bracket	(See Detail)	1
V	Tail Vise Cleat	1½ x 2½ x 14	1
W	Filler Block	(See Detail)	1
Drawer Carcase			
A	Side	¾ x 14⅝ x 13⅛	2
B	Front & Rear Rails	¾ x 2 x 36⅛	8
C	Side & Drawer Rails	¾ x 2 x 11⅜ (Includes tenons)	16
D	Drawer Dividers	¾ x 3⅞ x 14⅝	6
E	Carcase Back (Optional)	¼ x 37⅛ x 13⅛	1
F	Drawer	(See Detail)	9

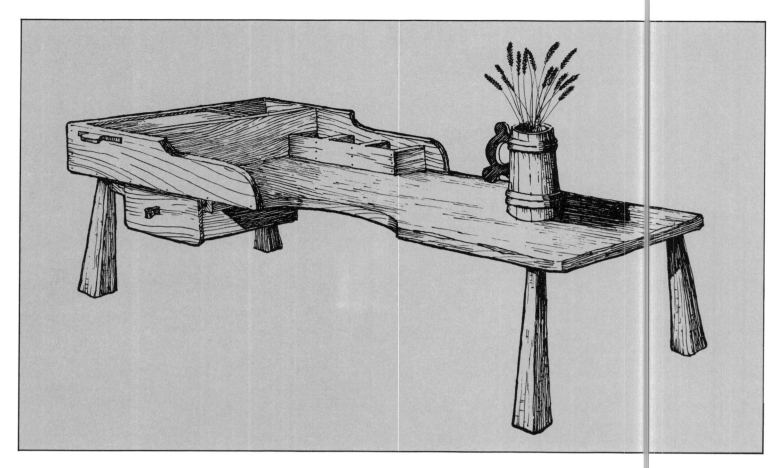

Cobbler's Bench Coffee Table

If Early American is your favorite furniture style, you may want to consider this for your next project. It's a fine example of an old time cobbler's bench, with overall dimensions that make it ideal for use as a modern day coffee table.

Start construction with the bottom piece. You probably won't find a board that's 18″ wide, therefore it will be necessary to edge-glue two or more narrow boards to get the needed width. Glue and clamp firmly, allowing to dry overnight, then trim to finish size of 5/4 (1⅛″ actual) x 18 x 42. Lay out the curve as shown on the grid pattern, then cut out with a jig saw.

The four legs are 15⅛″ long and square tapered. They measure 2″ at the base, narrowing down to 1¼″ at the top. The tenon is about 1 3/16″ long. To make the leg, cut a piece of 2″ square stock a bit longer than necessary. Use a lathe to turn the ¾″ dia. tenon. Allow extra length on the tenon for later trimming. If you don't have a lathe, the tenon can also be hand made with rasp. Trim to final length and bevel the leg bottom so it sits flat on the floor, then use a sharp plane to cut the tapers.

After cutting the two cleats to size (5/4 x 3 x 16) make the splayed leg drilling jig, following the three-step direction. A ¾″ bit is used to bore the vertical hole through the squared block. Align the jig so that the center of the drill bit will start 1½″ in from the edge of the cleat (see drawing). Also align the jig so that it's centerline is at 45 degrees to the cleat edges. When properly aligned, clamp in place and drill tenon holes with ¾″ bit. Repeat procedure for other three holes.

The two sides are made from ¾″ x 5″ x 16″ stock. Refer to the grid pattern to cut the curve. Also a ½″ x 3½″ slot is cut in one of the sides. The slot starts ½″ from the edge and ¼″ from the top.

The back and main divider can be made next. The back measures ¾ x 5 x 18, while the main divider measures ¾ x 3⅛ x 18. Note that each has a ¼″ x ½″ x 11¼″ long stopped dado located ¼″ down from the top edge. The slide itself is cut ½ x 3½ x 13½. Next, make the ½ x 3⅛ x 3 slide box divider and the 2″ high small dividers.

Before assembly, give all parts a thorough sanding, making sure to remove all planer marks. Clean up any saw marks on the curved cuts. Use a spokeshave or drawknife to give an "antiqued" edge to the four legs.

Begin assembly by joining the four legs to cleats. Apply glue to both leg tenons and cleat holes, then mate together. Rotate leg so that bottom bevel will sit flat on floor. Allow to dry overnight, then trim any excess tenon that protrudes through cleat top. Now the cleat and leg assembly can be joined to the bottom with 1¾″ x #10 wood screws. Note that the cleat is located 1″ from the back, front and side edge of the bottom piece.

Attach the two sides and the back to the bottom with glue and 2″ finishing nails set below the surface. Be sure the slotted side is in front. Next, add the main divider and slide box divider, again using glue and finishing nails. Check the sliding top for a good fit, and make adjustments as necessary. The small dividers can now be glued in place as shown in the drawing.

Make two drawer slides (see detail) and attach to the underside of the bottom with 1½″ x #8 wood screws. The drawer itself has a ¾″ x 4 x 8 front, with ½″ thick sides and back. The bottom is ¼″ plywood. The leather drawer pull is a nice detail, quite appropriate for the bench of a cobbler. Simply cut a narrow slot in the drawer front, then loop a 1″ strip of leather and insert through the opening. Use a couple of small tacks to secure it in place.

Final sand all surfaces, giving corners and edges a good rounding to simulate years of wear. Be sure to remove glue smudges. Apply a stain that reproduces the look of old pine (Minwax Early American is one). Allow to dry, then complete the project with two coats of polyurethane varnish.

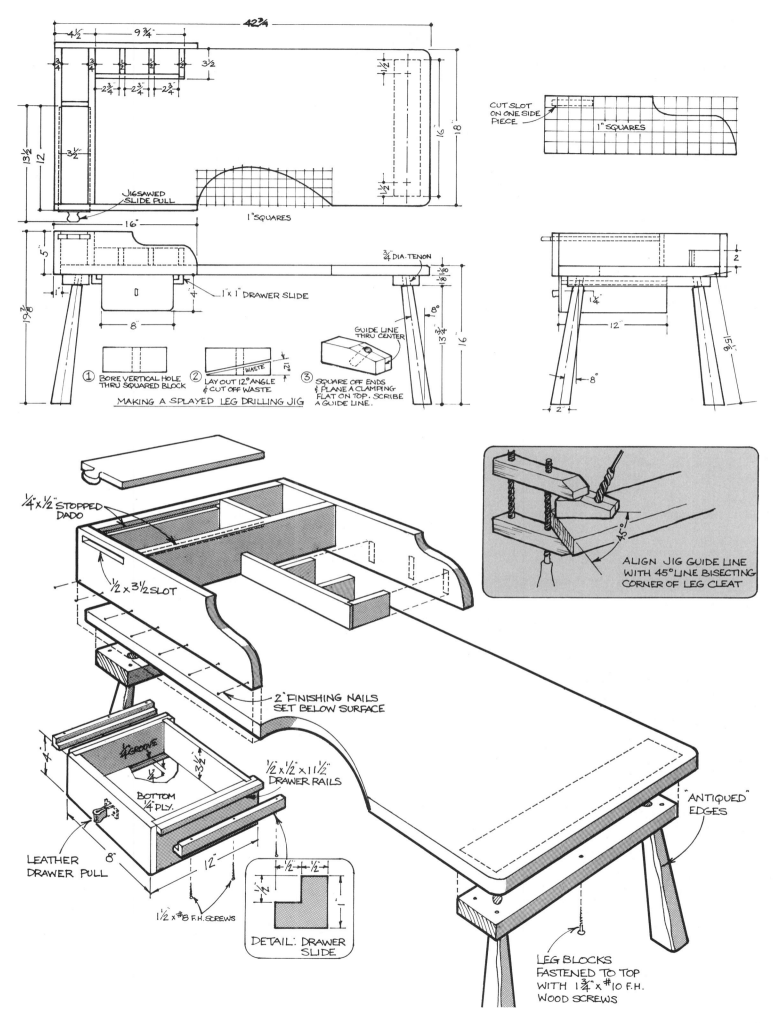

42¾

4½   9¾   3½

3½   13½   12

2¾   2¾   2¾

JIGSAWED SLIDE PULL

1" SQUARES

CUT SLOT ON ONE SIDE PIECE

1" SQUARES

16   18

1½   1½

16"

5"

19⅛

1"   8"

¾ DIA. TENON

8°   13¾   16

3⅛   4   1 x 1" DRAWER SLIDE

2   1½   12   15⅝   8°   2"

WASTE

12°

GUIDE LINE THRU CENTER

① BORE VERTICAL HOLE THRU SQUARED BLOCK

② LAY OUT 12° ANGLE & CUT OFF WASTE

③ SQUARE OFF ENDS & PLANE A CLAMPING FLAT ON TOP. SCRIBE A GUIDE LINE.

MAKING A SPLAYED LEG DRILLING JIG

¼" x ½" STOPPED DADO

½ x 3½ SLOT

ALIGN JIG GUIDE LINE WITH 45° LINE BISECTING CORNER OF LEG CLEAT

45°

2" FINISHING NAILS SET BELOW SURFACE

4   GROOVE   3½

BOTTOM ¼ PLY.

½ x ½" x 11½" DRAWER RAILS

"ANTIQUED" EDGES

LEATHER DRAWER PULL

8"   12"

½ x #8 F.H. SCREWS

½   ½   ½

DETAIL: DRAWER SLIDE

LEG BLOCKS FASTENED TO TOP WITH 1¾" x #10 F.H. WOOD SCREWS

19th Century Cherry Table

by Thomas A. Gardner

The photo shows a cherry table of about 1850 vintage. Nicely proportioned, with its elegant turned legs, this piece is of a style sometimes referred to as "Country" furniture.

While the table is entirely of cherry wood, other hardwoods may be substituted for reproduction. The second choice would be mahogany. As for structural details, dowel joints can be substituted for the apron and rail tenons and lap joints used instead of drawer dovetails.

The legs are turned from 2 inch stock to finish at 1⅞ inches square at the tops. Most turning dimensions are shown in the leg detail. When turning is completed, this writer prefers to apply a sealer before removing the turning from the lathe. This protects the surface from damage and prevents glue marks that are hard to remove.

Next, cut side and back aprons A and E to rough length, including tenons at each end. While ⅞ inch stock is called for, ¾ inch material may be substituted but other adjustments will have to be made.

All six double apron tenons can be cut with the same saw settings. Use a piece of scrap to check blade height for the ¼ inch depth of the shoulders. Make two long shoulder cuts on each apron. The tenon length is completed by drawing the apron away from the fence and making repeated passes over the blade, first on one side and then on the other until a full length tenon has been made. The upper shoulder is made using the same procedure. Waste between tenons is removed with backsaw and chisel. When completed, sand the aprons and apply a sealer.

Parts D1 and D2 are next cut and tenoned as shown. The two parts are alike and joined to front legs with shoulders facing down.

The next step is the fitting of the aprons and drawer rails to the legs. To prevent errors, mark each surface of the legs with corresponding marks on the aprons and rails. Use a mortise gauge to lay out mortises; remember that the aprons should be flush with the outside surface of the legs. This departs from the usual practice of having the aprons inset slightly. Mortises can be cut with a router, or by drilling holes the entire length of the mortise and finishing with a chisel.

Before making the top and drawer, the carcase should be completely finished and assembled. First, fit all parts together temporarily to check joints for fit and squareness. As a safety factor when gluing, use the following method. Glue back legs to their apron and front legs to the upper and lower rails, without clamping. Do not set aside to dry, but immediately fit the front legs and aprons to the back legs *without glue*. Clamp and check for squareness. If square, the unglued parts are separated and glue is applied. Clamp and again check for squareness. This procedure prevents any leg from twisting out of alignment under clamping pressure. Excess glue is easily removed from the previously sealed surfaces.

Cutting and fitting of drawer guides (B) and runners (C) is a simple job. Guides are glued and nailed to the aprons. The runners are then glued and nailed to the guides.

Construction of the drawer is next. The drawer front is of ⅞ inch stock while the sides and back are of ⅜ inch hardwood. One suggestion in fitting dovetails . . . slightly bevel the sides of the pins and they will slide into place easier.

Cut grooves on the sides and the back of the drawer front to hold the drawer bottom. This groove should be started ¼ inch up from the bottom edges and sizes for an easy fit of the ¼ inch plywood bottom.

Before assembling the drawer, cut the false beading on the front. This can be done with a mortising gauge or inlay router. Glue and assemble all parts, checking for squareness and flatness. The drawer bottom should slide easily into place. Secure it with a few nails up into the drawer back. The original drawer pull is of brass but a 1 inch dia. turned cherry pull would be fine.

Several pieces are jointed and edge glued to make up the top. After drying, cut to finish size and round the front and side edges. To allow the top to expand and contract with seasonal changes in humidity you'll need to cut a pair of ¼ in. wide by ½ in. long slots in the upper rail as shown. Also it will be necessary to make two pair of slotted glue blocks (see detail) and attach them to the side and back aprons. The top is joined to the base with 1½ in. x no. 8 round head wood screws and washers. There's not much room to drive the screws, so it will be helpful to use a box wrench and one of those removable screwdriver tips.

With the construction completed, thoroughly sand first with 100, then 180 or 150 and finally with 220 grit paper. Then rub down with steel wool. Most antiques were either shellaced or varnished. This piece calls for a varnish finish.

For many woodworkers, there is no better varnish than the polyurethanes. They are water and alcohol resistant and very durable. The first coat acts as a sealer and should be thoroughly sanded with 220 or 340 grit then steel wooled. Follow with one or two coats of satin varnish (two for the top). Lightly sand between coats with #600 wet or dry paper and 4/0 steel wool. Finish with a coat of hard wax.

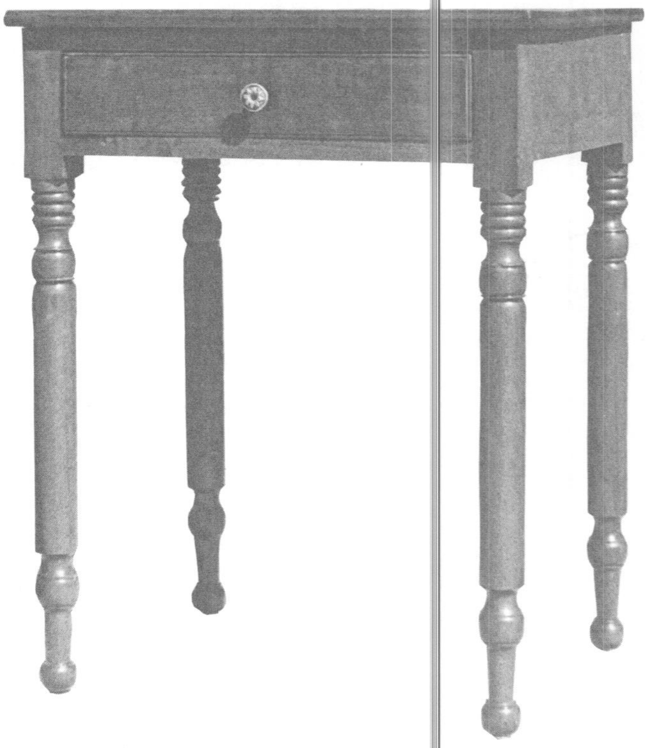

Bill of Materials (All Dimensions Actual)

Part	Description	Size	No.
A	Side Apron	⅞ x 5¼ x 15 (Incl. 1″ long tenons)	2
B	Drawer Guide	1 x 2 x 13	2
C	Runner	⅞ x 1 x 13⅞	2
D1,D2	Upper & Lower Rails	⅞ x 2 x 18¾ (Incl. 1″ long tenons)	2
E	Back Apron	⅞ x 5¼ x 18¾ (Incl. 1″ long tenons)	1
F	Leg	See Detail	4
G	Top	¾ x 17⅜ x 21¾	1
H	Drawer	See Detail	1

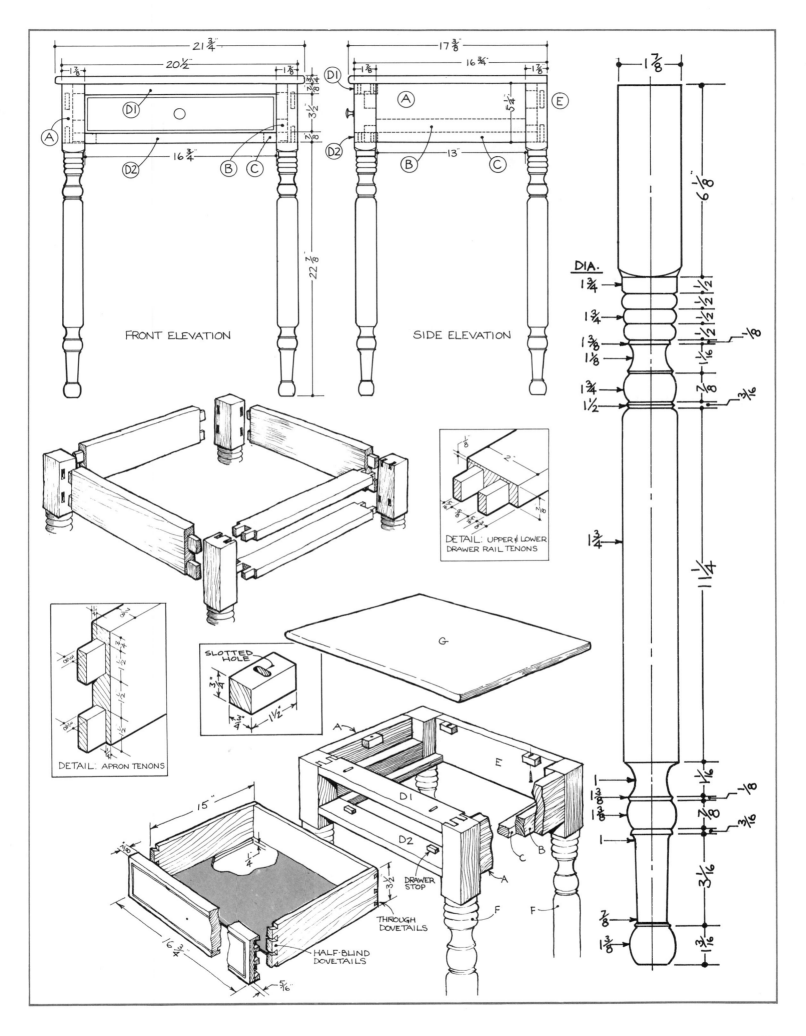

FRONT ELEVATION

SIDE ELEVATION

DETAIL: UPPER & LOWER DRAWER RAIL TENONS

DETAIL: APRON TENONS

SLOTTED HOLE

DRAWER STOP

THROUGH DOVETAILS

HALF·BLIND DOVETAILS

DIA.

11

Kitchen Utensils

This assortment of wooden utensils can be a useful addition to any kitchen. To keep them handy, we've included a hanger rack that holds all items except the French rolling pin.

The oven rack push-pull makes it easy to push-in or pull-out a hot oven rack. Make from a piece of maple, ¼″ thick x 1″ wide x 18″ long. A ⅜″ dia. hole in the handle permits it to hang on the rack.

To make the tenderizer, use a table saw to start the grooves, then file to the shape shown. Note that there are two sets of grooves, each one at right angles to the other.

The French rolling pin is a straight-forward turning job. Start with 1¾″ square maple and turn to dimensions shown. Use the spaghetti fork to pull a hefty load of spaghetti from the pot. Make from ⅜″ thick maple, cutting to shape shown. Then, add ten dowel pins and hanger hole. The stirring paddle is also made from ⅜″ maple stock.

After sanding, Behlen's Salad Bowl Finish (available from Woodcraft Supply Corp., 41 Atlantic Ave., Woburn, MA 01888) can be applied as directed. This finish is approved by the U.S. Food and Drug Administration for use on products that come in contact with food.

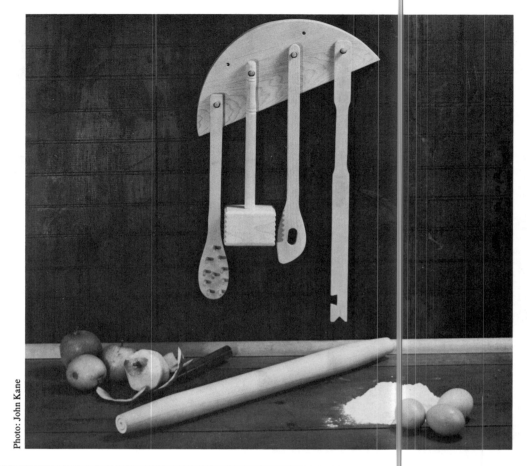

Photo: John Kane

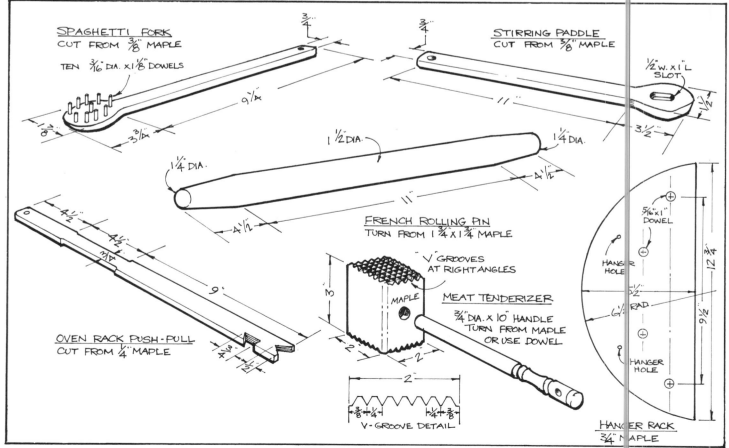

SPAGHETTI FORK
CUT FROM ⅜″ MAPLE

TEN ³⁄₁₆″ DIA. X 1⅛″ DOWELS

STIRRING PADDLE
CUT FROM ⅜″ MAPLE

½″ W. X 1″ L SLOT

9¾″

11″

3½″

1½″

FRENCH ROLLING PIN
TURN FROM 1¾ X 1¾ MAPLE

1½ DIA.

1¼ DIA.

1¼ DIA.

4½″

4½″

4½″

11″

"V" GROOVES AT RIGHT ANGLES

MEAT TENDERIZER

¾″ DIA. X 10″ HANDLE TURN FROM MAPLE OR USE DOWEL

3

MAPLE

2

2

2

V-GROOVE DETAIL

⅜ ¼ ¼ ⅜

OVEN RACK PUSH-PULL
CUT FROM ¼″ MAPLE

4½

4½

¾

9″

¾

½

5/16″ X 1″ DOWEL

HANGER HOLE

HANGER HOLE

6½″ RAD.

12¾

9½

HANGER RACK
¾″ MAPLE

The dark richness of walnut in contrast with the light color of maple results in the interesting look of this contemporary styled book rack. It's sturdy, easy to adjust, and will hold just about any size book.

Start by cutting 3 pieces of maple and 2 pieces of walnut to ¾" thick x 1" wide x 14¼" long. Edge glue these 5 pieces, alternating the maple and walnut as shown in the drawing. Make sure the grain runs in the same direction for all pieces. After allowing to dry overnight, a good sharp plane will do a nice job removing glue and smoothing the surface. Any slight planer marks can be removed with a cabinet scraper. The board can then be cut into two 7 inch long pieces.

Referring to the drawing, lay out the 4¼" long taper as shown. Cut out waste stock with a band or saber saw. For a good clean look, this piece must have edges that are completely free of scratches or sawblade marks. Make sure the edges are given a complete sanding, starting with coarse grade paper, then working along to medium and fine grades. It may take a little more time, but the effort will be well worth it.

After cutting the ¾" x 1½" x 5" ends, bore ½" dia. x ½" deep holes for the dowel stock. Apply a ½" radius to both upper corners, then sand all surfaces thoroughly. Assemble parts as shown, then complete the project with two coats of tung oil finish.

Photo: John Kane

Laminated Bookrack by Harvey E. Helm

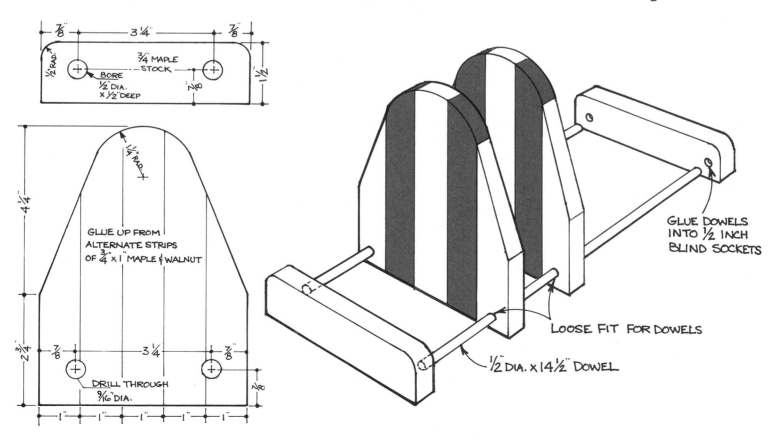

7/8   3¼"   7/8
½ RAD.
¾" MAPLE STOCK
BORE
½" DIA.
x ½" DEEP
½"
8/0

4¼"
¼" RAD.
GLUE UP FROM ALTERNATE STRIPS OF ¾" x 1" MAPLE & WALNUT
3¼"
¾" 2¼"
7/8   3¼   7/8
DRILL THROUGH 9/16" DIA.
8/0
1"   1"   1"   1"

GLUE DOWELS INTO ½ INCH BLIND SOCKETS
LOOSE FIT FOR DOWELS
½" DIA. x 14½" DOWEL

Pine Schoolhouse Desk

Photo: John Kane

This small desk-bench unit was inspired by the old-fashioned schoolhouse desks now commanding high prices at antique shops. Built of easily obtained 5/4 inch pine (1⅛" actual thickness) along with a few pieces of ¾ inch stock, it's proportioned for children of about 8-11 years and provides a convenient surface for both schoolwork and play. It's also an attractive piece of furniture for a child's room.

Start by jointing and edge-gluing three lengths of 5/4 x 8 inch stock for the desk top. Clamp until dry and then trim to finish dimensions of 20 x 26¾ inches. Plane and sand the slab flat, and round off the front and end top edges.

The shaped uprights supporting the desk and seat are cut from 5/4 x 10 inch and 5/4 x 8 inch stock respectively. Lay out a 1 inch grid pattern on cardboard of approximate size and enlarge one half of the profiles. Cut along your penciled profile and use this half-template to trace the shape on the workpieces.

Before cutting the curves, lay out and cut the rabbet at the top ends of the large upright. Also lay out and cut the dadoes to hold the bookshelf and footrest. These cuts can be easily done with a table saw and dado head or by making repeated passes over an ordinary blade.

The feet, which are also of 5/4 inch stock are next shaped as shown in Fig. 1, and dadoed to receive the seat and desk uprights. The bookshelf and footrest are next cut from ¾ inch stock. These are both cut to 9¼ x 22½ inches; however, the footrest is partially cut away along the front edge for a more decorative appearance.

Sand all parts well and glue and clamp feet, shelves and uprights together, maintaining squareness while counter-boring for ½ inch dia. plugs and drilling pilot holes for the screws fastening feet to uprights as shown in Fig. 3.

Cut the top brackets from ¾ inch thick pine and trim the ends to 36 degrees (see Fig. 4). Referring to the same detail, lay out, mark and drill the ½ inch dia. by 1¼ inch deep

counterbored screw hole on each end, then bore the ³⁄₁₆ inch shank dia. as shown. Also, locate and drill a ⅜ inch dia. by ⅝ inch deep dowel pin hole at the center of the bracket (7 inch from each end). The brackets can now be glued and screwed to the upright rabbets. Note that the screws are counterbored and covered with ½ inch dia. plugs.

Cut a backboard slightly long from ¾ inch stock for the rear of the bookshelf. Trim so it fits snugly between the uprights, flush with back and top edge of uprights. Secure with glue and finishing nails driven up through the book shelf.

Turn the assembly upside down and center it on the underside of the top, then locate the centerpoints of the two ⅜ inch diameter bracket dowel holes. Bore these holes ⅝ inch deep in the underside of the top to accept ⅜ inch dia. by 1¼ inch long dowel pins. Apply glue to the dowel pins and clamp the top to the brackets (don't glue any other area as the top must be free to expand and contract with seasonal changes in humidity. Next, drive the 1½ inch x no. 10 round-head wood screws and washers (Fig. 4). The shank hole is bored oversized (³⁄₁₆ inch) to allow some room for the top to move with those inevitable seasonal changes in width.

The top backboard is shaped from ¾ inch stock and fastened as shown in Fig. 3. The bench top is then cut to finish size, sanded and screwed to uprights. Finally, rout or gouge a 12 inch long by ¼ inch deep pencil groove near the back edge of top.

Use a plug cutter to cut ⅜" long plugs from the face grain of pine scraps or use birch dowel stock cut to length. The plugs may be trimmed and sanded flush or left protruding slightly and rounded off.

Go over the piece carefully, rounding off all corners to give it an antique appearance and to discourage splintering. After finish sanding, apply the stain and sealer of your choice.

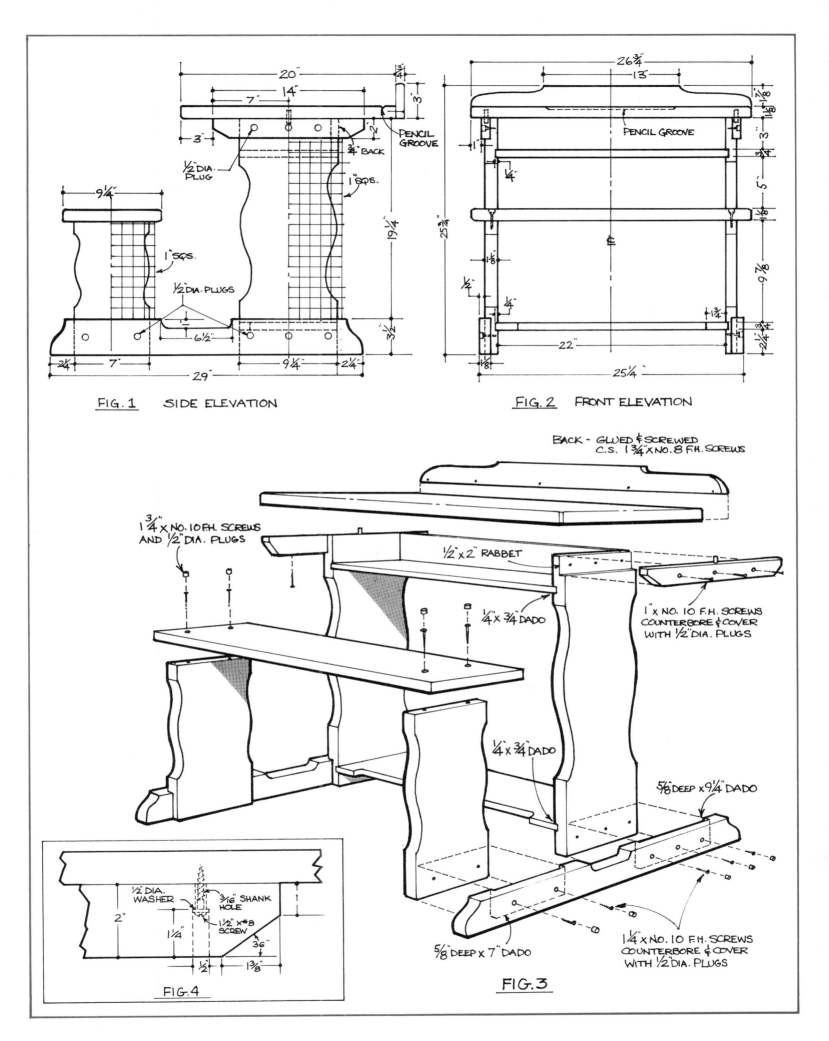

FIG. 1   SIDE ELEVATION

FIG. 2   FRONT ELEVATION

FIG. 4

FIG. 3

15

Photo: John Kane

While this may not be the safest bank to put money in, we think it has to rate as one of the most stylish. Actually, we like to think of it as a novelty item — a sort of storage and display station for your pocket change. It's designed to hold about $20.00 in quarters, although it also accepts pennies, nickels, and dimes. To remove your savings, simply turn the bank upside down and coins easily fall out the top slot.

A hardwood is the best choice for this project, and we selected walnut. The bank requires very little stock, so some of your scrap pieces may provide more than enough material.

Begin by resawing a piece of ¾" thick by 10-5/16" long stock to a thickness of 3/16". This will result in a piece 3/16" thick x ¾" wide x 10-5/16" long. Now, set up the table saw to cut this piece to a thickness of 3/32". This thickness is important, so try to cut it as accurately as possible. If cut too thin, the coins won't fit between the glass; if cut too thick, coins may slide over each other, rather than stand on edge. Using this technique, cut a total of two pieces 10-5/16" long, and one piece 8-5/16" long. These 3/32" thick x 3/16" wide spacers can now be epoxied between two pieces of 8-5/16" x 10-5/16" window glass as shown in the sketch (miter the corners where the spacers meet). Be sure to thoroughly clean the inside of the glass before assembly. The two 10-5/16" long spacers are glued along glass sides, and the 8-5/16" long spacer is glued along glass bottom.

The top, bottom and two sides can now be cut to dimensions shown, and a 3/16" deep groove cut lengthwise along the center of all four pieces. Make the groove width equal to the thickness of the window glass and spacer assembly. Now, use a 3/32 drill bit (or ⅛") and cut a series of holes forming the coin slot. A small file will clean up any rough spots.

Assemble all parts with glue, clamping firmly, and allow to dry overnight. After a thorough sanding, two coats of tung oil will complete the project.

Walnut Bank

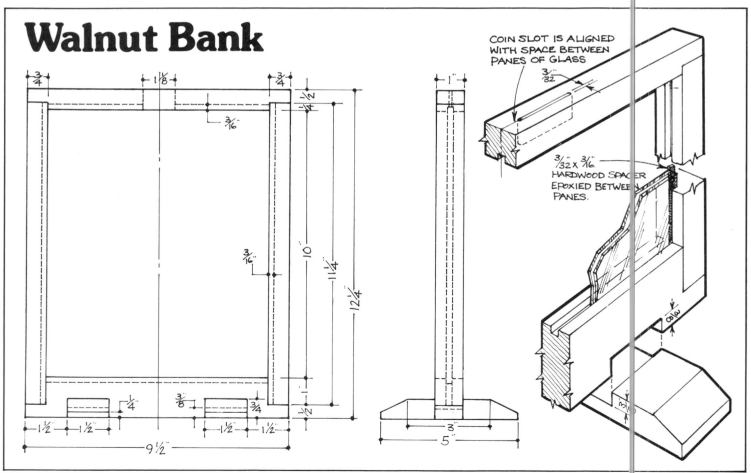

COIN SLOT IS ALIGNED WITH SPACE BETWEEN PANES OF GLASS

3/32

3/32 x 3/16 HARDWOOD SPACER EPOXIED BETWEEN PANES.

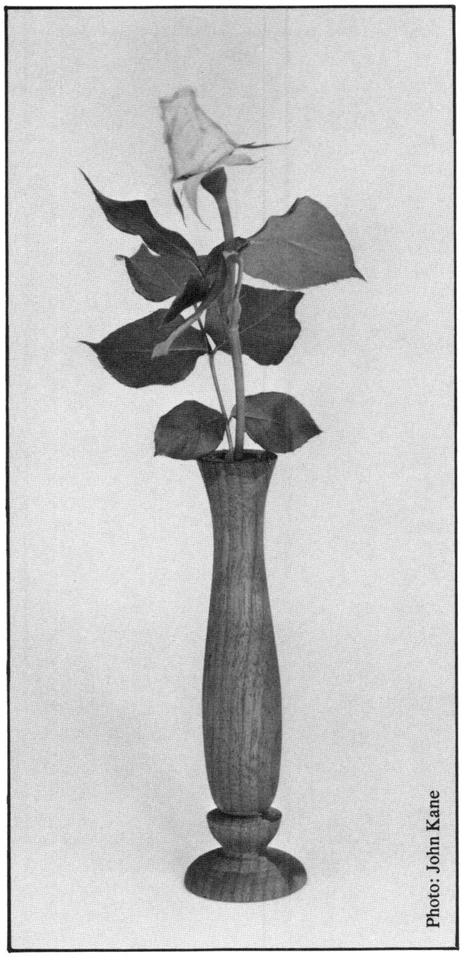

Photo: John Kane

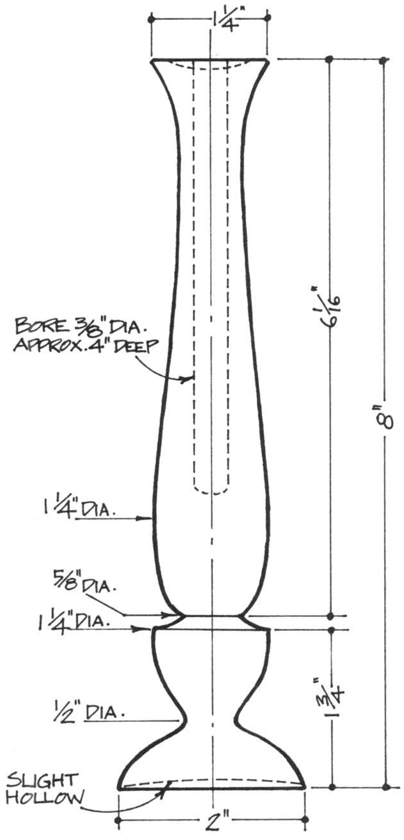

1¼"
BORE 3/8" DIA. APPROX. 4" DEEP
6 1/16"
8"
1¼" DIA.
5/8" DIA.
1¼" DIA.
½" DIA.
1¾"
SLIGHT HOLLOW
2"

Bud Vase

by Donald F. Stearns

Add a single red rose to the rich look of dark walnut, gracefully shaped, and the result is this elegant little vase. It makes a beautiful gift, perhaps one that will be treasured for years to come.

For those with some turning experience, it will not be hard to make. Start with walnut stock, about 2¼" square x 12" long. Mount in the lathe, keeping in mind that when turned, the top end of vase will face the head stock and the vase bottom will face the tail stock.

Reduce the square to a cylinder, then use the parting tool to establish each end of the vase. Use the skew to shape the flared base. Note that the base necks down to ½" dia., then expands to 1¼" dia. at a point 1¾" from the bottom.

Reduce the remainder of vase to 1¼" dia., then shape the elongated curve with a gouge. Turn waste stock on both ends to about ¼" dia. before giving the piece a thorough sanding. Now a skew or round nose scraper can be used to form a slight hollow at the base and top. Continue the hollowing of the base until the piece breaks free. Trim the ¼" dia. stub from the top and drill a ⅜" dia. hole 4 - 5 inches deep as shown. Final sand the vase before finishing with several coats of tung oil.

Grain Scoop

Wall decorations always make popular gift items. Using pine stock, this one is made in the form of a grain scoop and looks especially nice with a small arrangement of dried flowers.

A small piece like this often looks best with a light appearance, so we used 5/16" stock for all parts except the handles, but ¼" or ⅜" stock can also be substituted without any problem. If you don't have a power planer, sharpen up your hand planes and go to work on a piece of ¾" stock. A board about 8" wide and 7" long will take care of the side stock, and one 5¾" wide x 11½" long will suffice for the back, bottom, and front.

Cut all parts to dimensions shown, noting that each side leg has a ⅛" x 5/16" rabbet. If you use ¼" or ⅜" stock, adjust the rabbet to fit.

The handle is either lathe turned or handcarved to the dimensions shown. If you don't have a lathe, or prefer another style handle, we've included an alternate shape.

Sand all parts, then assemble with glue and countersunk finishing nails. After filling the nail holes, resand all surfaces before staining and finishing to suit.

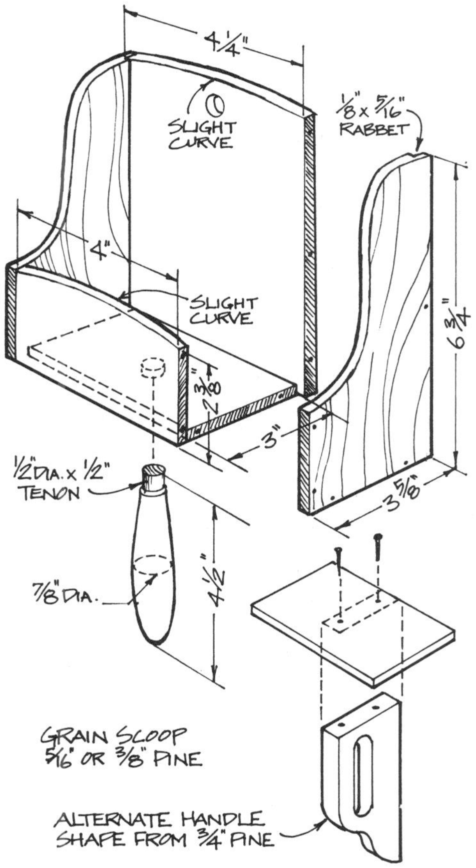

4¼"
SLIGHT CURVE
⅛" x 5/16" RABBET
4"
SLIGHT CURVE
3/8"
3"
6¾"
3⅝"
½" DIA. x ½" TENON
4½"
7/8" DIA.
GRAIN SCOOP 5/16" OR 3/8" PINE
ALTERNATE HANDLE SHAPE FROM ¾" PINE

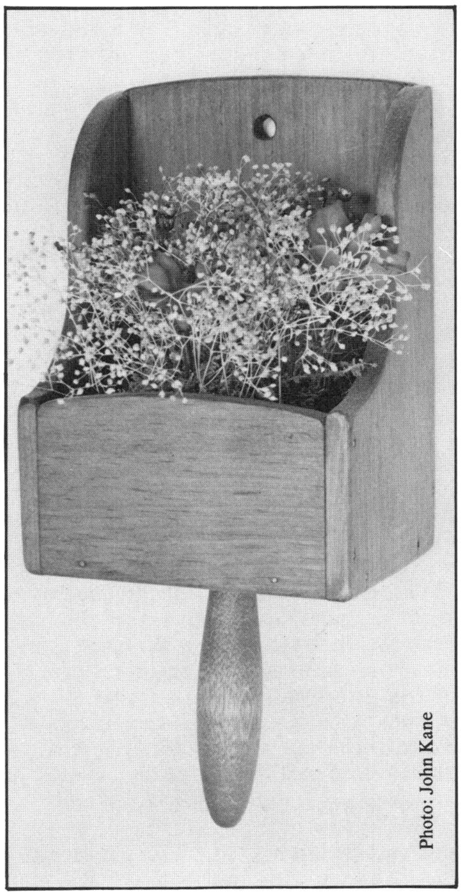

Photo: John Kane

17th Century Mantle Clock

by Roger E. Schroeder

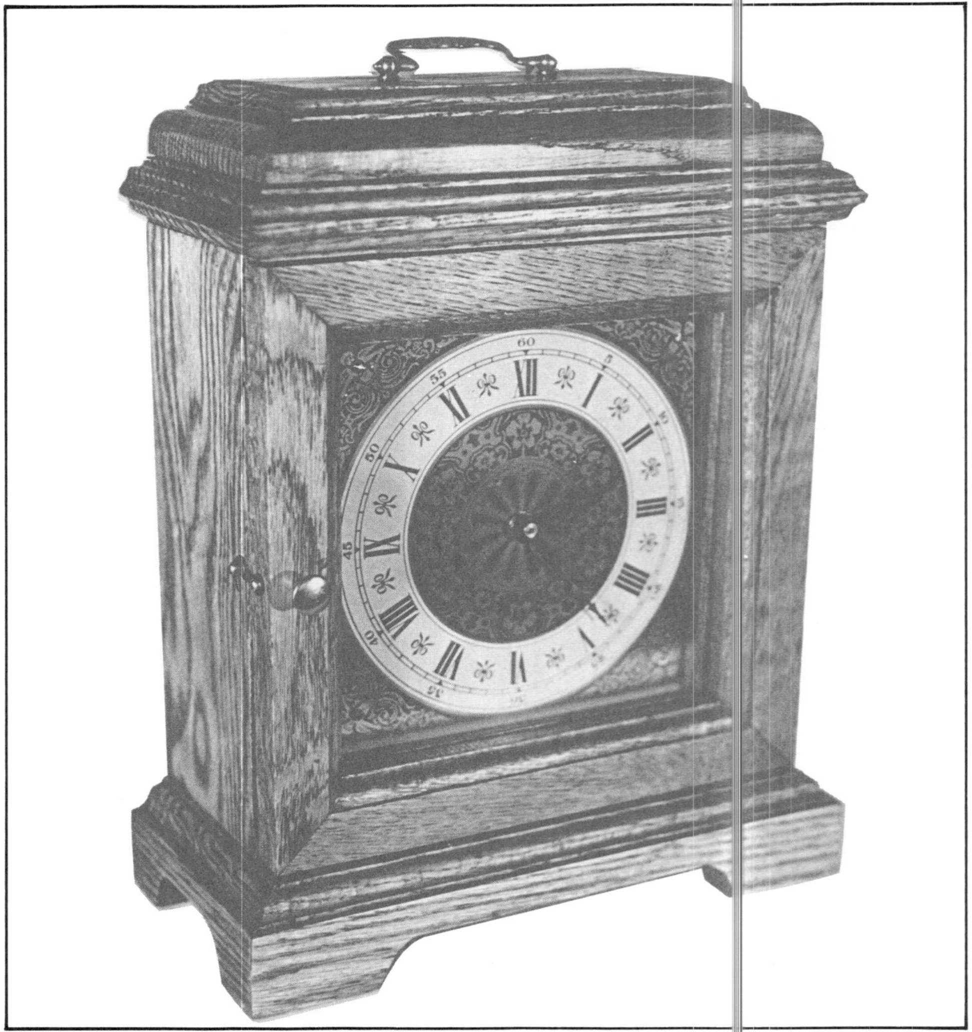

Clocks are achieving a growing popularity among amateur and professional woodworkers. This handsome clock can be completed in a weekend and will give a lifetime of satisfaction. Based on a late 17th century design, the one pictured is of oak, though almost any cabinet grade hardwood will give beautiful results.

I designed the clock so that little glue is used in its construction. Carefully placed wood screws keep the parts together, while glue holds only the mitered corners of the door and feet.

The project should be started by cutting to size the sides (A). A rabbet will have to be cut for the plywood back panel (I), also grooves for the plywood movement board (H), and mortises cut for the hinges. Once these operations are completed, parts B, C, D and E are made. Parts B, C and E are molded with a router and 5/32 inch Roman ogee bit while D is shaped with a ⅜ inch rounding bit. For all pieces I screw a scrap block to their undersides to be held in a vise. This allows for easier routing, especially on the half-inch pieces.

Secure the sides to the base, part B, with woodscrews. Insert the movement board into its grooves and temporarily attach part C. Before parts D and E are screwed together, holes will have to be drilled into part E for the bail handle. These handles usually have large-headed screws, so holes may have to be drilled into the top of D to accommodate the screw heads. It is not advisable to countersink them into the ½ inch thick part E.

Next, remove part C, clamp C, D and E together, and drill for two long wood screws that will hold all three parts together. Then reattach C to the sides, screw D and E together with four countersunk screws and attach them to C with the two screws countersunk into the bottom of C.

The feet can now be cut to size and shape, mitered and glued. I find corner clamps very useful for this operation. The assembled feet are then attached to the bottom of part B with wood screws that are countersunk ¼ inch. Care must be taken so that the screws do not go through the ogee curve. The back board can now be cut to size and secured with back locks or turnbuttons.

To make the door, rout the edge of a long ¾ inch board with the Roman ogee bit, then rip to size. When making the miters, I overcut each side, parts J, of the door by 1/16 inch. This allows for any error in the case construction. Extra wood is then removed with a hand plane or the jointer.

The glass for the door is not set into a recess but is instead held with a mitered retainer that has its own rabbet. I use a wide and long board, cut the rabbet and then rip the board. It would be wise to experiment with the depth of the rabbet so that the glass for the door does not rattle but is snug. The retainer is held with countersunk brass screws.

Attach the door to the case. Note that the 1½ inch hinges are mortised into the case sides and screwed flat on the inside face of the door.

The 8 inch square dial with a 6⅛ inch time ring plus a battery movement were purchased from Armor Products, P.O. Box 445, East Northport, NY 11731. A catalog costs $1.00.

A number of movements are available but I used a Model 22201 with a 31001 dial face and 804B hands.

The dial mounts to H with ½″ round head brass screws very near the corners so they will not be seen through the door opening. A 5/16″ dia. hole through the center of H will accept the threaded handshaft of the movement. A nut on the outside holds the movement tight.

If the door glass touches the end of the handshaft, a piece of cardboard between movement and the back of H should correct the problem.

The Woodworkers' Store, 21801 Industrial Blvd., Rogers, MN 55374 carries the flat door hook (D3052), knob (D3038), hinges (D3910), turnbuttons (D3055), and bail pull (E1120). Their catalog costs $2.00.

I finished the clock with McCloskeys dark oak stain, taking it apart to treat each piece separately. Several coats of tung oil were then applied.

Bill of Materials (All Dims. Actual)

Part	Size in Inches	No. Req'd
A	¾ x 4 x 10¼	2
B	½ x 5½ x 11¼	1
C	1⅛ x 5½ x 11¼	1
D	¾ x 5 x 10	1
E	½ x 4¼ x 8⅝	1
F	¾ x 1½ x 11⅝	1
G	¾ x 1½ x 5⅝	2
H	¼ x 9¼ x 10¼	1
I	¼ x 9¼ x 10¼	1
J	¾ x 1½ x 10¼	4
K	⅜ x ½ x 8	4

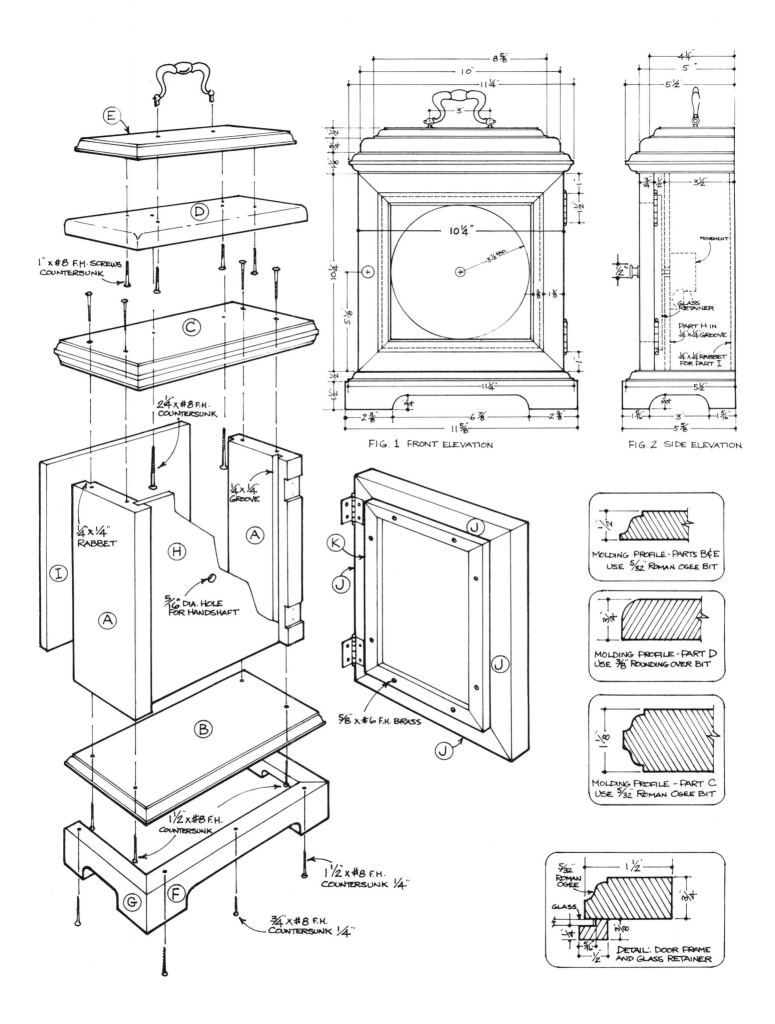

1" x #8 F.H. SCREWS
COUNTERSUNK

2 1/4" x #8 F.H.
COUNTERSUNK

1/4 x 1/4"
RABBET

1/4 x 1/4"
RABBET

1/4 x 1/4
GROOVE

5/16" DIA. HOLE
FOR HANDSHAFT

1 1/2" x #8 F.H.
COUNTERSUNK

1 1/2" x #8 F.H.
COUNTERSUNK 1/4"

3/4" x #8 F.H.
COUNTERSUNK 1/4"

5/8 x #6 F.H. BRASS

FIG. 1 FRONT ELEVATION

FIG. 2 SIDE ELEVATION

MOVEMENT

GLASS
RETAINER

PART H IN
1/4 x 1/4 GROOVE

1/4 x 1/4 RABBET
FOR PART I

MOLDING PROFILE - PARTS B & E
USE 5/32" ROMAN OGEE BIT

MOLDING PROFILE - PART D
USE 3/8" ROUNDING OVER BIT

MOLDING PROFILE - PART C
USE 5/32" ROMAN OGEE BIT

DETAIL: DOOR FRAME
AND GLASS RETAINER

5/32
ROMAN
OGEE

GLASS

19

Toy Truck

by Donald F. Stearns

You'll have to search pretty hard to find a toy store that has a truck equal to the size and durability of this one. It measures 7″ wide and almost 30″ long, big enough to haul those many things that only a small fry can think of. Made from pine scraps, it has been tested for nearly four years by my two grandsons...and has passed all tests.

Start work on the body (C) first. Using 4/4 stock (¾″ actual) cut to a width of 5¼″ and length of 12″. Referring to the detail, lay out dimensions as shown, then cut out with band or saber saw.

The four posts (G) are next. Rip 4/4 stock to ¾″ widths, then cut to 8⅜″ lengths. The doors (I) and panels (Q) are made as shown, resulting in a horizontal grain direction for the door and vertical grain for the panel. This small detail makes the door stand out from the panel and posts. If you're looking to save time though, make doors and panels from one piece (grain running vertically) then chisel a "V" cut around the perimeter of the door.

The hood (K) is full dimensioned in the detail. Cut to shape and give the rounded top a good sanding. Locate and drill ¼″ deep x ¾″ dia. headlight holes and ¼″ deep x ⅜″ dia. signal light holes. Later, headlights (N) and signal lights (O) will be glued in these holes.

Dimensions for the back (J) and dash (L) are given in the bill of materials. Bumper (P) is shown in the detail drawing. If you want to avoid rabbeting, cut one piece ⅜ x ¾ x 5, one piece ⅜ x ¾ x 6¼, then glue together. The fender (M) can be cut next. For added strength, run the grain in direction of arrow.

Axle boxes (parts R & S) are made from about a 14″ length of 1⅛″ square stock. Set the table saw blade to a depth of ½″ and form the ⅜″ wide groove by making repeated passes. Be sure to use a push stick to keep hands away from the blade.

The bed (D) and sides (E) are cut from 4/4 stock. To make the end (H) refer to detail, using a band or saber saw to cut the curve. Also detailed is the spring (V) and coupling (U). Note that the coupling has a hole drilled through it to accept a ½″ dia. x 2⅛″ long dowel pin. A chamfer helps reduce friction. Glue the dowel so that ½″ protrudes through both top and bottom of coupling.

Six wheels are next. The two front wheels (A), are made from ¾″ thick stock cut to 3½″ diameter. The four rear wheels are 1½″ stock and cut to same diameter.

Before assembly, give all parts a thorough sanding. If you plan to stain,

Photo: John Kane

this is a good time to do it. If it's done after assembly, you'll have to watch for glue squeeze out and smudges.

All parts are assembled using glue and countersunk finishing nails. Fill all countersunk holes. Note the springs (V) are attached to (D) with ¼″ blind dowel pins. Part U is doweled and glued to part D. The other end of the

dowel is left free to pivot in the ½″ dia. hole bored in the body (C). Do not use glue here.

Before final finish be sure to round off sharp corners and edges, then give all surfaces one more sanding. Two coats of polyurethane varnish followed by a rubdown with 4/0 steel wool completes the project.

Part	Bill of Materials Description	(All Dims. Actual) Size in Inches	No. Req'd
A	Wheels	¾ x 3½ dia.	2
B	Wheels	1½ x 3½ dia.	4
C	Body	See Detail	1
D	Bed	¾ x 5½ x 21¾	1
E	Side	¾ x 3¾ x 22½	2
F	Roof	¾ x 5 x 5½	1
G	Post	¾ x ¾ x 8⅜	4
H	End	See Detail	1
I	Door	¾ x 3 x 2½	2
J	Back	¾ x 3¾ x 5½	1
K	Hood	See Detail	1
L	Dash	¾ x 1½ x 3¾	1
M	Fender	See Detail	2
N	Headlight	¾ dia. x ½ long	2
O	Signal Light	⅜ dia. x ½ long	2
P	Bumper	See Detail	1
Q	Panel	¾ x 2½ x 3	2
R	Axle Box	1⅛ x 1⅛ x 3⅞	2
S	Axle Box	1⅛ x 1⅛ x 5⅜	1
T	Axle	⅜ dia. x 7″ long	3
U	Coupling	1⅛ x 2 x 2	1
V	Spring	See Detail	2

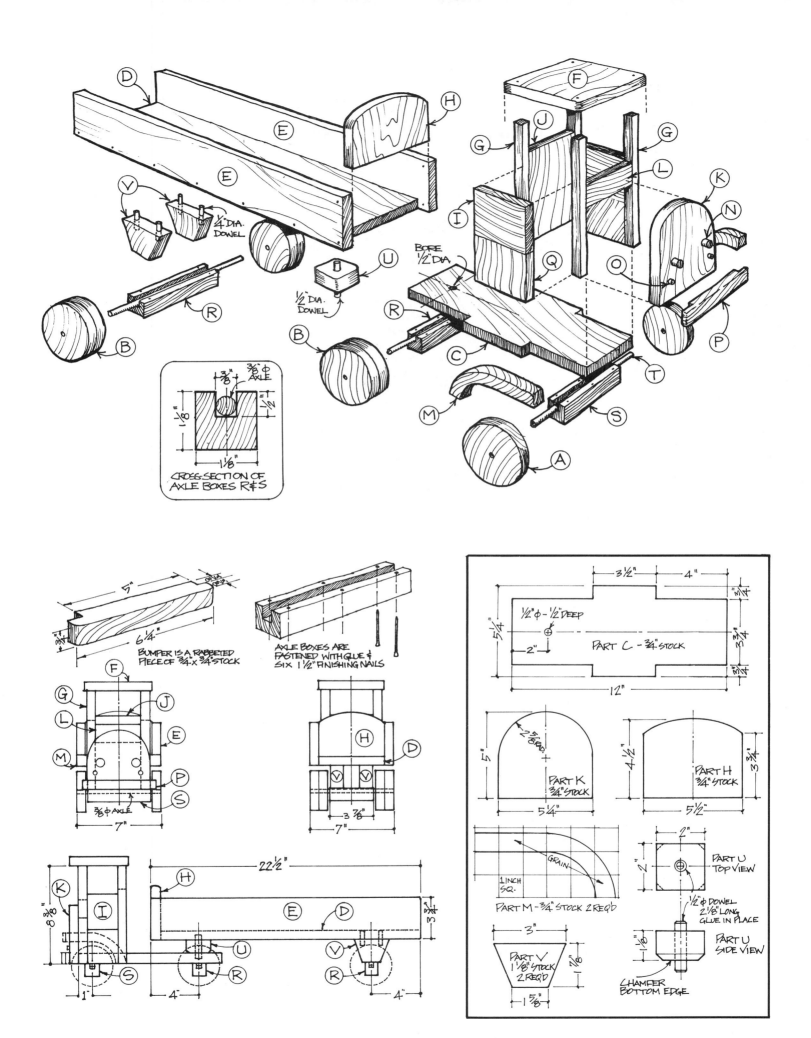

CROSS-SECTION OF
AXLE BOXES R & S

3/8" φ AXLE

BORE 1/2" DIA

1/4" DIA. DOWEL

1/2" DIA. DOWEL

5"

6 1/4"

3/4"

BUMPER IS A RABBETED
PIECE OF 3/4" x 3/4" STOCK

AXLE BOXES ARE
FASTENED WITH GLUE &
SIX 1 1/2" FINISHING NAILS

3/8" φ AXLE

7"

3 7/8"

7"

8 3/8"

22 1/2"

3 3/4"

1"

4"

4"

3 1/2"   4"

3/4"

5 1/4"

1/2" φ - 1/2" DEEP

2"

PART C - 3/4" STOCK

3 3/4"

3/4"

12"

2.5/8" RAD

5"

PART K
3/4" STOCK

5 1/4"

4 1/2"

PART H
3/4" STOCK

3 3/4"

5 1/2"

GRAIN

1 INCH
SQ.

PART M - 3/4" STOCK 2 REQ'D

3"

PART V
1 1/8" STOCK
2 REQ'D

7/8"

1 5/8"

2"

2"

PART U
TOP VIEW

1/2" φ DOWEL
2 1/8" LONG
GLUE IN PLACE

PART U
SIDE VIEW

1/8"

CHAMFER
BOTTOM EDGE

Letter Rack

Jigsaw addicts are going to enjoy this project. It's a nicely designed letter rack, with a pair of intricately shaped holders, making it quite a bit fancier than most you'll find.

Since the holders have some narrow sections, we used ¼″ pine plywood to provide added strength. The back is ½″ thick solid pine stock. Another good choice would be ½″ solid mahogany for the back and mahogany plywood for the holders.

Start with the back, cutting a piece of ½″ stock to 5¼″ x 20″. Using the drawing and its dimensions as a guide, lay out the shape as shown, then cut out with the jigsaw or saber saw.

Use the full size pattern to layout the holder, using the jig saw to cut out. To make the inside cuts, drill a ¼″ dia. hole in the waste stock, then remove blade from saw. Now feed the blade through the hole and reattach it to the saw.

Before assembly give all parts a good sanding, especially the holder edges. To join the holder and back, tap two clipped brads into each beveled strip, add glue, then use hand pressure to press the holder and strip together. The brad prevents them from slipping. Now glue and clamp both strip and holder to the back using a waste block as shown.

Final sand, and stain to suit.

Photo: John Kane

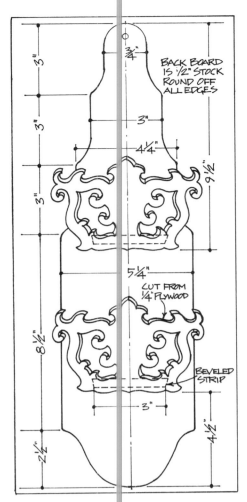

METHOD OF FASTENING LETTER HOLDERS TO BACK

Note Caddy

Photo: John Kane

Natasha is her name. She's an Afghan hound and though she may look a little goofy, she does her job very well. She will faithfully stand guard by your desk telephone, holding a roll of adding machine tape and a pencil for jotting down those easily forgotten messages.

The base is shaped from 3½ x 3½ inch squares, one of which is center-bored with a ⅜″ dia. bit. The other is drilled partially through to form a socket for the dowel axle. Clamp the two parts together when drilling to insure that the holes line up.

The dowel axle should fit the hole with enough friction to stay in place when the assembly is tilted but be loose enough that a slight rap on the rear will start it out.

Small tear-off bars glued and nailed on each side will keep the base together. These should be beveled to a sharp edge and small teeth cut with a triangular file.

The head and base front are drilled for a short pencil. Also, drill through head and into rear of base to insert heavy cotton twine for the ears and tail. Secure the twine with small pegs glued in and trimmed off. The twine is then unraveled and combed out.

Draw the face with waterproof india ink or enamel and apply a couple of coats of penetrating oil or just wax for a finish.

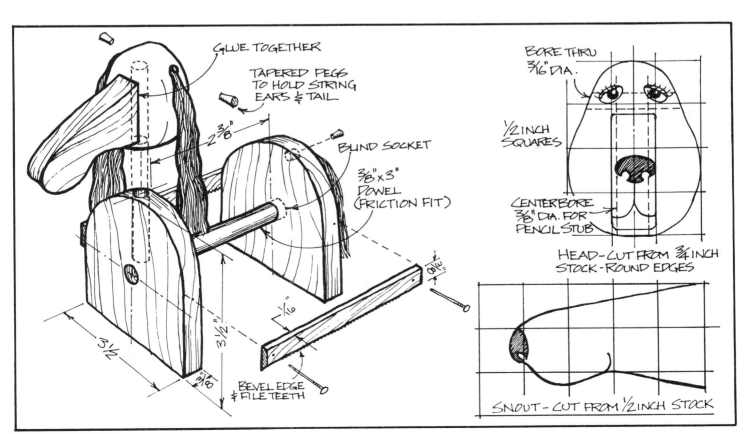

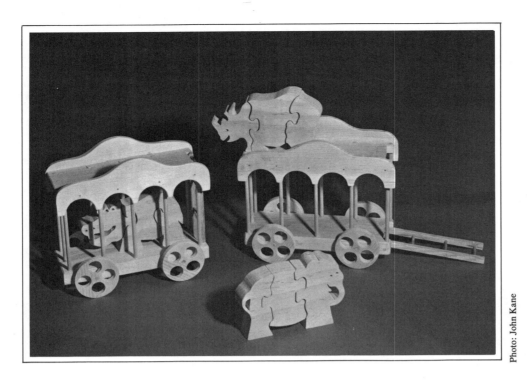

Photo: John Kane

Even though circus parades are a thing of the past, children will still enjoy playing with this delightful wooden toy.

The three animals are made from ¾" or 1⅛" thick stock. Transfer shapes from grid patterns, then use a jig saw with narrow blade to cut out.

Make wagon bottom from ¾ x 2½ x 7, the top ½ x 2½ x 7. A 1¾" wide x ⅜" deep notch is cut on both as shown. Clamp the top to bottom and drill through both for ¼" dowels.

Make the two curved aprons from ¼" thick x 4½ wide x 7½ long stock. Mark a centerline along its length, then drill four 1¼" dia. holes on the centerline, spaced as shown. Now rip down the centerline to form two matching pieces.

Cut wheels with a 2" dia. hole saw. Axles are ¼" dowel stock, while door pivot and bars are ⅛" dia. The door rails are likely to split if made from pine, so use hardwood here.

Give all parts a complete sanding before assembling with glue. When completed, the cage door should fit in the notched top with an easy friction fit. Final finish with a couple of coats of polyurethane varnish.

Circus Wagons – Animal Puzzles

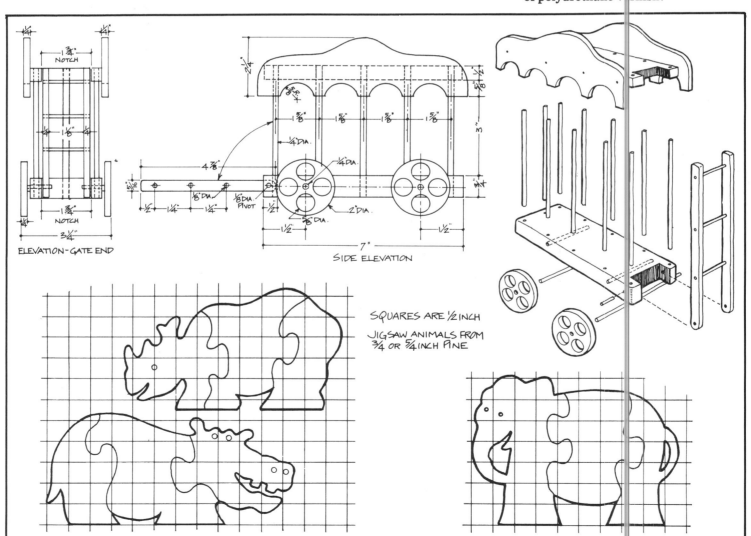

ELEVATION-GATE END

SIDE ELEVATION

SQUARES ARE ½ INCH

JIGSAW ANIMALS FROM ¾ OR 5/4 INCH PINE

Library Stool

Clean lines, solid construction, and the beauty of natural oak all combine to create this handsomely styled library stool. It's a fine example of contemporary furniture design, and from it one can begin to understand why this style of furniture continues to become more and more popular.

Start construction by edge gluing enough 4/4 stock to make the two sides and top. It's a good idea to lay out all boards so that the grain runs in the same direction when viewed from the edges. This makes for easier planing and smoother sanding later on. And don't forget that when viewed from the board ends, the direction of the annular rings should be alternated to minimize warp.

Now, the glued-up stock can be ripped to a finish width of 12″. Cut the two end pieces to 12″ lengths, then lay out and cut the curved front and ½″ deep mortises.

For best appearance, the edge-joint lines on the top should match up with those of the sides, just as they did before the glued-up stock was crosscut. With this in mind, rip the top into 2 pieces, each 4¾″ wide x 14½″ long, then cut a ⅜ x ⅜ rabbet and round off inside corners as shown. Two aprons can be cut 3″ wide x 14½″ long and also rabbeted. Make this a good tight joint so it won't show.

After cutting the 2″ wide x 15½″ long stretchers, each apron can be glued to its mating top half at the rabbet joint. Use glue and several clamps, taking special care to make sure the joint is perfectly square. When dry the apron ends and sides are drilled for dowel pins.

Sand all parts thoroughly, then assemble with glue and clamps and allow to dry overnight. Four counterbored screws fix the stretchers to the top. A router equipped with a ⅜″ rounding over bit is used to round the top outside edge. Other edges are sanded to a light radius. Now all edges and surfaces are given a complete final sanding before finishing with two coats of satin polyurethane varnish.

Photo: John Kane

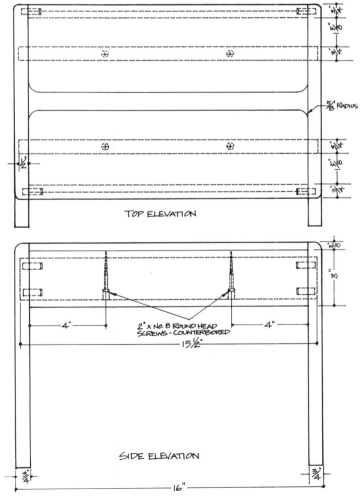

TOP ELEVATION

⅜″ RADIUS

2″ x No. 8 ROUND HEAD SCREWS - COUNTERBORED
15½″

SIDE ELEVATION

4″   4″

¾″   ¾″

16″

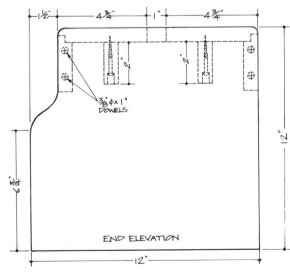

1½″   4¾″   1″   4¾″

⅜″ ⌀ x 1″ DOWELS

12″

END ELEVATION

12″

Ratchet Table Lamp

An 18th century ratchet candlestand provided the inspiration for this attractive combination end table and reading lamp. The ratchet device permits the lamp height to be varied from 38 to 50 inches from the floor, thus converting the piece to a floor lamp. And it's as interesting to build as it is to look at.

Oak was used for our model but maple, birch or cherry can be substituted. Although the posts and ratchet bar are of 1⅛ inch stock, thinner one inch (13/16″ actually) can be used. For stability, the feet should be about 2 inches thick and can be laminated from 1 inch stock.

Start by cutting feet to length, then lay out and cut the half-lap notches centered on each piece. Cut these for a snug fit. Lay out and cut two mortises to take the post tenons. Sand feet and join with glue.

The two posts are next cut slightly long and tenons formed on each end. Leave upper tenons a bit long so they can be trimmed flush later. Chamfer the posts as shown.

The ratchet bar is cut to length and width and a ⅜″ x ¾″ deep groove is cut, centered along its length. Drill a ⅜″ dia. x 2″ deep hole in the top in line with the groove. Connect groove and hole by drilling another ⅜″ hole into the back of the groove and angled up to intersect the nipple hole near its bottom.

Lay out and cut the ratchet teeth. Before starting each angled cut, chisel a small notch to help start the blade.

A ⅜″ x ⅜″ filler strip is cut to fit snugly in the long groove flush with the outer surface. Tap the strip in place temporarily and cut the tenon at the end of the bar. Remove the strip and feed lamp cord into the angled hole and out the top of the bar. Tie a loose knot in the cord so it won't slip back down while you glue the filler strip in place.

The notched spreader which is mortised to the end of the ratchet bar and keeps it centered between the posts is cut next. Notch it to fit around posts and mortise it to receive the tenon. Also cut and bevel the upper plate which is mortised to fit the post tenons and the ratchet bar. The mortise for the ratchet bar should be cut so that the bar slides easily. The cam assembly is made from ⅜″ dia. dowel and hardwood resawed to ⅜″ thickness. This is installed after assembly of the stand.

Carefully sand all parts and temporarily join posts to base with the spreader between them. Add the beveled top plate and ratchet bar to ascertain that all parts fit well and the bar moves easily.

If all looks well, cut the table support cleats and screw them to the posts. Make sure they are level and 22 inches from the floor. Glue lower post tenons into base and peg them as shown. Also glue and peg the ratchet bar to its spreader. Do not glue the upper tenons into the top plate until after the table top has been fitted.

The top consists of two boards which, after jointing, are 8½ and 7½ inches wide. Cut the boards to rough length and, using the assembled stand as a guide, carefully lay out the locations of the posts and ratchet bar on the jointed edge of the wider board. Notch this board to fit around the uprights. The post notches should be a tight fit while the ratchet bar notch is a bit oversize. Edge-join the boards with glue and ⅜″ dowel pins and clamp until dry.

Trim top to finished size and after removing the upper plate, drive the top down over posts and fasten it to the cleats. The beveled plate can now be glued to post tenons.

The cam is attached by drilling a 7/16″ hole, centered on one post and 6 inches above the table top. Assemble the cam as shown in the exploded view. Note that one dowel is 3 inches long and protrudes to serve as a handle. The cam sides should be parallel and snug against the posts. All dowel ends except the handle are trimmed flush after gluing.

A pair of nuts on the 1½″ nipple will permit you to use a wrench to screw it about ½ inch into the top of the ratchet

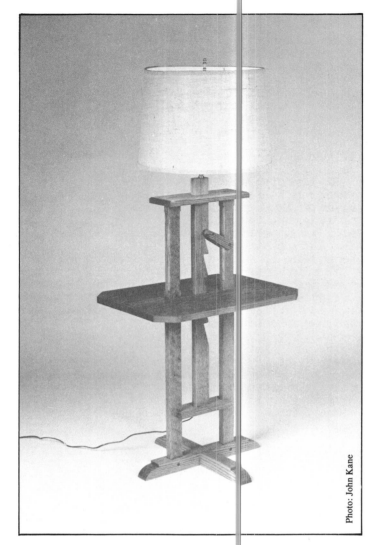

bar. Add lamp hardware as shown. The small opening at the top of the groove can be filled with a wood plug glued in place.

After a final sanding, apply stain if desired. We used one light coat of Minwax Provincial oil stain as the natural oak was quite light. This was followed by two coats of urethane varnish applied to all parts. The final coat was rubbed down with 4/0 steel wool.

Bill of Materials		
(All Dims. Actual)		
Description	Size in Inches	No. Req'd
Foot	2 x 2 x 18	2
Post	1⅛ x 1¾ x 34½ (includes tenons)	2
Ratchet Bar	See Detail	1
Spreader	¾ x 3 x 8	1
Upper Plate	¾ x 4½ x 12	1
Cam	See Detail	2
Support Cleat	¾ x 1½ x 14	2
Top	¾ x 16 x 22	1

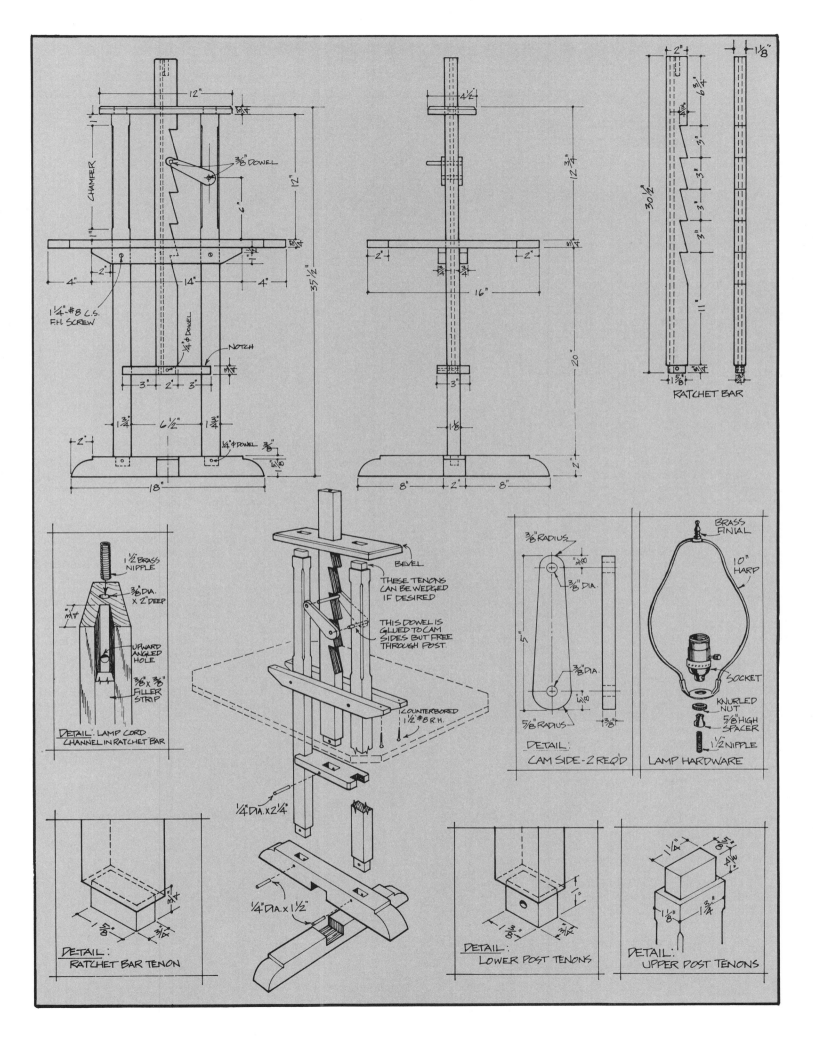

RATCHET BAR

CHAMFER

3/8" DOWEL

12"

6"

1 1/4"#8 C.S. F.H. SCREW

NOTCH

1/4"ϕ DOWEL

3"

4"   2"   14"   4"

3"   2"   3"

1 3/4"   6 1/2"   1 3/4"

2"

1/8"ϕ DOWEL   3/8"

18"

35 1/2"

4 1/2"

12"

16"

3/4"   3/4"

2"   2"

3"

1 1/8"

20"

8"   2"   8"

2"

2"   1 1/8"

6 1/4"

4 1/4"

3"

3"

3"

3"

3"

30 1/2"

1 5/8"

11"

1 1/2" BRASS NIPPLE

3/8" DIA. X 2" DEEP

UPWARD ANGLED HOLE

3/8" X 3/8" FILLER STRIP

DETAIL: LAMP CORD CHANNEL IN RATCHET BAR

BEVEL

THESE TENONS CAN BE WEDGED IF DESIRED

THIS DOWEL IS GLUED TO CAM SIDES BUT FREE THROUGH POST.

COUNTERBORED 1 1/2" #8 R.H.

1/4" DIA. X 2 1/4"

3/8" RADIUS

3/8" DIA.

3/8" DIA.

5"

5/8" RADIUS   3/8"

DETAIL: CAM SIDE - 2 REQ'D

BRASS FINIAL

10" HARP

SOCKET

KNURLED NUT

5/8" HIGH SPACER

1 1/2" NIPPLE

LAMP HARDWARE

3/4"

5/8"   3/4"

DETAIL: RATCHET BAR TENON

1/4" DIA. X 1 1/2"

1 3/8"   3/4"   1/2"

DETAIL: LOWER POST TENONS

1 1/4"

1 1/8"   1 3/4"

DETAIL: UPPER POST TENONS

27

18th Century Trestle Table

by Paul Levine

The 17th century was a time of deep unrest and turmoil in Europe. Religious persecution in Swiss Alsatia and Palatinate Germany forced the emigration of Amish and Mennonite peoples to Pennsylvania where they had been invited by William Penn in 1682.

Living in secluded areas, guarding their fragile cultural heritage, these industrious Germanic people soon learned to adapt to their new country.

They lived, as many early settlers did, in small cabins with one large room. This room served as a place to cook, eat, sleep and pass the time with friends. In this cramped lifestyle, pieces of furniture had to serve multiple purposes. Settles became beds, chair backs would fold down to become tables, and tables would drop leaves to become smaller and get tucked away.

The table shown in the photo can be disassembled and stored away. Made of American black walnut sometime before 1750, its medieval character served the gentle and simple ways of the country people generally referred to as Pennsylvania Dutch.

Although the table looks massive in the photo, and indeed has a certain rugged beauty, an examination of the dimensional drawings will show that it is in fact a small table. The original was made entirely of American black walnut, but the use of oak, maple or even pine will be authentic and considerably less expensive.

Begin with the legs (B). Make a full size pattern and transfer this onto the stock which should be at least 1⅛ inches thick. A bow saw with a fine blade is ideal for cutting the curves as their large size and detailed curvature may be a problem for some bandsaws. Don't forget to leave enough material at the end for the tenons.

The outside rail D and feet A come next. Note that although the curves are identical, part D is shorter. Also note that the rails consist of two pieces D and E, glued together. On the end elevation view (left side), the dotted lines showing parts D & E have been made solid, making it easier to lay out their profiles. Mortises for the leg tenons are then laid out and cut into the feet and top rail assemblies.

The top (H) comes next. These tables usually had tops made of one wide board but you will probably have to edge-joint and glue up two or more boards to achieve the width. The decorative edge on the top can be added with a molding plane or a router with rounding over bit.

Set the top on the leg assemblies so that part D is an equal distance from the ends of the top and measure for the stretcher (G) length. Allowing for the two long tenons, cut the stretcher and

Photograph courtesy The Metropolitan Museum of Art, gift of Mrs. Robert W. deForrest, 1933

again detail the corners with a plane or router.

After making the tenons and wedges (F), temporarily assemble the table and locate the dovetail troughs at each end of the top just outboard of the D rails. These can be easily cut with a router and dovetail bit. Cleat C is cut to fit these troughs across the full width of the top. If the dovetail routine seems too difficult, cut part C flat on top, counterbore them and screw them to the top. Use three screws per rail, one in the center and one near each end. The end screw holes should be elongated to allow for seasonal movement of the top.

The top can now be set on the leg assembly and holes drilled through parts C and D for the four ¾ inch diameter pegs (I) which secure the top to the leg assembly. These pegs can be

lathe turned as were the originals, or whittled.

The finishing touch is the drawer. Early drawers had large dovetails and bottoms of ¾ or ⅞ inch stock set into rabbets in front and sides. Not authentic, but far more practical is the use of ¼ inch plywood for the bottom panel as shown. The drawer runners M are glued and screwed to the sides to fit in the grooved rail assemblies.

Finishing of the table will depend upon the type of wood used but in general, the finish should be of a low luster type; either well rubbed varnish or perhaps one of the penetrating oils such as Watco Danish Oil. Be sure to give the underside of the top the same treatment as the topside. A brass pull similar to the style shown completes the project.

Bill of Materials (All Dims. Actual)			
Part	Description	Size	No. Req'd
A	Foot	2 x 2¾ x 25¼	2
B	Leg	1⅛ x 15½ x 24⅝ (includes tenons)	2
C	Cleat	1⅛ x 2⅜ x 26½	2
D	Outside Rail	1⅛ x 2¾ x 24	2
E	Inside Rail	1⅛ x 2¾ x 21	2
F	Wedges	½ x 2 x 5	2
G	Stretcher	2 x 2½ x 33½ (includes tenons)	1
H	Top	1⅛ x 26½ x 41¼	1
I	Pegs	¾ dia. x 6″ long	4
J	Drawer Front	⅞ x 5½ x 23	1
K	Drawer Back	¾ x 4¾ x 23	1
L	Drawer Side	¾ x 5½ x 18⅛	2
M	Drawer Runner	⅞ x ⅞ x 17	2

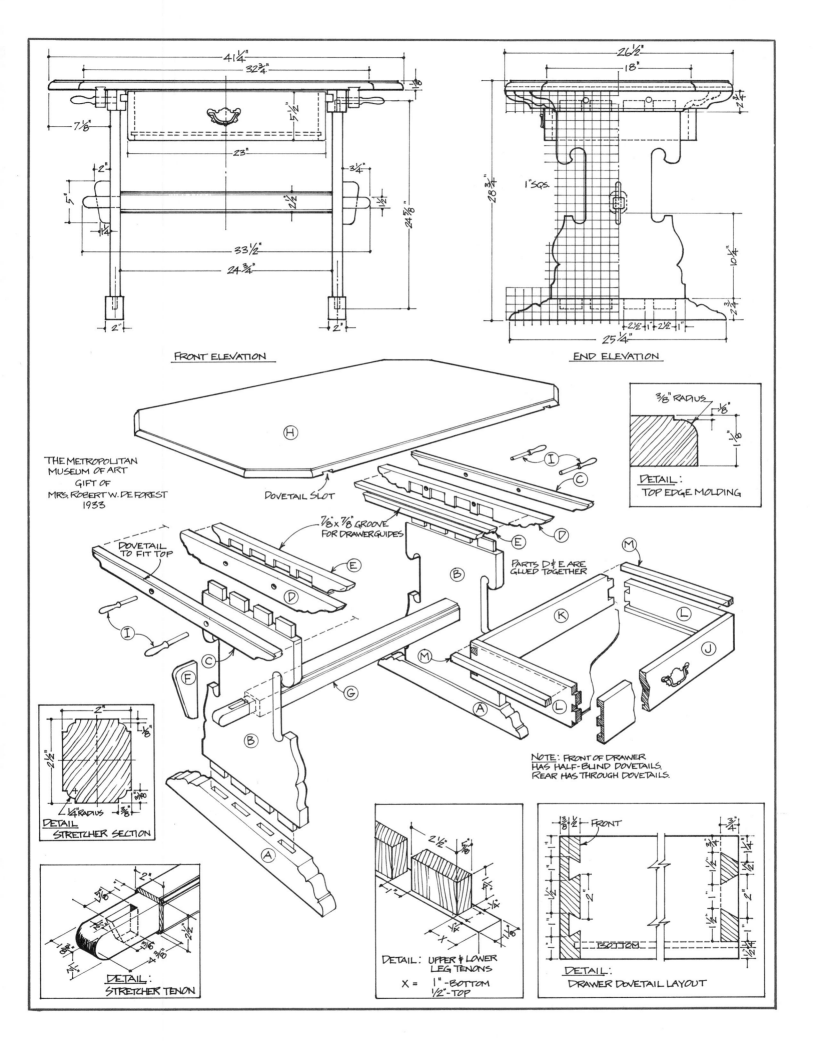

FRONT ELEVATION

END ELEVATION

THE METROPOLITAN
MUSEUM OF ART
GIFT OF
MRS. ROBERT W. DE FOREST
1933

Dovetail Slot

DETAIL:
TOP EDGE MOLDING

3/8" RADIUS

DOVETAIL
TO FIT TOP

7/8 x 7/8 GROOVE
FOR DRAWER GUIDES

PARTS D & E ARE
GLUED TOGETHER

NOTE: FRONT OF DRAWER
HAS HALF-BLIND DOVETAILS.
REAR HAS THROUGH DOVETAILS.

DETAIL
STRETCHER SECTION

1/4 RADIUS

DETAIL:
STRETCHER TENON

DETAIL: UPPER & LOWER
LEG TENONS

X = 1"-BOTTOM
    1/2"-TOP

DETAIL:
DRAWER DOVETAIL LAYOUT

FRONT

BOTTOM

1"SQS.

29

Quilt Rack

by Larry Miller

Photo: John Kane

With today's interest in quilting, there are many households that have several beautiful quilts sitting in storage closets and chests where no one is able to see or appreciate the time and handiwork they represent. The maple quilt rack shown here was developed after my grandmother expressed an interest in having a place to display her beautiful quilts.

From 2″ square stock, turn two spindles to dimensions shown. The two lower rungs (A) are made next, each turned to 1″ dia. from 1⅛″ square stock. Use the parting tool to establish the 24⅞″ length between shoulders, then finish by turning ⅜″ dia. x ¾″ long tenons each end. Using a diamond point chisel, four light cuts will form the decorative bead at the center. Repeat the same techniques to make the upper rung (F), except note that shoulder to shoulder length is 24″, and tenon should be made ½″ dia. x 1″ long. The stretcher (B) can now be made from 1″ (¾″ actual) x 3½″ x 24″ stock.

Next cut the arms (C) and legs (E) from 5/4 x 4″ x 12″ stock. For maximum strength, the grain direction should be the same as the arrows on the drawing. Before assembly apply a ¼″ radius to the exposed edges of arms, legs, and stretcher - then give all parts a thorough sanding. Drill ⅜″ dia. holes in part (C) as shown.

The stretcher (B) is attached to (D) with ⅜″ dowels. Be sure that these dowels do not interfere with dowels that join legs (E). Also, a ½″ dia. hole is drilled in the spindle for (F).

Now attach legs (E) to part (D) with ½″ dowels. To insure that all four legs will sit flat on the floor, take extra care and use a doweling jig when drilling holes. Clamping is difficult because of the lack of parallel flat surfaces, so a clamping jig cut to the shape of the leg should be used. If care is exercised when originally cutting out the arms and legs, the scrap can be used as the clamping jig.

Assemble part (A) to arms (C), then join this sub-assembly to the spindle (D). A clamping jig will also help here.

Final sand the entire project. The finish is your choice, but maple looks beautiful when given at least two coats of Watco Danish Oil finish, then waxed.

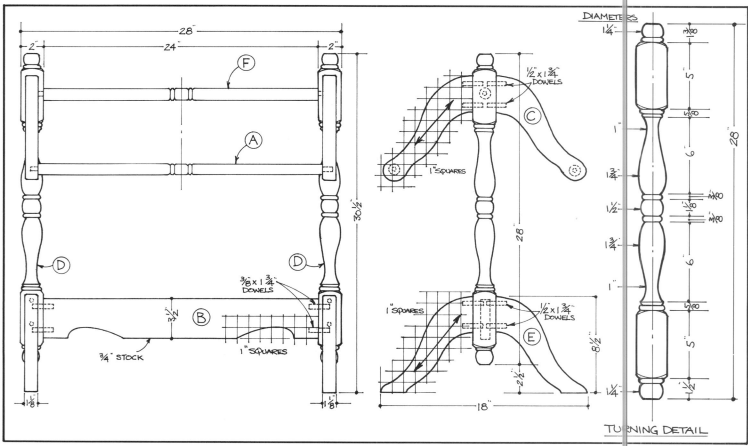

18th Cent. Shelves

The design of this classic piece is based on a colonial original. Solidly constructed from ¾" pine, there are three good size shelves that provide plenty of display area. It's an enjoyable project that will add a handsome look to just about any room in the house.

Make the two sides first, cutting each one to ¾" thick x 5½" wide x 34" long. Standard lumberyard 1 x 6 stock (which actually measures ¾" thick x 5½" wide) can be used here. Lay out and mark the location of the three shelf dadoes, then cut them ¾" wide x ¼" deep. It's best to cut the dadoes slightly less than the ¾" shelf thickness, so that after the shelves are sanded, the fit will be perfect. The dadoes can be cut by making repeated passes with the table or radial saw blade, or by using a dado head cutter. Also, a router will do the job well.

Now, the curves can be transferred from the drawing to the stock. Use a saber saw, bandsaw or coping saw to cut to shape, keeping the sawblade on the waste side of the line.

The shelves can now be cut to length and width, and the front corners nipped off at 45 degrees as shown in the detail. If you wish to use 5½" wide stock throughout, simply make the front edge of the shelf flush with the side curve.

Now sides and shelves can be given a thorough sanding. Make sure any planer marks are removed. Also, especially concentrate on the curved front edges of the sides.

Minwax Early American is a good choice of stain for this project. Apply two coats, let dry, then finish with two coats of satin polyurethane varnish.

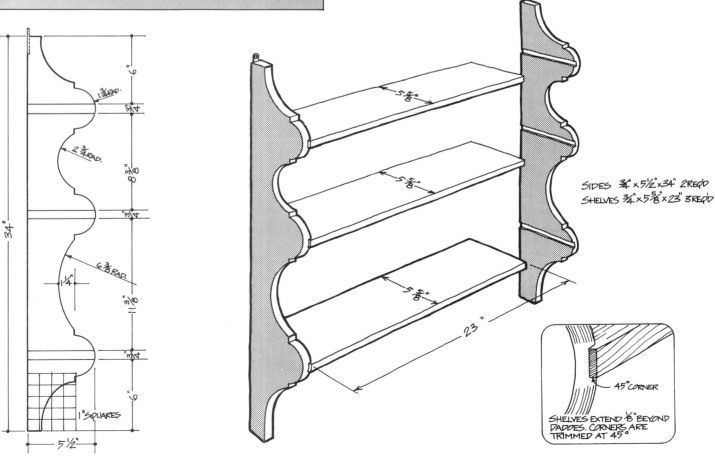

SIDES ¾" x 5½" x 34" 2 REQ'D
SHELVES ¾" x 5⅝" x 23" 3 REQ'D

45° CORNER

SHELVES EXTEND ⅛" BEYOND DADOES. CORNERS ARE TRIMMED AT 45°

Hand Mirror

With pleasing lines and a gracefully curved handle, this stylish mahogany hand mirror will make a most attractive and useful gift.

Start with good flat ¾" stock, about 15" long and at least 7½" wide. Using the grid pattern, lay out and mark the entire profile as shown, then locate and mark the center point of the glass cutout circle. At this center point, drill a ¼" dia. x ¼" deep hole for gluing a ¼" dia. x ½" long dowel pin. This pin will serve as a bearing point for the router to cut a perfect circle.

Use a ¼" dia. straight bit in the router and set for a depth of 3/16" - ¼". We used a Sears router with a base diameter of 6", resulting in a 6½" diameter circle. If your router has a different base diameter, make dimensional changes as necessary.

To make the cut, bear edge of router base against pin and

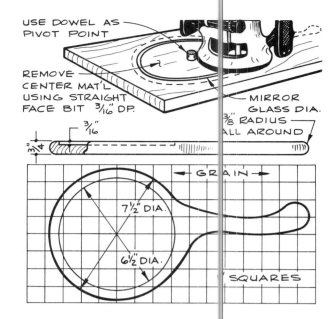

slowly lower bit into the wood. Keep the base firmly against the pin as the router makes the complete circle. Now the pin can be cut flush with surface and the router used free hand to remove the remaining material.

A bandsaw or saber saw will cut the handle and frame profiles. Give edges a good rounding, especially the handle. A complete sanding is essential. Stain if desired, followed by 2 coats polyurethane. Have a glass shop cut a ⅛" mirror to fit, and glue in place with mirror adhesive. Be careful not to use just any adhesive as it may affect the mirror silver.

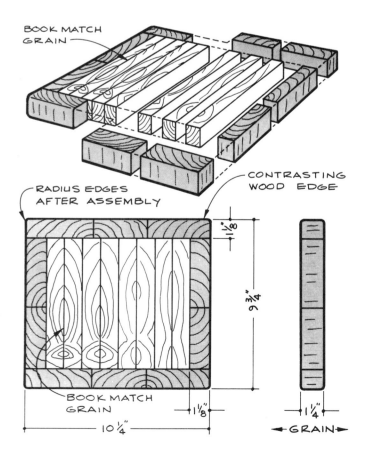

Cutting Boards   by Paul Levine

I make these attractive boards from scrap stock and have found them to be good sellers. Oak, maple, ash, or teak are all suitable wood choices. Cut 1" stock to 7½" wide x 11¼" long. Crosscut the stock into eight 1¼" strips, keeping them in order as cut. The 11¼" length results in a bit of scrap. Each piece will measure 1" x 1¼" x 7½".

To bookmatch the grain, twist the first piece, end-grain up, with a counter-clockwise rotation. Twist the second piece, end-grain up, with a clockwise rotation. Continue until all pieces are end-grain up and matched.

Glue with Elmer's Glue-All. When dry, even edges, then add the end-grain frame. When frame dries, belt sand surfaces flush. Further sand by hand, ending with 320 grit paper. Apply Salad Bowl Finish, available from Woodcraft Supply, 41 Atlantic Ave., P.O. Box 4000, Woburn, MA 01888.

Tic-Tac-Toe

Tic-Tac-Toe enthusiasts will like this one. With a mahogany playing board and small drawer for storing the playing pieces, it makes a rather unique set - one that should sell well at craft fairs and gift shops.

Make the mitered base first. You'll need about a 25" length of ¾" thick x 1" wide mahogany stock. Cut the mitered corners, then use the dado cutter to cut ¼" deep x 3½" wide step. Apply glue and clamp (several elastic bands make a good clamp).

After cutting the two sides and back, start work on the ½ x 6 x 6 top. Lay out the location of the horizontal and vertical lines as shown. Now, set up your router with a ⅛" dia. straight bit (set for a ⅛" deep cut) and a guide plate. Adjust the guide plate to locate the grooves as shown, then make the cut, stopping ¾" in from the edge. Drill holes as shown, adding a slight chamfer to each one.

The playing pieces are ¾" dia. dowel stock cut ¾" long. The "X's" are stained dark, the "O's" left natural.

Assemble with glue and small finishing nails. For a final finish we applied two coats of pure tung oil.

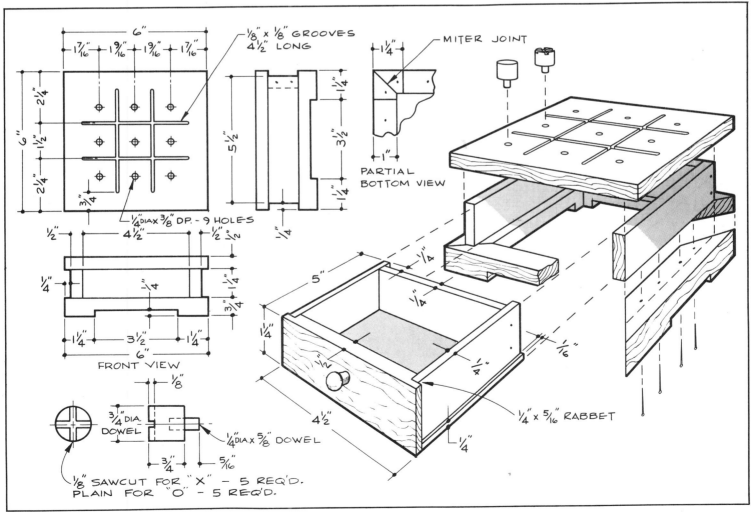

1/8" x 1/8" GROOVES 4 1/2" LONG

MITER JOINT

PARTIAL BOTTOM VIEW

1/4" DIA x 3/8" DP - 9 HOLES

FRONT VIEW

3/4" DIA. DOWEL

1/4" DIA. x 5/8" DOWEL

1/8" SAWCUT FOR "X" - 5 REQ'D.
PLAIN FOR "O" - 5 REQ'D.

1/4" x 5/16" RABBET

Vanity

by Robert A. McCoy

Did you ever finish a project and wonder what to do with the small pieces of stock that are left over? You may be surprised to learn that this lovely vanity was built using not much more than just such scrap parts. It's an enjoyable project to build — for yourself, as a gift, or for sale. We keep ours on top of a chest of drawers, using it as a dressing mirror and to accommodate an assortment of watches, tie tacks, combs, rings, keys, and other small items.

Construction is well within the capability of the beginner of quality woodworking. The drawing shows almost all joints to be dowels. Advanced woodworkers may prefer to make other types of joints but the vanity has little strain so dowel joints are adequate. Woods suggested are the common cabinet hardwoods — walnut, cherry, birch, maple or other suitable hardwood. All stock is surfaced to ¾" except for the 1⅛" center drawer front, the ½" feet, and the ¼" back panel. It is much easier to lay out the curved pieces on paper or light cardboard than to work directly on the wood.

Begin by cutting the top and bottom of the base unit to size (¾ x 8 x 20 for the top, ¾ x 8 x 18½ for the bottom). Referring to Fig. 3, lay out and mark the serpentine pattern, then cut out with a band saw or saber saw. After cutting the drawer dividers and base sides to size, lay out and bore all dowel holes. Use a doweling jig to drill one hole, then locate the matching hole with center markers. Use care to avoid cutting through the top. A brad point wood bit, which has a short spur point, will be useful here. Now, a ¼" x ¼" rabbet for the back panel can be cut in the top, bottom, and ends.

Give all parts a thorough sanding before assembling for a dry fit. When satisfied that everything fits, glue and clamp the unit together. Remember that the drawer dividers are set ¼" in from the back in order to accept the back panel.

To make the feet, lay out the pattern as per Fig. 4, then cut to shape and apply a ¼" radius routed cove as shown. To get the two front feet, measure in 2½" from each end and cut off. To get the back feet, measure 1¾" from each side of the centerline and cut off. Sand, glue, and clamp to the base.

To make the drawers, refer to the exploded view and to Fig. 5. Don't cut the drawer front curves until after the drawers are assembled. Slide assembled drawer units into the base, then use the curved base front as a template and transfer the curves to the top edge of the drawer front. Use a band saw to cut out the curves. Now, with drawers in place, sand all curved front surfaces.

A drum sander will also be helpful here.

The mirror unit poses no difficult problems. All pieces are cut according to the templates and the mirror frame is assembled first. The mirror frame is made from three pieces which must be fitted carefully with 5/16" dowels. Make a dry assembly to be sure everything fits. When satisfied, clamp using a band or web clamp. If these clamps are not available, place a clamp tightly on each side of the joint and clamp against the two clamps.

Now use a router with a ¼" rabbeting bit to cut a ¼" x 11/32" deep rabbet all around for the mirror glass. Also, a ¼" rounding over bit can be used to round the front edges as shown. The arms that hold the mirror frame are sanded and rounded over using the same bit.

Lay the mirror frame, and the arms that will hold it together, on a flat surface and adjust the pieces so that there is no more than 1/16" clearance where they are joined together. A brass washer will fill this space when assembled. Measure the distance between the arms at the base and cut the stretcher that joins them. (The drawing shows a half-lap joint but a mortise and tenon or dowel joint may be substituted). If you have been very accurate so far it should measure the

same as the drawing indicates. If not, a slight adjustment may be necessary. The two arms can now be glued to the stretcher. After the glue has dried, lay the pieces together and locate where the threaded inserts are to be placed, then drill a hole through each arm for the threaded knob shaft.

Now drill a hole in the mirror frame (in line with the arm hole) for the threaded insert. These inserts are available from the Brookstone Co., 127 Vose Farm Rd., Peterborough, NH 03458. A wooden knob can be epoxied to an 8-32 threaded rod.

A glass shop will cut the ⅛" mirror to shape. It is held in place with ¼" plywood (5/32") tacked to the frame with brads or screws.

Final sand all surfaces of both the base and mirror frame. Most of the good cabinet woods do not require a stain; however if a stain is desired it should be done at this time. Some woods finish better if a filler is used, oak for example.

The choice of finishes is a matter of personal taste, but if a nice grained wood is used a clear finish is recommended. I generally prefer a clear polyurethane finish which, when properly done, produces a smooth hard finish which wears well and is easy to maintain.

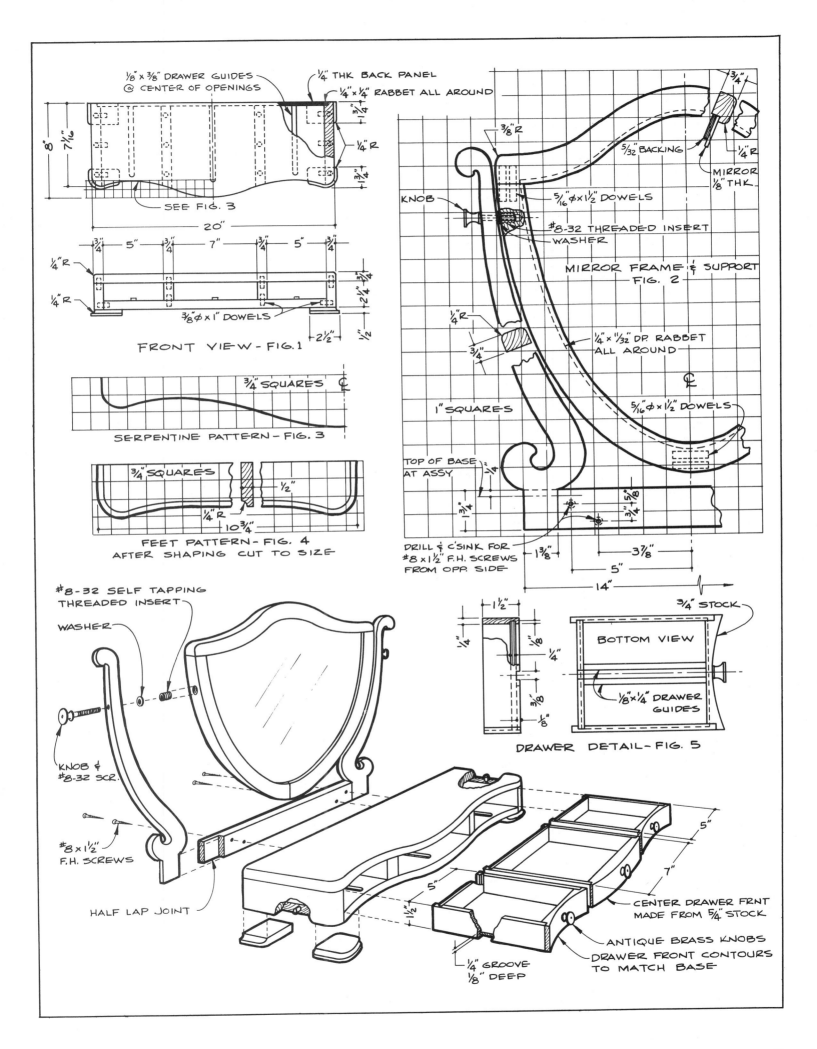

⅛" x ⅜" DRAWER GUIDES
@ CENTER OF OPENINGS

¼" THK BACK PANEL

¼" x ¼" RABBET ALL AROUND

8"

7 1/16"

¾"

¼" R

¾"

SEE FIG. 3

20"

¾" 5" ¾" 7" ¾" 5" ¾"

¼" R

¼" R

2¼" ¾" ¼"

½"

⅜" Ø x 1" DOWELS

2½"

FRONT VIEW - FIG. 1

¾" SQUARES

SERPENTINE PATTERN - FIG. 3

¾" SQUARES

½"

¼" R

10 ¾"

FEET PATTERN - FIG. 4
AFTER SHAPING CUT TO SIZE

¾"

⅜" R

5/32" BACKING

¾"

¼" R

MIRROR
⅛" THK.

KNOB

5/16" Ø x 1½" DOWELS

#8-32 THREADED INSERT

WASHER

MIRROR FRAME & SUPPORT
FIG. 2

¼" R

¾"

¼" x 11/32" DP. RABBET
ALL AROUND

1" SQUARES

5/16" Ø x 1½" DOWELS

TOP OF BASE
AT ASSY

¼"

¾"

3" 5/8"
¼"

DRILL & C'SINK FOR
#8 x 1½" F.H. SCREWS
FROM OPP. SIDE

1 ⅜"

3 ⅞"

5"

14"

#8-32 SELF TAPPING
THREADED INSERT

WASHER

KNOB &
#8-32 SCR.

#8 x 1½"
F.H. SCREWS

HALF LAP JOINT

1½"

¼"

1"

¼"

3/8"

1/8"

¾" STOCK

BOTTOM VIEW

⅛" x ¼" DRAWER
GUIDES

DRAWER DETAIL - FIG. 5

5"

7"

5"

½"

¼" GROOVE
⅛" DEEP

CENTER DRAWER FRNT
MADE FROM 5/4 STOCK

ANTIQUE BRASS KNOBS

DRAWER FRONT CONTOURS
TO MATCH BASE

Pine Shaker Cupboard

Many elements of fine Shaker design can be found in this charming pine cupboard. Although not an exact reproduction, our plans are based on an authentic Shaker piece — and we have made only minor dimensional and construction changes. For example, the top molding on the original was probably cut using several special molding planes. To reproduce it, we revised the design slightly to permit the use of standard moldings. The result is an unusual and attractive detail that is reasonably easy to make.

Our method of applying beading to the door rails and stiles is also a bit unusual in that it results in a mitered bead. Normally this is not easy to do, at least not with a molding head cutter, but we managed to work out a technique that makes the operation fairly simple.

A project like this looks best if knots are kept to a minimum, especially in front, so choose your pine carefully. If possible, select door panel stock that has pleasing wood figure. Notice ours is cut so that the figure is centered on the panel, and that the lower panel is a continuation of the upper one. Of course, there's no hard and fast rule that says you must do it this way, but we do feel it can add a great deal of interest to a piece.

Start construction by edge-joining enough stock to take care of two sides (B), four shelves (C), and the top (E). Two or three boards will have to be joined to get the needed width.

The front pieces (A) are cut to length and width, then mortised for a ⅜" thick x 1½" wide x 1¼" long tenon. Cut the leg curve, then use a Sears Craftsman, ¼" 3-bead molding

head cutter (No. 9-2352) to apply a bead along the outside edge. Part D is now cut 2½" wide x 14½" long, including the ⅜" thick x 1½" wide x 1¼" long tenons on each end.

Make the frame-and-panel door next. Note that steps 1 - 4 summarize the method used to cut the mitered rails. If you don't have a molding head cutter, you can still produce the effect of a panel beading. Simply cut the panel (part K) rabbet about ⅞" wide. This extra room provides a place to glue a ¼" half-round molding around the panel. For a clean look, be sure to miter the corners of the molding.

To bead the panels as we did, refer to the bill of materials and cut door stiles (G) and rails (H, I, and J) to overall length and width (rail length includes tenons). Now, noting the door rail tenon details, cut tenons as shown, then use the molding head cutter to apply a ¼" bead (step 1) on parts G, H, I, and J as shown. Next, a ¼" wide x ⅜" deep groove (step 2) is routed along the same parts. Notice that the groove does not extend along the entire length of part G, but rather is stopped short to keep the groove from running out the ends.

Use a miter square with a 45-degree angle (step 3) to lay out the 5/16" miter cuts on the rails, then cut out on the waste side of the line with a backsaw. To insure a perfect 45-degree angle, construct the jig as shown (step 4). Locate the jig exactly on the miter line and use a sharp chisel to pare excess stock.

Lay rails (H, I, and J) in position on parts G. Using the rails as templates, mark the exact location of the mortise and miter cuts on parts G. Cut the mortises first, then use the backsaw and chisel to remove most of the miter cutout. Now, again use the special jig to pare the miter.

Select panel stock (K) and cut to size, then form a ¼" x ½" rabbet around the edge. After giving all parts a complete sanding, the door can be assembled with glue and clamps. It's most important that the door be both square and flat, so pre-assemble the parts and check it over. After gluing and clamping, check it once again, and make adjustments as necessary.

After a thorough sanding, the rest of the cabinet can be assembled. The shelves are glued in dadoes and further secured with two countersunk wood screws. Use plugs to cover holes. Attach the back with screws driven into the shelves. Glue and finishing nails, countersunk and filled, hold the top and the top molding to the carcase.

Final sand all parts, then stain to suit. We used two coats of Minwax Provincial wood stain, followed by two coats of Minwax Antique Oil finish.

Bill of Materials	(All Dimensions Actual)		
Part	Description	Size	No. Req'd
A	Front	¾ x 4 x 51	2
B	Side	¾ x 14¼ x 51	2
C	Shelf	¾ x 13½ x 19	4
D	Case Rail	¾ x 2½ x 14½ (inc. 1¼" long tenons)	1
E	Top	¾ x 14¼ x 19¼	1
F	Back	¾ x 9⅝ x 45⅛	2
G	Stile	¾ x 2½ x 43	2
H	Top Rail	¾ x 3 x 10⅛ (includes tenons)	1
I	Center Rail	¾ x 5 x 10⅛ (includes tenons)	1
J	Lower Rail	¾ x 4 x 10⅛ (includes tenons)	1
K	Panel	½ x 7⅝ x 16⅛	2

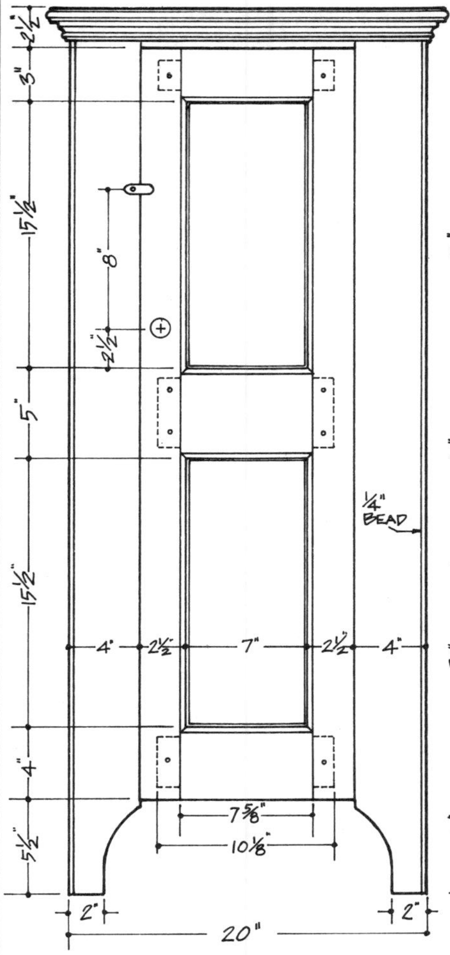
2½"
3"
15½"
8"
2½"
5"
15½"
4"
5½"
4" 2½" 7" 2½" 4"
¼" BEAD
7⅝"
10⅛"
2" 2"
20"

FRONT ELEVATION

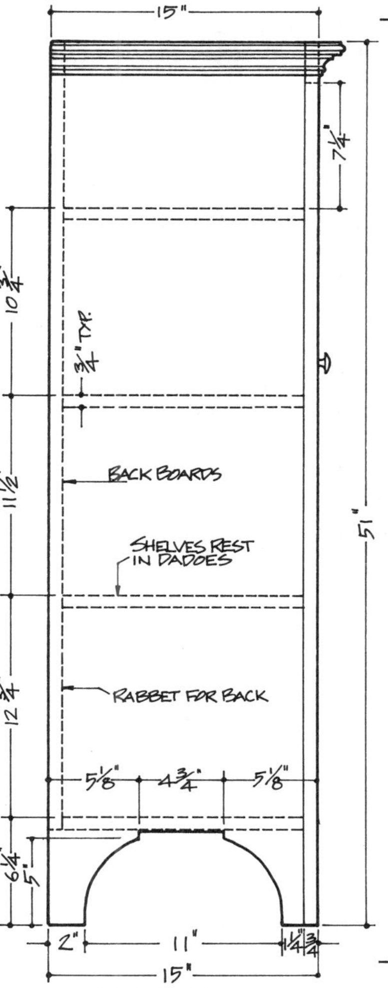
15"
7¼"
10¾"
¾" TYP.
BACK BOARDS
11½"
SHELVES REST IN DADOES
51"
RABBET FOR BACK
12¾"
5⅛" 4¾" 5⅛"
6¼"
5"
2" 11" 1¼ ¾
15"

SIDE ELEVATION

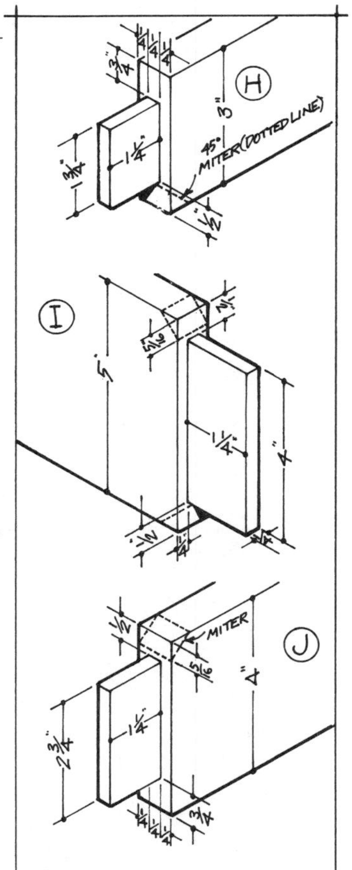
H
45° MITER (DOTTED LINE)
I
J
MITER

DETAILS:
DOOR RAIL TENONS
(GROOVES & MOULDING CUTS NOT SHOWN)

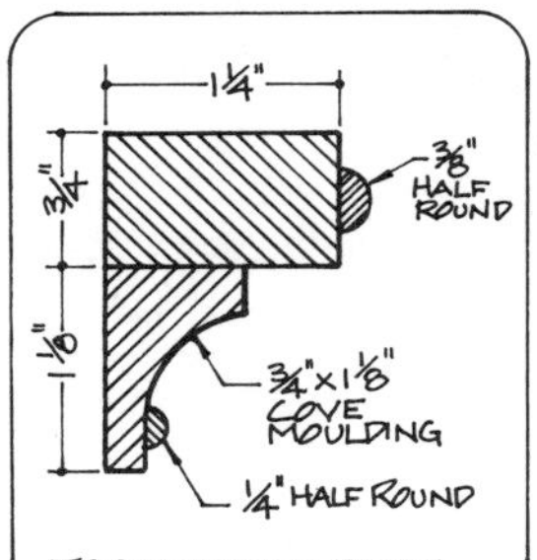
1¼"
⅜" HALF ROUND
¾" x 1⅛" COVE MOULDING
¼" HALF ROUND

TOP MOULDING DETAIL

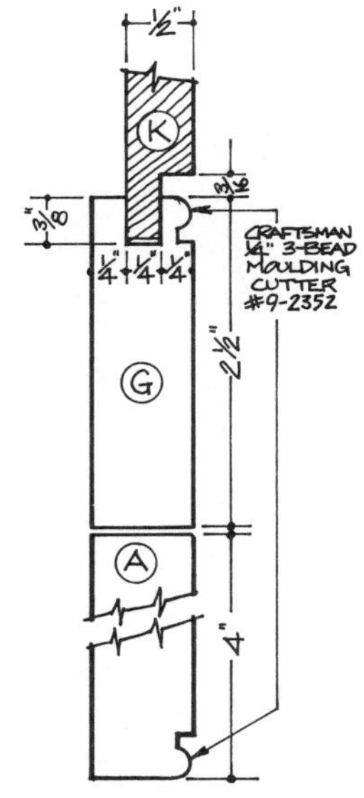
½"
K
CRAFTSMAN ¼" 3-BEAD MOULDING CUTTER #9-2352
G
2½"
A
4"

SECTION THRU STILES AND DOOR PANEL

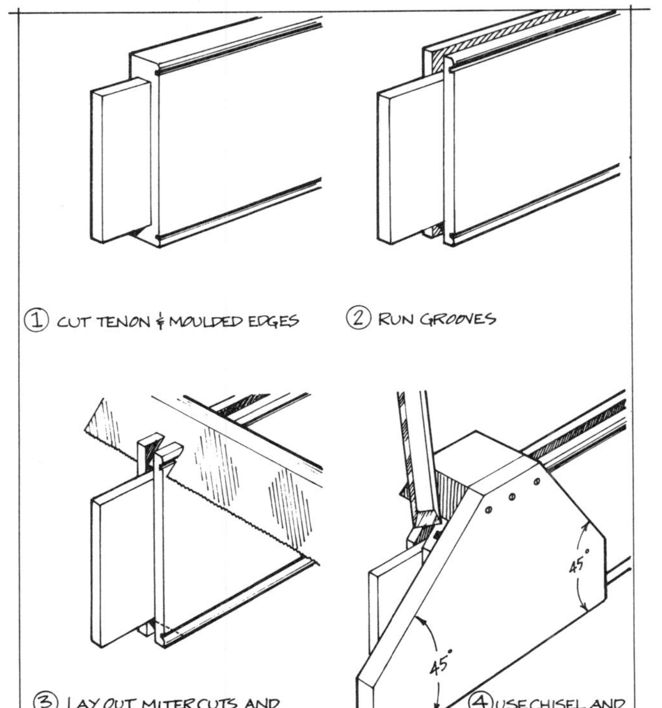
① CUT TENON & MOULDED EDGES
② RUN GROOVES
③ LAY OUT MITER CUTS AND CUT ON WASTE SIDE OF LINES WITH BACKSAW.
④ USE CHISEL AND JIG TO PARE MITER.
45°
45°

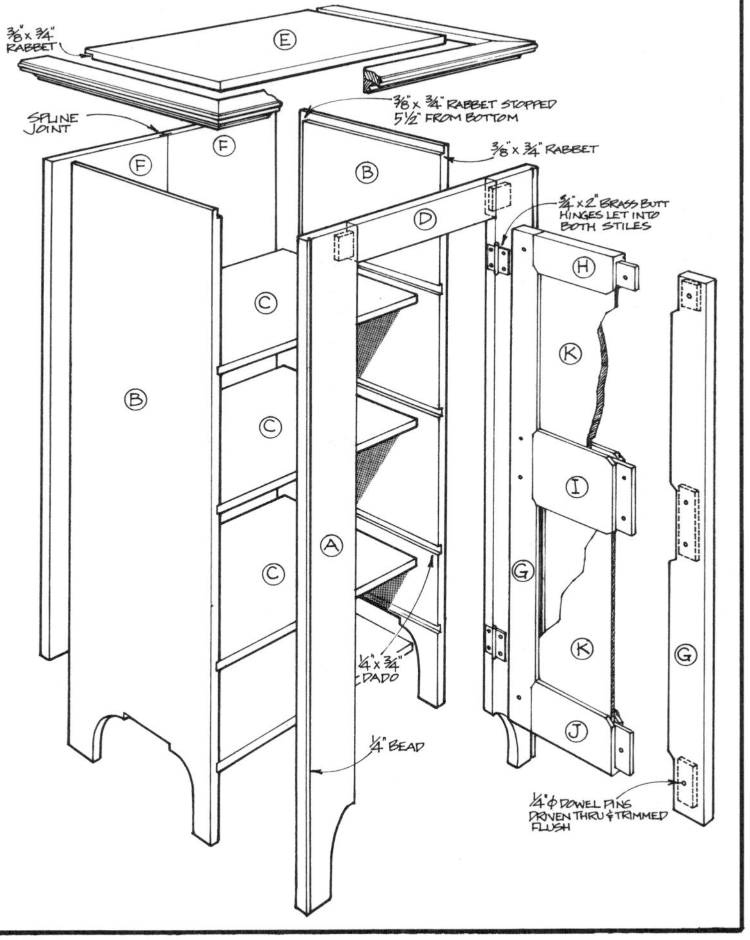
⅜" x ¾" RABBET
E
⅜" x ¾" RABBET STOPPED 5½" FROM BOTTOM
SPLINE JOINT
F
B
⅜" x ¾" RABBET
D
¾" x 2" BRASS BUTT HINGES LET INTO BOTH STILES
H
C
K
I
A
G
¼" x ¾" DADO
J
¼" BEAD
¼" ϕ DOWEL PINS DRIVEN THRU & TRIMMED FLUSH

Contemporary Cabinet

by Paul Levine

I love wood. Its great strength and beauty give me a feeling of warmth. I enjoy being in a room of wooden objects, wooden paneling, and wood floors.

Over the years each different species of wood that I've worked has shown me its own personality. Some are sweet smelling and tasting, like cherry and vermillion, some are very clean working, and finish very smooth and pleasant to the touch, like birch and maple. Then again, some woods are ornery like zebra and African rosewood.

When I look at a board laying in a pile, I will sometimes see irregularities in the grain that produce a striking appearance. To me these boards beg to be made into furniture.

Such was the case one day when I saw the mineral stains in a maple board. I took the board home and resawed it, and bookmatched it into two panels. These panels sat in my shop for months until I decided what wood to use for the frame, and what type of cabinet to build around them.

In this cabinet the frame for the maple panels, the carcase, and the stand are African rosewood. The reveals, or feet are ebony. The lines of

this cabinet are simple and straight-forward and the woodwork is completely unornamented, with the exception of the exposed dovetails. The construction involves frame and panel, for the doors and back; through dovetails, for the carcase; and mortise and tenon, for the frames and stand. I originally intended to make four small drawers for the inside but later decided to leave the open pigeon holes.

Before plywood became available, and before modern glues, large solid areas were created using frame and panel construction. Horizontal rails, and vertical stiles were joined together using a variety of mortise and tenon joints, to create frames. The empty spaces in this lattice would then be filled in using thin panels.

Often the frame became a showcase for unusually attractive panels. Butt, crotch, stump, and burls were resawed, or veneered, and sometimes matched into panels. Today if you wish to utilize any of these you will have to find them and dry them yourself but the results you will get are worth it. If you wish to use dry lumber that has an interesting figure for panels, you still have many choices.

Maple frequently has mineral

stains, many from sugaring and worms. There are many varieties of two toned woods that will provide interesting color patterns when flat sawn, like ash, apple, cherry and pear.

To resaw boards for panels a band saw is the best machine. For narrow panels you can use a table saw. If you don't have either of these machines you can still make the panels. If you saw the wood when it is still green it will be much easier to work, and you can use a log saw. Since the panels are usually short, 18" to 30", this is really not much work. The disadvantage here is that you will not see the dried down colors, and you will have to wait until the pieces dry before you can work them. They may warp, and you may end up having to resaw them again.

If you dry the wood first, the job of resawing on these short lengths is still not a very big one. Great care must be taken, even with kiln dried wood, to let the resawn pieces reach equilibrium before you incorporate them into a piece of furniture. If your shop is dry and the wood is wet, when you open up the board it will curl towards the fresh sawn side. On the other hand if you buy kiln dried hardwood, and your shop is damp the outside of the board will pick up some moisture before sawing, and then when you resaw the inside will take on moisture, and the wood will curl away from the fresh sawn side.

Don't lay these panels down ever again. Since they are thin even small changes in shop humidity can cause a board that only has one side exposed to warp.

The panels can be used directly in frames. If you wish to bookmatch them before making up the door, joint the edge to be matched with a jointer or plane, and butt joint them. With today's adhesives this will be a strong joint, and more than adequate for the load. I clamp the joint up tight and make sure that it is clamped on both sides (with pipe clamps) to prevent the pressure from warping the panel, i.e. buckling up or down.

After the glue is dry take off the clamps and scrape off the excess glue. Plane the panel down with a hand plane or again on the jointer. If you choose a highly decorative wood for the panel it's best to leave the frame plain. I rabbeted the edges of the panels to fit into grooves in the frame so that the panel surfaces would be just slightly lower than the frames. This was done so that the frame could contain this wild pattern.

The frames should be given the same attention as the panels. If you choose an interesting pattern for the panel play down the grain in the frame. I chose rosewood because it picked up the colors in the panel. The top and the bottom rails are one continuous piece. The stiles are resawn pieces so that their grain matches exactly. Note that rails are ⅛ inch thicker than stiles.

After I made the frames and assembled the doors dry, I left them to stand at one end of my shop for a few more months. In this manner I let the doors grow on me. Several times I switched the panels from one frame to the other, or turned them upside down. When I finally decided upon the correct (for me) orientation of the panels and frames, the design of the whole cabinet had grown in my mind. I let the doors determine the rest of the cabinet because they are such a strong element. The job of the rest of the cabinet is to frame, support, and contain the doors.

The joints on the frames for the doors are slip joints, which are very easy to make. Although there are other stronger versions of the mortise and tenon joint, this one is quick and very forgiving.

I cut the slip joint on the band saw. I first cut the open mortises on the rail stock, leaving the stock ⅛" longer than final measure so that I can sand them flush. I regulate the depth of cut with a stop block behind the blade. As with almost every machine joint I cut, I make a trial cut first. If the measurements are just what I want them to be, I cut up the stock. Next come the tenon cuts on the stiles. Again I will make trial cuts, first for depth, and then for the width of the tenon. When the tenon will just fit in the open mortise with hand pressure only, I cut up the tenons.

The frame can be assembled to check for fit, and appearance. If you have cut a tenon too big for the open mortise, you can use a plane or a chisel to pare it down to a snug fit. If the tenon is too small, cut a piece of veneer and glue it onto the tenon with the grains parallel.

After the frame joints are corrected groove the inside of the rails and stiles to receive the panels. This can be done with a plane or a router. The grooves should be carried on to the tenons for a distance of about ⅜" from the shoulders or just take a ⅜" square notch out of each tenon to provide clearance for panel corners. The groove for the panel should provide for a very small amount of clearance at the top and bottom. Theoretically if the expansion rates for the frame wood and the panel wood are the same no extra is necessary. Leave about 1/16" for ease of fit. The rate of expansion on most domestic hardwoods is 1/10 of a percent for length only. That is to say for an 18" hardwood panel to go from green to dry the shrinkage will be only about 1/64".

On the other hand the rate of expansion or contraction of most domestic hardwoods across the grain is about 4% for radial shrinkage, to 10-12% for tangential shrinkage. That means a panel of about 12" in width will shrink almost 1¼" going from green to dry.

This translates into an allowance of about ⅛" on each side of each panel allowing for as much as 20% change in humidity. The wood will not change as fast as the atmosphere. For the wood to adjust fully to a 20% change it would take at least six months.

The doors can now be assembled with glue; remember however not to glue the panel into the frame. The panel must be allowed to expand into the deep groove provided for it without tearing the frame apart. If you put one drop of glue at the top center and bottom center of each panel it will suffice to hold the panel in place and stop it from rattling.

In setting out to finalize your design for the cabinet, you should allow for some trimming down of the doors to fit the space. On these doors I allowed 1/16".

The back of the cabinet is also of frame and panel construction, however the rails and stiles are of equal thickness. For the back there is one continuous frame across with a middle stile, called a muntin. If the frames were to contain glass panels, these stiles would be called mullions. This muntin is mortised at the ends, and fits over notches or dadoes cut on each side of the rails. The panels are thicker than those of the door and are made of African rosewood, book-matched and jointed.

For the top, bottom and sides of the carcase solid slabs were used. The pieces are chosen from straight grained flat stock, and then are jointed and planed. The top and the bottom are wider than the sides so that they overhang the doors, and further reinforce the containment of the panels.

The carcase pieces are rabbeted in the back to receive the back frame. Housings, or grooves across the grain are made to receive the partitions. The carcase is then dovetailed together. The carcase should be glued face up on a flat surface, and care should be taken to see that the bottom, top, and sides are square. If they are not square you can square it up by shifting the clamps.

Let the glue dry in all of these assemblies thoroughly, before any further machining. The back panel may be glued in place (that is the frame and panel assembly). The doors can now be fitted to the front of the cabinet. The hinges used here are straight brass knife hinges. You will have to predrill all screw holes. In African rosewood the screw holes will have to be larger than usual or you will twist off the heads of the screws in this very dense wood.

The stand can now be built and using the dimensions of the cabinet, continue the line of the edges straight down to the floor. It was a common practice with Shaker furniture to have the outside edge of the tapered legs plumb. Taper the two inner edges as shown in the drawings. The stand is

(continued on next page)

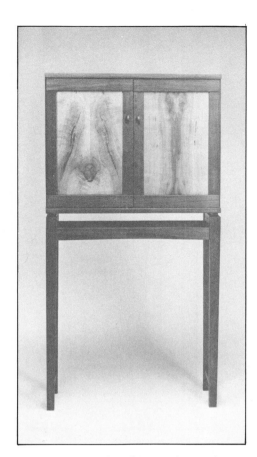

Front view of cabinet shows book-matched panels of doors.

Rear view displays framed panels of book-matched rosewood. Note that, unlike doors, stiles run from top to bottom with rails butting against them.

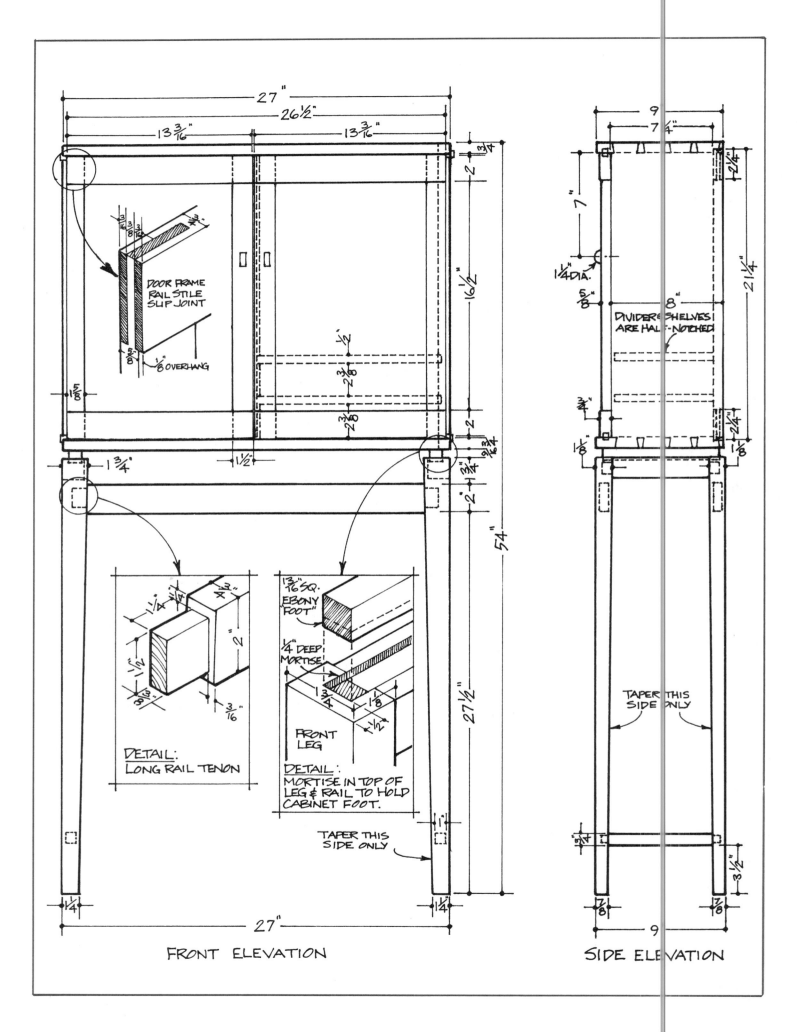

27"

26½"

13 3/16"   13 3/16"

3/4

2

DOOR FRAME
RAIL STILE
SLIP JOINT

3/16 3/8 3/4

1/8 OVERHANG

5/8

1/8

16½"

1/2

2 3/80

2 3/80

1½"

3/4
9/64

3/4
2

2

54"

1 3/4"

DETAIL:
LONG RAIL TENON

1/4

1/4

3/4

2

1/2

3/8

3/16

13/16" SQ.
EBONY
FOOT"

1/4" DEEP
MORTISE!

3/4   1 1/8

1/2

FRONT
LEG

DETAIL:
MORTISE IN TOP OF
LEG & RAIL TO HOLD
CABINET FOOT.

27½"

1/4   1/4

1"

TAPER THIS
SIDE ONLY

27"

FRONT ELEVATION

9

7 1/4"

2 1/4

7"

1/4 DIA.

5/8

8"

DIVIDER & SHELVES
ARE HALF-NOTCHED

3/4

21½"

2 1/4

1/8   1/8

2 1/4

TAPER THIS
SIDE ONLY

3/4

3 1/2"

7/8   7/8

9

SIDE ELEVATION

assembled with mortise and tenon joints.

You can cut your tenons using a router, band saw, table saw, or by hand. I used a radial arm saw with a stopping block to cut the single tenons, and the band saw to cut the double tenons. The mortises were made by drilling a line of holes to the correct depth and then finishing up with a mallet and chisel.

For ease in transporting, I attached the case to the stand with four screws through the top side rails of the stand. Driving screws in rosewood and ebony is not easy even with oversize pilot holes. Use #10 2¼″ sheet metal screws. These screws are hardened and can bite without breaking. An alternative, as shown in the drawings, is to use hardwood dowel pins glued into the bottom of the case and through the ebony feet.

My choice for a finish was influenced by the desire to let the full natural beauty of the wood make itself apparant to both the senses of sight and touch. For that reason, I chose to use a penetrating oil of the synthetic resin type rather than a surface finish such as urethane varnish.

Several coats were initially applied; each being allowed to soak in for about five minutes before wiping off the excess. After the final coat had dried for a couple of days, I gave the piece a rubdown with 4/0 steel wool to even out the soft sheen.

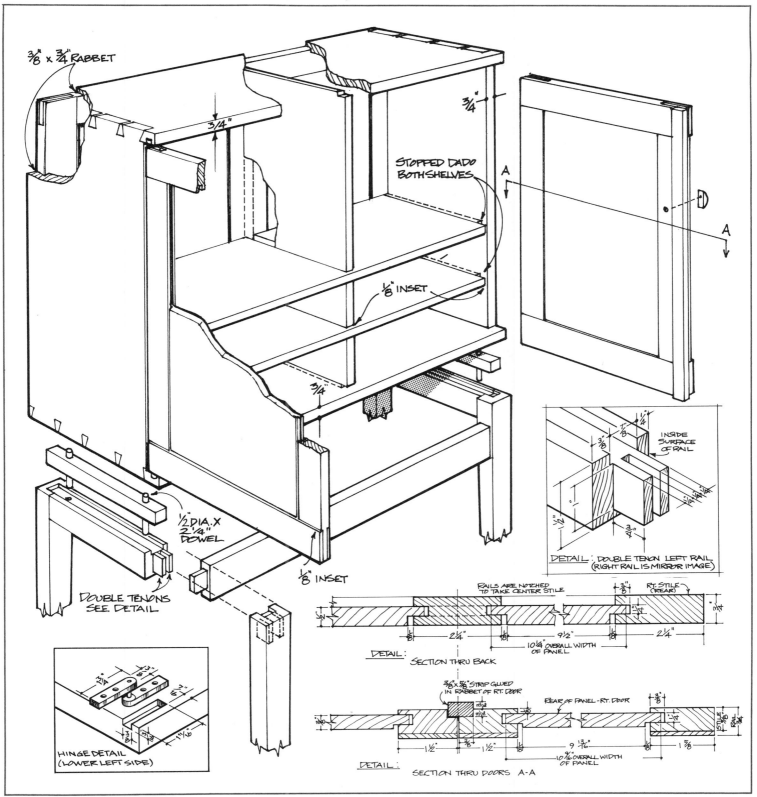

Black Forest Clock
by Roger E. Schroeder

dark or close-grained wood such as walnut or cherry could be substituted. I used a single piece that measured 12 inches wide so no glue joints would show. Having sketched the design on a piece of tracing paper, I transferred it to the wood with carbon paper. Only one side of the front need be sketched since the design is symmetrical and the tracing paper can be reversed, allowing the design to be duplicated on the opposite side.

A saber or jig saw will be needed for cutting the front out and a band saw will facilitate many of the cuts. Before carving, take a router and run it with a ½ inch round-over bit around the dial and pendulum opening.

I'm a strong proponent of Swiss-made carving tools. The steel is not brittle and it holds an edge better than any other. However, I do recommend frequent stropping on a piece of leather during the carving.

Outlining the leaves can be accomplished with a V-parting tool. This can also be used to give a slight undercut to the leaves for effect. The areas around the leaves can be reduced in depth using a #3 gouge. The leaf veins and crosshatched lines can also be done with the veiner.

To give more delicacy to the leaves, I removed wood on the reverse side of the front up to where the case would hold it, leaving between ¼ and ⅜ inch of wood.

Handmade dovetails are not as difficult to make as they look and make for an attractive case. Refer to the side section view for the dovetail dimensions and layout.

After the sides, top, and bottom have been cut and joined, triangular glue blocks are glued to the four inside corners of the case. Four roundhead wood screws are used to secure the carved front to the glue blocks. Properly locate and tack the dial face to the ¼" thick dial board, then tack the dial board to the back of the carved front.

A router is used to cut a ¼" x ¼" rabbet for the back panel. Square the rounded corners with a straight chisel. The ¼" thick back panel can now be cut to size.

Now put the movement in place and secure it with the center nut. After adding a "C" sized battery, the back panel can be put in place with screws on back blocks. A hanger is mortised into the back of the case to complete the assembly.

Final finish consisted of an application of brown mahogany paste filler. For best results, follow the manufacturer's directions for both the preparation and use of the filler. Following this, I applied several coats of pure tung oil, rubbing down the final coat with a clean, soft cloth.

Made of mahogany, this impressive looking clock features a case joined with hand cut dovetails and a front carved with an oak leaf and fruit motif. The result is a unique wall piece — one that can be enjoyed for many generations to come.

The dial, hands, and a quartz battery operated pendulum movement are all available from Klockit, P.O. Box 629, Lake Geneva, WI 53147. For the movement, order part no. 11904. Specify part no. 66953 for the hands, which are included free with the movement order. The movement comes complete with a 14" long brushed brass pendulum and bob. While the dial face shown is no longer available, a similar dial face is Klockit's no. 26129.

It's best to begin by carving the front of the clock. Though a South American mahogany was used, another

Bill of Materials	(All Dimensions Actual)	
Description	Size	No. Req'd
Case Side	¾ x 4¾ x 20	2
Case Top	¾ x 4¾ x 8¼	1
Case Bottom	¾ x 4¾ x 8¼	1
Case Back	¼ x 7¼ x 19	1
Corner Block	1½ x 1½ x ¾	4
Dial Board	¼ x 6¾ x 7	1
Carved Front	13/16 x 11 x 20	1
Movement & Pendulum	Klockit #11904	1
Hands	Klockit #66953 black	Pair
Dial	Klockit #26129	1

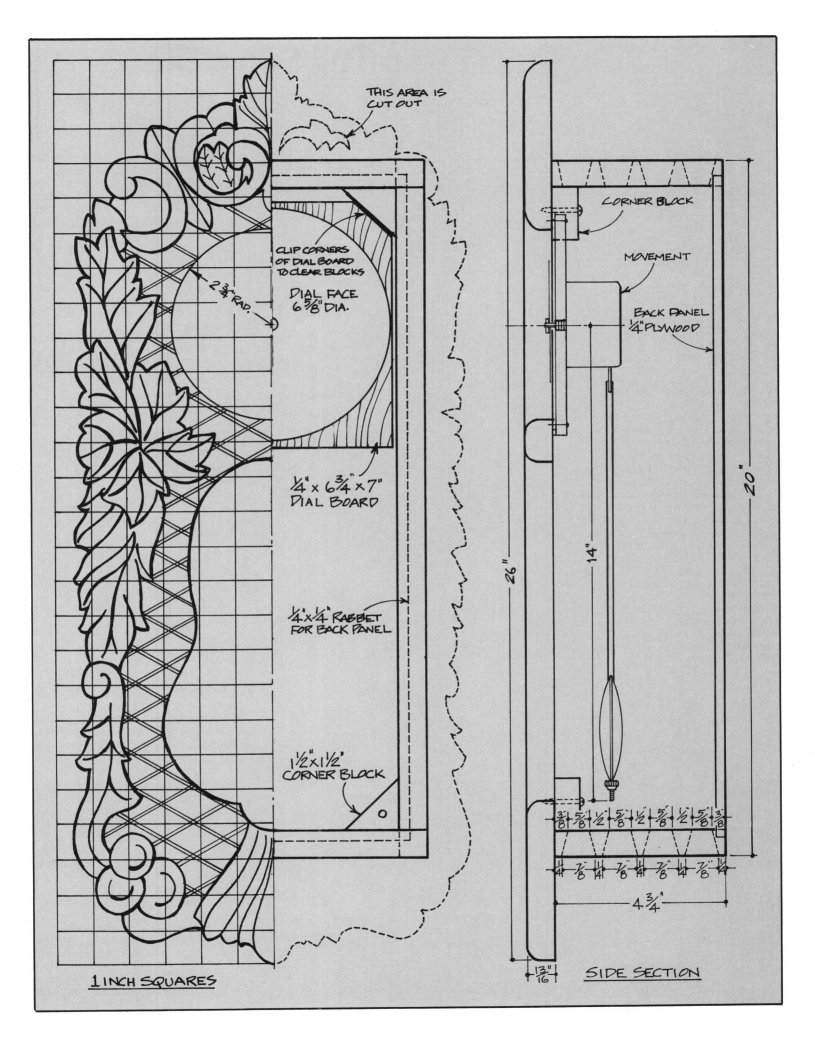

THIS AREA IS CUT OUT

CLIP CORNERS OF DIAL BOARD TO CLEAR BLOCKS

DIAL FACE 6⅝" DIA.

2¾" RAD.

¼" x 6¾" x 7" DIAL BOARD

¼"x ¼" RABBET FOR BACK PANEL

1½"x1½" CORNER BLOCK

1 INCH SQUARES

SIDE SECTION

CORNER BLOCK

MOVEMENT

BACK PANEL ¼" PLYWOOD

26"

14"

20"

³⁄₈" ⅝" ½" ⅝" ½" ⅝" ½" ⅝" ³⁄₈"

¼" ⅞" ¼" ⅞" ¼" ⅞" ¼" ⅞" ¼"

4¾"

13⁄16"

3 Projects From The Scrap Bin

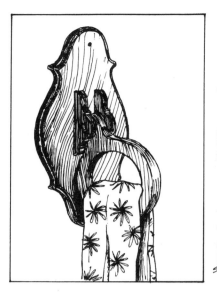

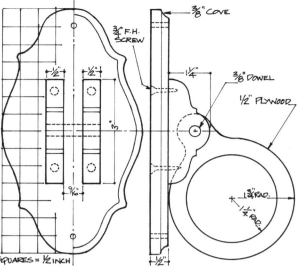

SQUARES = ½ INCH

TOWEL RING

Here's a pleasant change from the usual plated steel or molded plastic towel holders. Use it in the bath with small hand towels or for dish towels in the kitchen. For adequate strength, the ring should be hardwood plywood, with the back and hinge made from matching solid stock. Mahogany, walnut, or birch are good choices.

After cutting parts to size, sand all surfaces and then use a router to apply a ⅜" cove around the back. Assemble hinge halves to the back with glue and wood screws. The plywood ring pivots on a ⅜" dowel, with dowel ends glued to hinge halves.

Final sand all parts, using special care to thoroughly round off edges on the ring. Two coats of polyurethane will complete the project.

MATCHBOX

Hang this small box by the fireplace or woodstove and you won't have to go searching for a match when it's time to start the fire. It provides lots of space to store a generous supply of wooden matches.

Cut the back, sides, and front to size from ⅜" thick pine. A small triangular block is also cut to serve as a bottom. Sand all parts thoroughly.

Assemble sides to front and back with glue and small finishing nails. Apply a thin coat of glue to the triangular bottom and assemble to the bottom as shown.

Final sand all surfaces and edges, then apply a stain of your choice. Final finish with 2 coats of polyurethane varnish, followed by a rub down with 4/0 steel wool.

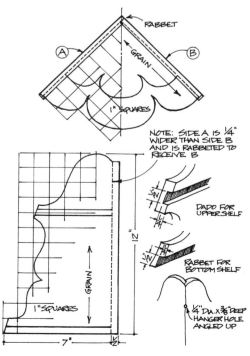

HANGING MATCH BOX ⅜ INCH PINE

NOTE: SIDE A IS ¼" WIDER THAN SIDE B AND IS RABBETED TO RECEIVE B

DADO FOR UPPER SHELF

RABBET FOR BOTTOM SHELF

¼" DIA. x ⅜ DEEP HANGER HOLE ANGLED UP

CORNER SHELVES

This charming wall shelf is a scaled down version of a lovely antique piece. Made from ½" pine, it can be completed in just one or two evenings in the workshop.

Parts A & B are cut from ½" thick by 12" long stock. Note that side A has a ¼" deep by ½" wide rabbet on one end, which means that side A must be cut ¼" wider than side B. Also note that sides A & B also have a ½" wide dado and rabbet cut for the shelves. A jig or saber saw will cut the curved scrollwork.

Now, using the grid pattern provided, cut out the top & bottom shelves as shown. Be sure to give the sides and shelves a thorough sanding, taking special care to smooth the curved surfaces.

Assemble all parts, final sand, then stain to suit. Two coats of polyurethane will complete the project.

Child's Rocker

Worn out small fry will find this rocker a cozy place to rest tired legs...at least for a few minutes. The design is based on a composite of several early 18th century rockers, and the result is a piece that's solidly constructed yet reasonably easy to build. It's dimensioned to fit a child of about kindergarten age, so if you have a younger or older child, you may want to revise the dimensions a bit. Pine is used for all parts.

Start by cutting the sides to size (4/4 x 12⅜ x 22¼). It will probably be necessary to edge join 2 or more boards to get the 12⅜" width. Using the detail as a guide, lay out and cut the tenons as shown, then lay out and cut the ¼" deep x ¾" wide seat dado. Bevel the back edge to the angle shown, then lay out and cut all remaining curves.

The back is cut to 4/4 x 13 x 20 and again edge gluing will probably be needed. Cut hand hole and top curve as shown. The rocker is cut from 5/4 x 4 x 23 stock. Lay out and cut mortises, then cut curved shapes as shown. Next the seat is made from 4/4 x 12¼ x 14½ stock. Cut to the angle shown to fit against side dadoes.

Before assembly give all parts a complete sanding. Use special care on the curved edges, making sure to remove all rough spots.

Assemble the side tenons to rocker mortises. Secure in place with ¼" dia. dowel pins. The seat is secured to the sides with glue and wood screws, countersunk and covered with wood plugs. Attach back with glue and countersunk finishing nails.

Give all surfaces a final sanding, making sure to remove any glue squeeze-out. Stain to suit, then apply two coats of polyurethane varnish. Allow to dry, then rub down with 0000 steel wool.

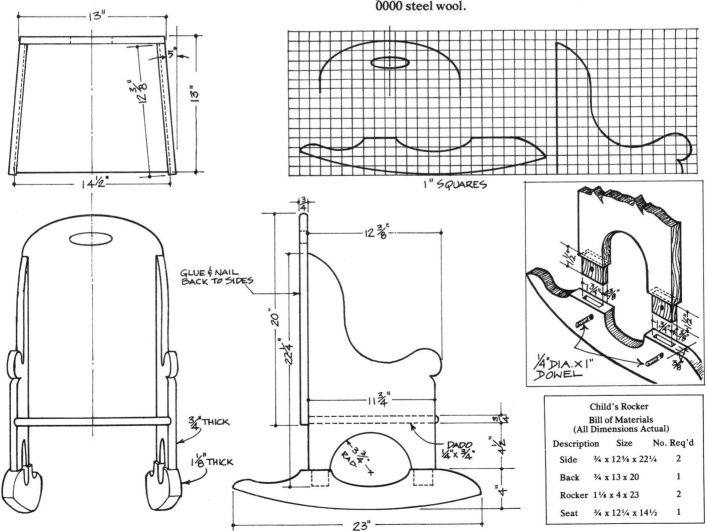

1" SQUARES

GLUE & NAIL BACK TO SIDES

¾" THICK

1⅛" THICK

¼" DIA. x 1" DOWEL

DADO ¼" x ¾"

¾ RAD.

Child's Rocker Bill of Materials (All Dimensions Actual)		
Description	Size	No. Req'd
Side	¾ x 12⅜ x 22¼	2
Back	¾ x 13 x 20	1
Rocker	1⅛ x 4 x 23	2
Seat	¾ x 12¼ x 14½	1

Push-Pull Toy

Children will love the action of this toy. As it's pushed or pulled, the cam action makes the four funny faced poppets move up and down. Kids can be pretty tough on a toy like this, so hardwood is best. We used walnut for the frame and shoes, and butternut for all other parts. The contrasting color tones add an interesting look.

Make the two wheels from 9″ square blanks. Mark the location of the four 2⅛″ dia. cut-outs, then use an expansion bit to drill the holes. Now cut the blank to a 7″ dia. Splitting is likely to occur if the cut-out holes are drilled after the wheel is cut to the 7″ dia.

Build the frame next. For added strength the end should be half-lapped as shown. Assemble with glue, then clamp securely and check for squareness. The four cams are simply ½″ stock cut to 2½″ dia. The poppet head, shaft, shoe, and all other parts are made as shown. Sand well before final assembly. The push-pull rod and handle are added last.

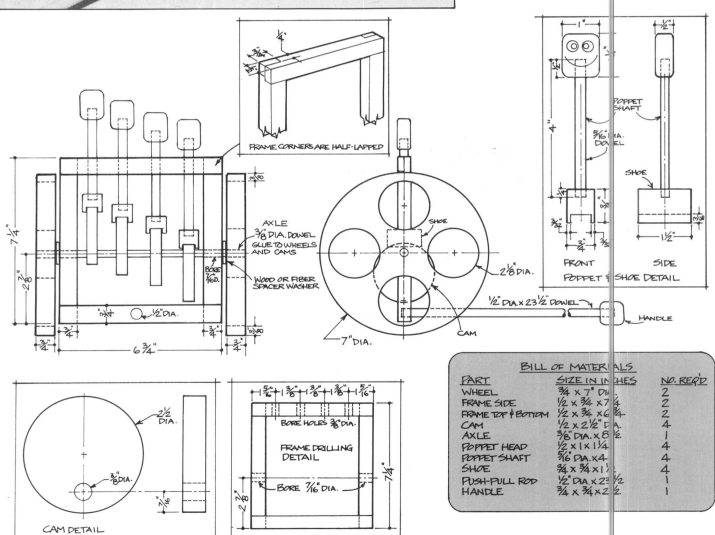

FRAME CORNERS ARE HALF-LAPPED

AXLE
⅜″ DIA. DOWEL
GLUE TO WHEELS
AND CAMS

BORE 7/16 I.D.

WOOD OR FIBER
SPACER WASHER

½″ DIA.

7¼″

2⅞″

6¾″

¾″ ¾″ ¾″

3/80 3/80

SHOE

2⅛″ DIA.

7″ DIA.

CAM

½″ DIA.x 23½″ DOWEL

POPPET
SHAFT

5/16 DIA.
DOWEL

SHOE

4″

3/32″

¾″ ⅜″

FRONT

SIDE

POPPET & SHOE DETAIL

HANDLE

CAM DETAIL

2½″ DIA.

⅜″ DIA.

7/16″

FRAME DRILLING DETAIL

5/16″ 3/8″ 3/8″ 3/8″ 5/16″

BORE HOLES ⅜″ DIA.

BORE 7/16 DIA.

7¼″

2⅞″

BILL OF MATERIALS		
PART	SIZE IN INCHES	NO. REQ'D
WHEEL	¾ x 7″ DIA.	2
FRAME SIDE	½ x ¾ x 7¼	2
FRAME TOP & BOTTOM	½ x ¾ x 6¾	2
CAM	½ x 2½″ DIA.	4
AXLE	⅜ DIA. x 8½	1
POPPET HEAD	½ x 1 x 1¼	4
POPPET SHAFT	5/16 DIA. x 4	4
SHOE	¾ x ¾ x 1½	4
PUSH-PULL ROD	½ DIA. x 23½	1
HANDLE	¾ x ¾ x 2½	1

Half-Round Table

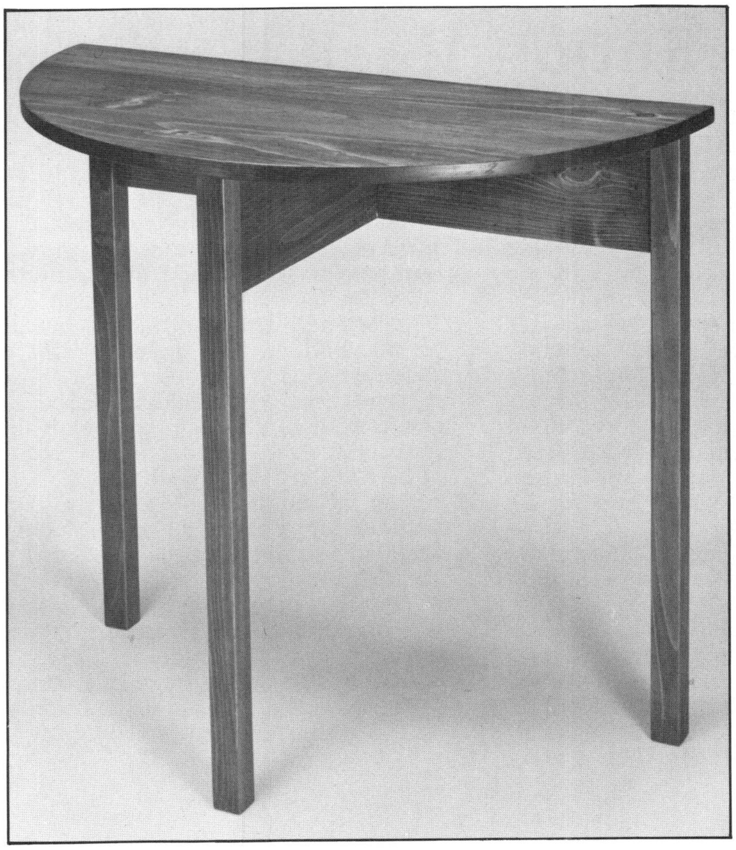

We based the design of this lovely pine table on an authentic colonial piece. It's been simplified somewhat by substituting dowel joints in place of mortises and tenons; however, more advanced woodworkers will probably choose to use the latter technique. No matter what way it's built though, the resulting table will be a very charming example of colonial style furniture.

Begin with the legs. If you can't get 1¼" stock, they can be made by face gluing two pieces of 1" (¾" actual) x 5 x 27½ stock. Use enough clamps to insure good surface contact. After drying, rip the piece to 1¼" widths. This results in a leg measuring 1¼" x 1½". To get a 1¼" square leg, rip ⅛" from each side of the 1½" wide surface. Now, trim each leg to a finish length of 27¼".

Cut the center apron (¾ x 5½ x 11¾) and rear apron (¾ x 5½ x 25½) to size, then add the rear apron dado as shown. Now the legs and aprons can be drilled for ⅜" x 1½" long dowel pins.

The top is made by edge joining enough stock to get the needed width. Lay out the 15" radius, then cut to shape. A quick compass can be built using a thin strip of wood. On one end a brad serves as a pivot point. Measure 15" from the brad and drill a small hole for a pencil point.

Before assembly, give all parts a complete sanding. At this point, we added a coat of Minwax Special Walnut wood finish. When dry, glue and clamp all dowel joints, then check to be sure all parts are square.

The top is joined using glue blocks as shown. To be sure that the top fits firmly to the aprons & legs, we actually located the blocks about 1/16" below the top edge of the aprons.

Finish with 2 coats of Minwax Antique Oil Finish, then final rub with 0000 steel wool.

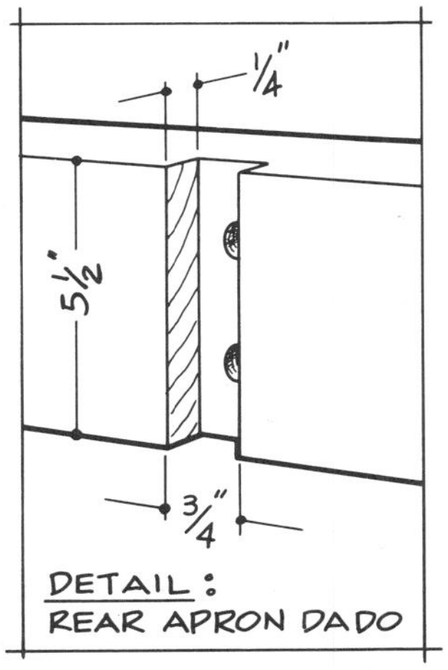

1/4"
5 1/2"
3/4"
DETAIL: REAR APRON DADO

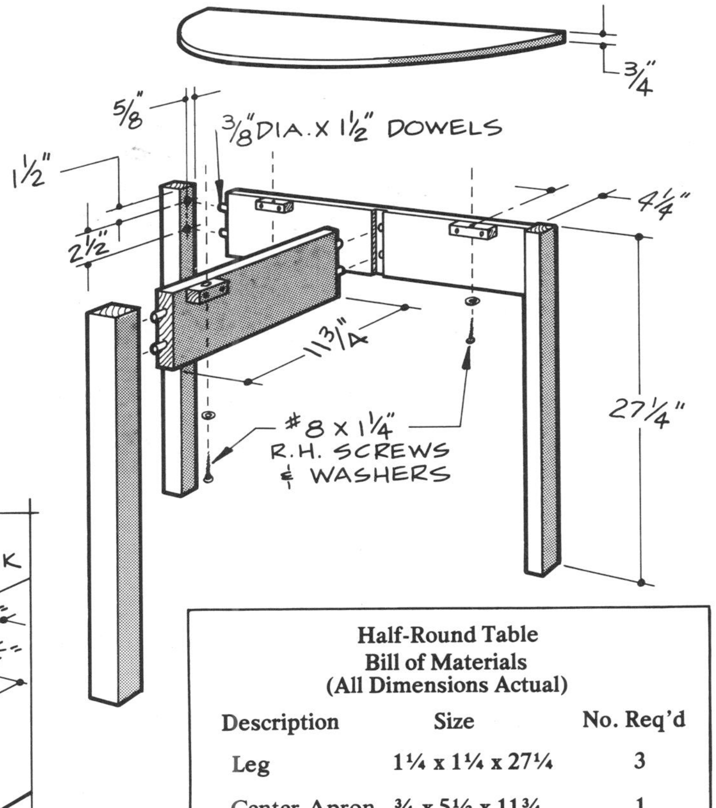

3/4"
5/8"
3/8" DIA. X 1 1/2" DOWELS
1 1/2"
2 1/2"
4 1/4"
11 3/4"
27 1/4"
#8 X 1 1/4" R.H. SCREWS & WASHERS

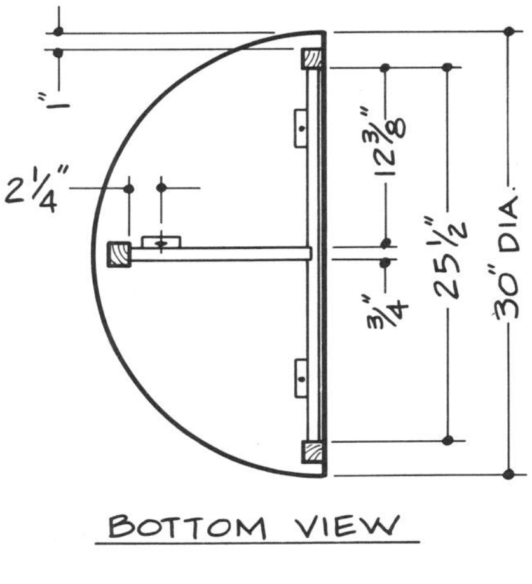

1"
2 1/4"
12 3/8"
3/4"
25 1/2"
30" DIA.
BOTTOM VIEW

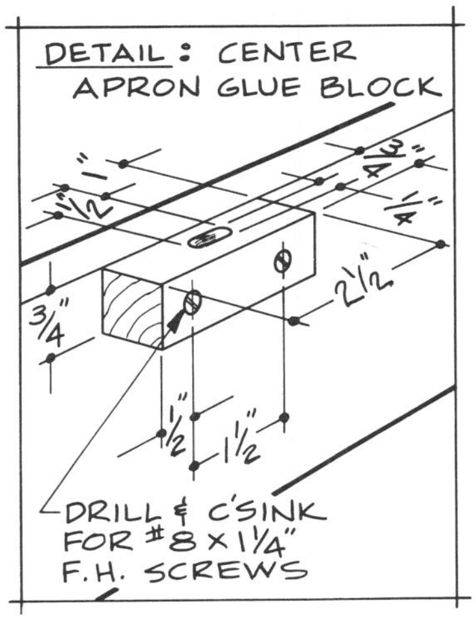

DETAIL: CENTER APRON GLUE BLOCK
1"
1/2"
4 3/4"
1/4"
3/4"
2 1/2"
1/2"
1 1/2"
DRILL & C'SINK FOR #8 X 1 1/4" F.H. SCREWS

Half-Round Table Bill of Materials (All Dimensions Actual)		
Description	**Size**	**No. Req'd**
Leg	1¼ x 1¼ x 27¼	3
Center Apron	¾ x 5½ x 11¾	1
Rear Apron	¾ x 5½ x 25½	1
Top	¾ x 15 x 30	1
Glue Block	See Detail	3

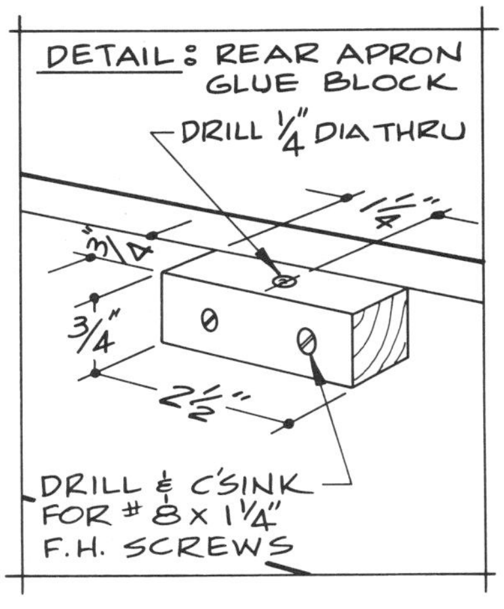

DETAIL: REAR APRON GLUE BLOCK
DRILL 1/4" DIA THRU
1 1/4"
3/4"
3/4"
2 1/2"
DRILL & C'SINK FOR #8 X 1 1/4" F.H. SCREWS

Spoon Rack

by Paul Levine

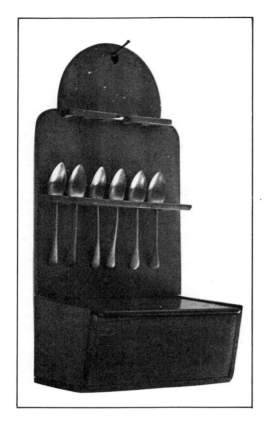

This beautiful, clean statement in wood hangs in a small warm kitchen. The room is well lit, with two large windows overlooking a garden. To add to the cozy feeling, a large fireplace dominates the adjacent wall.

From this description it is hard to imagine that upon walking out into the garden one discovers that this house is sandwiched between two skyscrapers. This is the Abigail Adams Smith Museum, located at 421 East 61st Street in New York City. Now restored to a tranquil home setting and filled with American furniture, this warm house and the warm people who care for it invite you into another time.

With its simple elegant lines, the spoon rack graces this setting as it did when first made in the early 1800's. To make a replica of this antique for your very own, use ½" pine and cut all pieces to shape, remembering that the back, sides, and front are cut full width or depth to allow for jointing.

After the back has been shaped and bored for the hanging hole, notch it to receive the sides. These will later be nailed into the back. Lay out and cut dovetails at the front corners. If you have never made this joint, this is a good place to learn because pine is soft and easy to work. The front is shorter than the sides by the thickness of the lid. Although the front slopes inward to the bottom, the dovetail joint is made as though the joint were to remain vertical. After sanding, assemble the front, back and sides with glue and nails. Check to see that the sides are square to the back and let dry.

Cut the bottom to size, then glue and nail into place. The spoon holders can also be applied at this time, nailing through the back.

The lid is the last piece to be added. It's rounded at the front and left to protrude over the edge to allow for ease of opening. The hinge mechanism is two dowels driven through the sides and into the lid as shown.

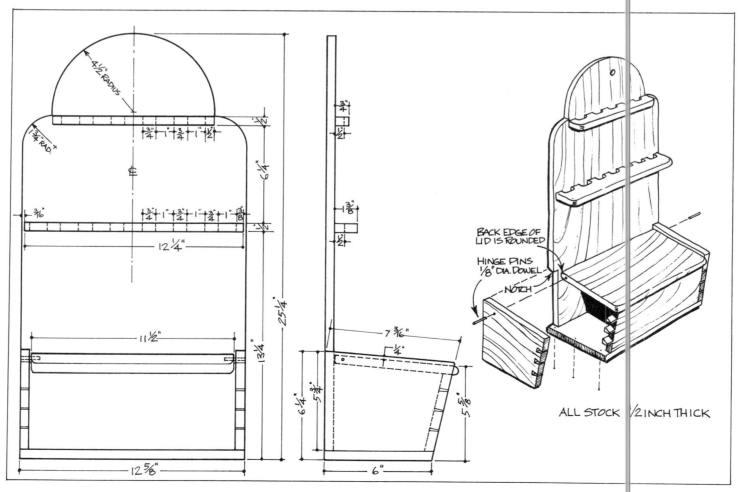

BACK EDGE OF LID IS ROUNDED

HINGE PINS ⅛" DIA. DOWEL

NOTCH

ALL STOCK ½ INCH THICK

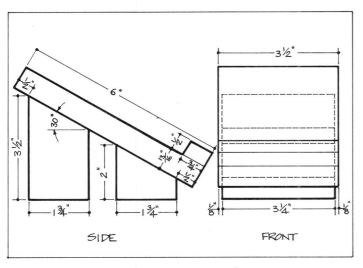

SIDE   FRONT

Calculator Stand

by Alan C. Sandler

Here's a pleasant alternative to the usual plastic type calculator stands. Many find this is a useful desktop accessory because it makes it easier to read and operate the calculator. The contemporary style has a lot of appeal, and solid hardwood construction adds weight and sturdiness. We used maple for ours, but just about any hardwood will be suitable.

The top is made from a piece of stock measuring 1" (13/16 actual) x 3½" x 6". This is sized for our calculator which measures 3" x 5", however if yours is considerably larger or smaller, you'll want to adjust the dimensions to suit. The ½ x 13/16 x 3½ lip can be made by ripping 4/4 stock to a width of ½".

The two posts are made from 8/4 (1¾ actual) stock cut to

the dimensions shown. Before assembly give all parts a complete sanding. Use 220 grit paper for final sanding.

Referring to the sketch, glue posts to top as shown. With a joint that's difficult to clamp, such as this, it's a good idea to use glue that has good "tack" qualities. Aliphatic resin (Titebond) or hide glues are good choices.

Final sand to remove sharp edges, then finish with 2 coats tung oil.

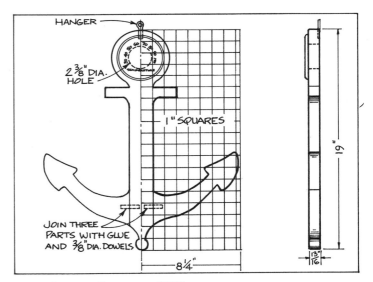

Anchor Thermometer

by Roger E. Schroeder

An excellent project for about any scrap from pine to walnut, this anchor weather station will hold a thermometer or any other round weather instrument. Made of 4/4 cherry wood and finished with a walnut stain and tung oil, it comprises three pieces of wood: two arms and a center, held together with ⅜ inch dowels and glue. A 2⅜ inch dia. hole is made for the reduced back of the thermometer which is force-fitted, and a hanger is mortised into the back of the anchor. Both the 4" dia. thermometer and hanger are available from Armor Products, Box 445, East Northport, NY 11731. A catalog costs $1.00.

Plant Stand

Just about any houseplant can be beautifully displayed in this attractive stand. It features a removable upper box, making it easier to transport the plants for such jobs as repotting or watering. Pine, maple, or oak are all suitable wood choices.

Begin with the legs (A). The 1½″ thickness can best be obtained by face gluing two pieces of 1 x 8 x 23½ stock. Use enough clamps to insure good surface contact. After drying, rip the piece to 1½″ widths to result in 1½″ square legs. Also trim to a finish length of 23″.

Cut the front and rear aprons (B) and side aprons (C) to size. The side stretcher (D) and the main stretcher (E) can also be cut and notched as shown. Now lay out, mark, and drill ⅜″ dia. dowel holes for parts A, B, C, and D as shown. Note that aprons (B) & (C) are inset ⅛″ while lower aprons (D) are centered on the leg.

The 12″ wide top (F) will probably require edge joining narrower stock in order to gain enough width. Glue and clamp the boards overnight, then cut to a finish length of 19½″.

Cut parts G, H, and I as per the Bill of Materials. Use freehand to trace the simple handle curve on part H, then use a band or saber saw to cut to shape.

Give all parts a complete sanding, then dry fit parts B, C, & D to A. If the fit up looks good, glue and securely clamp the joints, making sure everything is square. Part E can now be glued to D as shown.

The top is joined with four glue blocks (K), see detail. Note that the blocks are slotted to allow for movement of the top. The upper box, parts G and H, are joined with glue and dowel pins as shown. The ½ x ½ bottom support cleats are glued and screwed in place to support the plywood bottom. The plywood is not fastened, but instead drops in place to facilitate easy removal and cleaning. Dowel pins are glued to the top (F) as shown. These then fit into (but are not glued to) corresponding holes in part G.

Final sand all parts, rounding off any sharp edges. Stain to suit, apply 2 coats polyurethane, then rub down with 0000 steel wool.

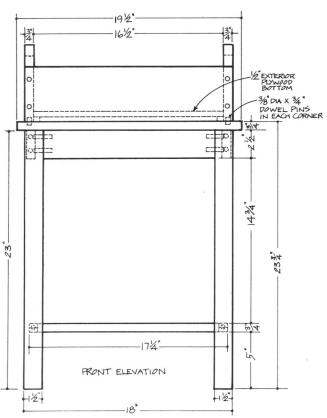

FRONT ELEVATION

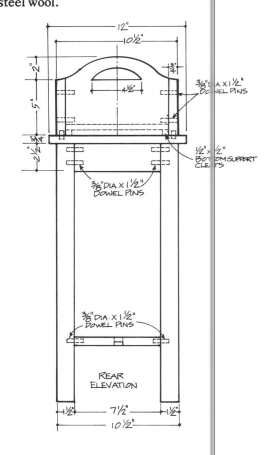

REAR ELEVATION

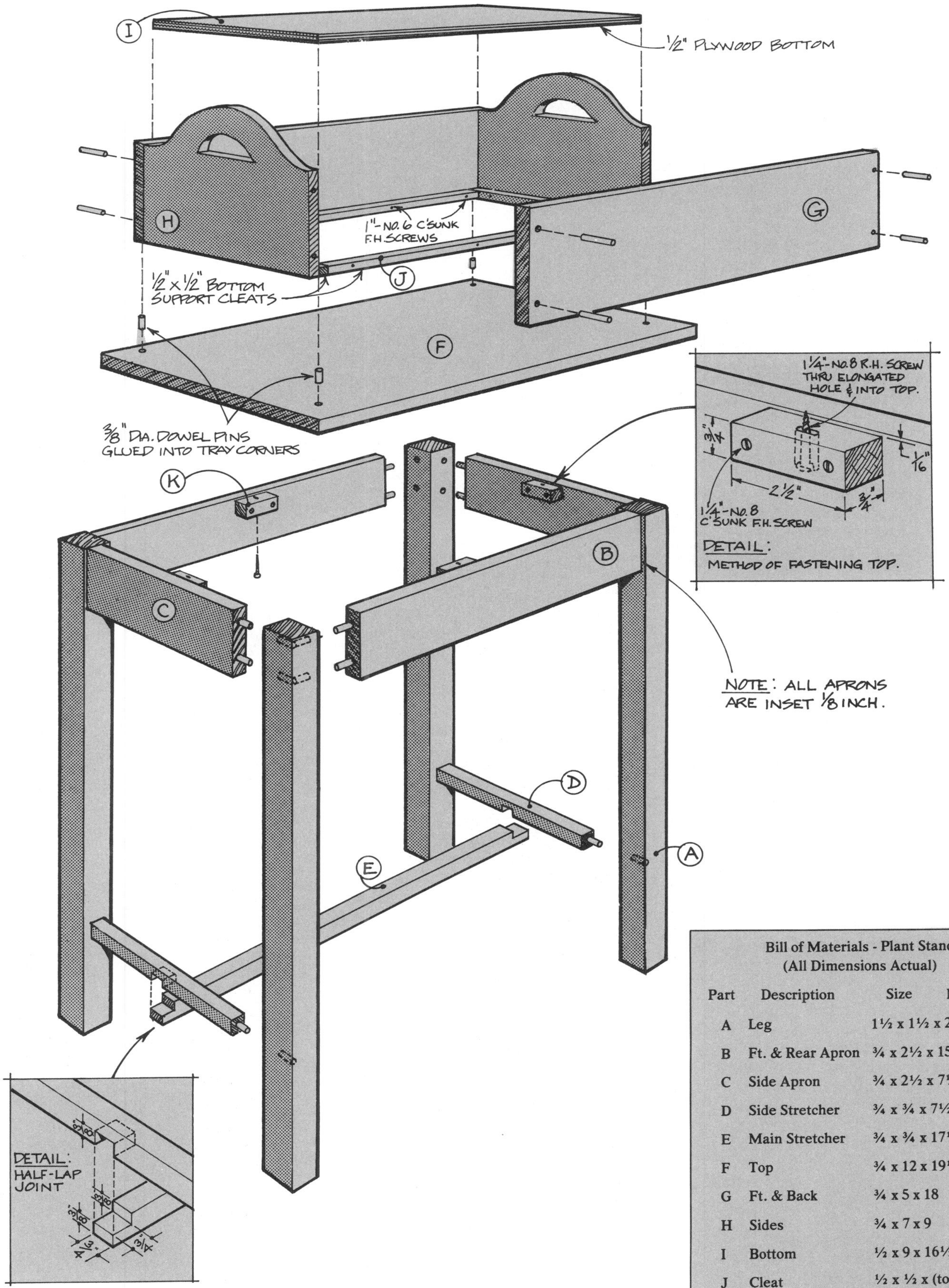

I
½" PLYWOOD BOTTOM
H
G
1"-NO. 6 C'SUNK F.H. SCREWS
½" x ½" BOTTOM SUPPORT CLEATS
J
F
⅜" DIA. DOWEL PINS GLUED INTO TRAY CORNERS
K
B
C
NOTE: ALL APRONS ARE INSET ⅛ INCH.
D
A
E
1¼"-NO. 8 R.H. SCREW THRU ELONGATED HOLE & INTO TOP.
¾"
1/16"
2½"
¾"
1¼"-NO. 8 C'SUNK F.H. SCREW
DETAIL:
METHOD OF FASTENING TOP.
DETAIL:
HALF-LAP JOINT
3/8
3/8
¾

Bill of Materials - Plant Stand (All Dimensions Actual)			
Part	Description	Size	No. Req'd.
A	Leg	1½ x 1½ x 23	4
B	Ft. & Rear Apron	¾ x 2½ x 15	2
C	Side Apron	¾ x 2½ x 7½	2
D	Side Stretcher	¾ x ¾ x 7½	2
E	Main Stretcher	¾ x ¾ x 17¼	1
F	Top	¾ x 12 x 19½	1
G	Ft. & Back	¾ x 5 x 18	2
H	Sides	¾ x 7 x 9	2
I	Bottom	½ x 9 x 16½	1
J	Cleat	½ x ½ x (to suit)	4
K	Glue Block	See Detail	4

Oak Writing Desk

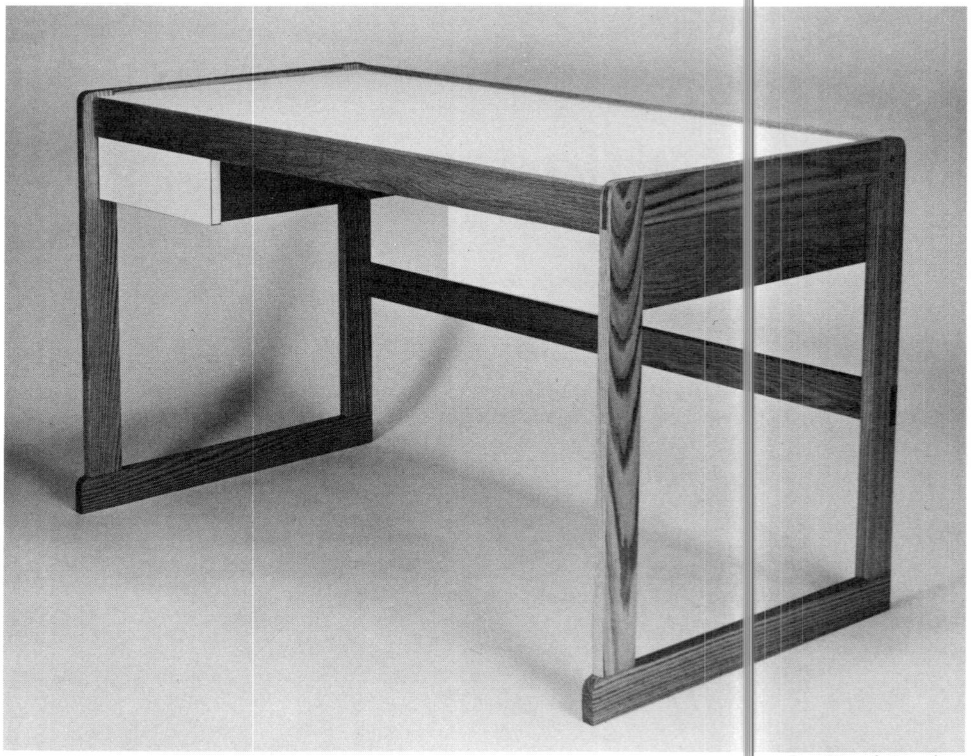

by Paul Levine

Those with a flair for contemporary styling will like this nicely proportioned desk. Solid oak stock is used for all visible wood surfaces. The top core (G), false front core (O), box top and bottom (J) and drawer bottom (N) are plywood. Parts G and O are covered with white plastic laminate.

Begin by cutting the four legs (A) to size. On one end, a ⅜ in. thick by 1½ in. wide by 2½ in. long tenon is made, while the other end is cut to form a ⅜ in. wide by 2½ in. deep open mortise. With this completed, set up the dado head cutter to cut the ¾ by 2½ in. notch in the two back legs. Now the end rail (B) tenons can be cut to fit the leg mortises. To look best, this joint must have a good tight fit, so use special care here.

The foot (C) is cut to length and width from ¾ in. thick stock. Note that the front and rear mortises are made to accept the leg tenons. Parts A, B, and C can now be glued together to form the side frames. Apply sufficient glue and clamp securely. When dry, round the top corners and the top front end of the feet to a ¾ in. radius, as shown.

Using stock that measures a full 1 in. thick, now cut the front rail (D) and rear rail (E) to size. In order to accept the laminated top, a ⅝ by ⅞ in. rabbet is applied to part D, and a ⅝ by 1¼ in. rabbet is applied to part E. It's best to cut the front rail slightly wider than 2½ in. and make the rabbet about 1 in. deep, however. Later, after the top is added, you'll be able to lightly plane the front rail perfectly flush with the laminate.

The ¾ in. thick plywood top core (G) is covered with white plastic laminate (H), although other colors can also be used if you prefer. It is important to laminate both sides of the top to equalize tensions. After the top has been laminated (with contact cement) and trimmed, it can be glued and clamped to the front rail (D) and rear rail (E). Lightly plane the front rail flush with the plastic laminate top, then round off the front edge with a router and ¼ in. rounding-over bit.

The side frames can now be joined to the top assembly (parts D, E, G, and H) with glue and woodscrews. As shown, the screws are counterbored and plugged. Plated screws are suggested because oak will sometimes corrode unplated steel. To support the top while the side frames were being attached, I clamped auxiliary legs (made from ¾ in. scrap pine) to the inside of all four legs. The length of the auxiliary legs was such that when the front and rear rails rested on them, the top was properly located in relation to the side frames. Two 5 ft. pipe clamps were spanned across the top, clamping the top assembly between the side frames and temporarily holding things together while the screws were drilled and secured. The stretcher (F) was also attached at this point.

Now make the two drawer box assemblies, consisting of parts I, J, and K, as shown in the drawer box detail. After rabbeting the back, make the ¼ by ¼ in. tongues on the top and bottom, and the corresponding ¼ by ¼ in. grooves in the sides. Note that the 5/16 in. deep by 1 in. wide drawer guide groove in the sides must be cut before the box is assembled. Pilot holes for the 1¼ in. long screws must also be located and drilled before assembly. To facilitate drilling these holes, turn the desk over and temporarily assemble and clamp in place one side, the top and the back. Repeat the process for the box on the other side of the desk.

Glue and assemble the boxes (make sure they are square) and mount them with the lag screws. We chose lag screws so a socket wrench could be used.

The drawers can now be constructed. Note the ⅜ in. deep by ⅛ in. wide tongue and groove joint (see drawer joint detail) with which the drawer front and back (L) are joined to the sides (M). The 3/16 in. deep by 1 in. wide grooves in the sides to accept the guides (P), and the ¼ in. deep by ¼ in. wide grooves in the front, back, and sides to accept the plywood drawer bottom (N) must also be cut before assembly. The bottom is rabbeted on all four sides to create the ¼ by ¼ in. tongue.

The false front core material (O) can be cut to size next. I used ½ in. thick plywood. Using the laminate (H), cover both sides, the edges and the ends. Note the bevel applied to create the black line detail around the false drawer fronts. Mount the fronts to the assembled drawers using ¼ in. threaded inserts and screws. I recommend drilling oversize ⅜ in. diameter holes through the drawer carcase front, which will allow some adjustment in the false fronts. Lastly, glue the drawer guides into the drawer guide grooves on the drawer sides. The drawer guide additional length will allow the drawers to be fully extended. *Note:* The false front is sized 12 5/16 in. long to allow some clearance at the desk sides. The 4⅜ in. width of the false front provides a small finger grip along the bottom edge with which to pull the drawer out. After sanding, I finished the desk with two coats of Watco Danish Oil.

Bill of Materials (all dimensions actual)

Part	Description	Size	No. Req'd.
A	Leg	¾ × 2½ × 28⅞*	4
B	End Rail	¾ × 2½ × 24*	2
C	Foot	¾ × 2½ × 24¾	2
D	Front Rail	1 × 2½ × 46½	1
E	Rear Rail	1 × 2⅞ × 46½	1
F	Stretcher	¾ × 2½ × 48	1
G	Top Core	¾ × 21¾ × 46½	1
H	Laminate	as needed	
I	Box Side	¾ × 5⅞ × 20⅛	4
J	Box Top & Bottom	½ × 11½ × 20⅛*	4
K	Box Back	¾ × 5⅞ × 12½	2
L	Drawer Front & Back	½ × 3½ × 10¾*	4
M	Drawer Side	½ × 3½ × 13	4
N	Drawer Bottom	½ × 10½ × 12½*	2
O	False Front Core	½ × 4¼ × 12 5/16	2
P	Drawer Guide	½ × 1 × 19	4

*Includes tenon or tongue.

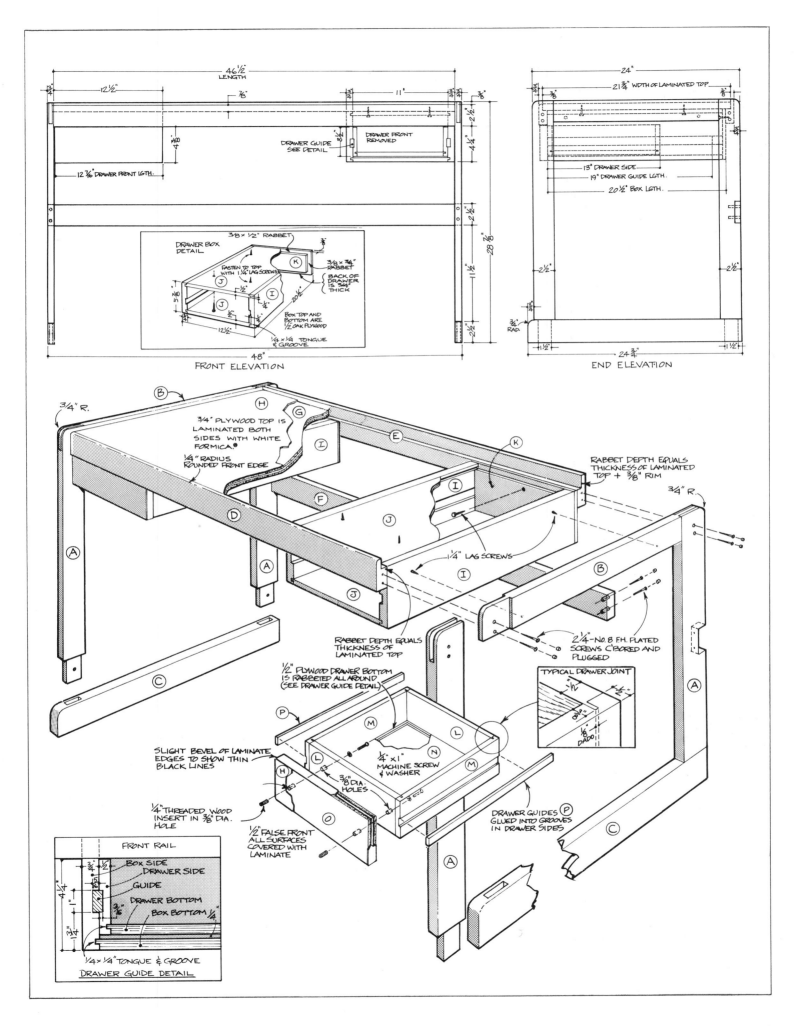

FRONT ELEVATION

46½" LENGTH

12½"

⅞"

11"

DRAWER GUIDE
SEE DETAIL

DRAWER FRONT
REMOVED

12 ³⁄₁₆" DRAWER FRONT LGTH.

28 ⅝"

48"

DRAWER BOX DETAIL

3/8 × 1/2" RABBET

FASTEN TO TOP
WITH 1¼" LAG SCREWS

K

3/8 × ¾"
RABBET

BACK OF
DRAWER IS ¾"
THICK

J

I

J

BOX TOP AND
BOTTOM ARE
½ OAK PLYWOOD

12½"

¼ × ¼ TONGUE
& GROOVE

END ELEVATION

24"

21¾" WIDTH OF LAMINATED TOP

13" DRAWER SIDE

19" DRAWER GUIDE LGTH.

20½" BOX LGTH.

2½"

2½"

¾"
RAD.

1½"

24 ¾"

1½"

¾" R.

B

H

G

E

K

3/4" PLYWOOD TOP IS
LAMINATED BOTH
SIDES WITH WHITE
FORMICA®

I

RABBET DEPTH EQUALS
THICKNESS OF LAMINATED
TOP + 3/8" RIM

¼" RADIUS
ROUNDED FRONT EDGE

F

¾" R.

D

A

I

J

A

I

1¼" LAG SCREWS

J

B

2¼"–No.8 F.H. PLATED
SCREWS C'BORED AND
PLUGGED

A

RABBET DEPTH EQUALS
THICKNESS OF
LAMINATED TOP

½" PLYWOOD DRAWER BOTTOM
IS RABBETED ALL AROUND
(SEE DRAWER GUIDE DETAIL)

TYPICAL DRAWER JOINT

⅛"
DADO

SLIGHT BEVEL OF LAMINATE
EDGES TO SHOW THIN
BLACK LINES

P

M

L

C

L

N

M

¼" × 1"
MACHINE SCREW
& WASHER

H

3/8 DIA.
HOLES

¼" THREADED WOOD
INSERT IN 3/8" DIA.
HOLE

O

½" FALSE FRONT
ALL SURFACES
COVERED WITH
LAMINATE

DRAWER GUIDES
GLUED INTO GROOVES
IN DRAWER SIDES

P

A

FRONT RAIL

4¼"

BOX SIDE
DRAWER SIDE
GUIDE
DRAWER BOTTOM
BOX BOTTOM ¼"

1"

¾"

¼ × ¼" TONGUE & GROOVE
DRAWER GUIDE DETAIL

18th Century Chair Table

By and large, houses in colonial America were rather small, oftentimes just one or two tiny rooms. With small houses and small rooms, space was at a premium, so colonists had to be very practical when choosing furniture. The chair table is a good example of that practicality. It served two functions. At mealtime it was used as a table, right in the middle of a room. When the meal was over, it was opened as a chair and pushed out of the way against a wall.

The advantages of the chair table can still be enjoyed by many of us today. Anyone with a space problem can put it to use, particularly those with small homes or apartments. It truly is a timeless furniture style.

The sides (A) can be made first. If you can't get 10½" wide stock you'll have to edge-join two or more boards to get the needed width. Cut to width and length (including tenons), then lay out and mark tenons as shown in the details. Use the dado head in conjunction with a table or radial saw to cut the tenon cheeks. A back saw and sharp chisel will finish the job. Make all cuts with care. Also cut the ¼" deep x ¾" wide seat dado.

Arm rests (C) and feet (B) can be made next. Cut to overall length and width, then lay out mortise location. To cut mortises, drill a series of adjacent ¾" diameter x 1 9/16" deep holes. This removes most of the material. What's left can be cleaned up with the chisel. After mortises are completed, the curved profiles (as shown on the grid pattern) can be cut.

The back (D) is made from 1" (¾" actual) stock. As with the legs, you'll have to edge-join several boards to get the 16½" width. Note that it has a 1⅛" x 3½" notch at both upper corners, allowing the back to fit around arm rests (C). After completing both notches, the curved profile can be cut out.

The seat (E) can be cut next. If your local lumberyard carries 1" x 12" stock try to select a board that has a minimum of cup. If they only carry narrower stock, you'll once again have to join them.

Part (F), the cleats, are made from 1⅛" stock and cut to dimensions shown in both the side elevation and detail of the rear pivot hole location. Next, locate and drill the pivot and locking holes.

The 28" wide by 36" long top (G) can now be made. Edge-join boards as necessary, trim to length and width, then cut the corners to 30 degrees as shown.

At this point, before assembly, it's a good idea to give all components a thorough sanding job.

Assemble sides (A) to arm rests (C) and feet (B). Be sure to apply sufficient glue to both mortises and tenons.

Clamp securely and allow to dry overnight. When dry, drill ¼" dia. holes for dowel pins as shown. Cut pins a little long, then trim and sand flush.

The seat (E) is glued to the dado in side (A) and further secured with two countersunk woodscrews. The countersunk holes are then plugged and sanded flush. The back (D) can now be attached with glue and three countersunk and plugged woodscrews each end.

Each cleat is fixed to the top with three wood screws. Since the top will want to expand and contract in width due to seasonal humidity changes, it's best not to use glue here. The wood screws will allow some movement of the top and minimize the chance of cracking. Locate the cleat so that there is about ⅛" of "play" between the cleat and the arm rest.

Now, with the top resting in proper position on the arm rest, mark the location of the arm rest pivot and lock holes. After drilling holes, pegs can be made as shown in the detail.

Final sand all surfaces. Round off sharp corners, taking particular care to smooth curved edges. We stained our piece with 2 coats of Minwax Early American wood finish. After allowing the stain to thoroughly dry, we applied two coats of Minwax Antique Oil Finish. A light rub down with 0000 steel wool completed the project.

Chair Table			
Bill of Materials (All Dimensions Actual)			
Part	Description	Size	No. Req'd.
A	Side Board	1⅛ x 10½ x 21 (Inc. tenons)	2
B	Foot	1⅛ x 5 x 20	2
C	Arm Rest	1⅛ x 4 x 14½	2
D	Back	¾ x 16½ x 28½	1
E	Seat	¾ x 11 x 26¾	1
F	Cleat	1⅛ x 1½ x 24¾	2
G	Top	¾ x 28 x 36	1
H	Pivot & Lock Pegs	See Detail	4

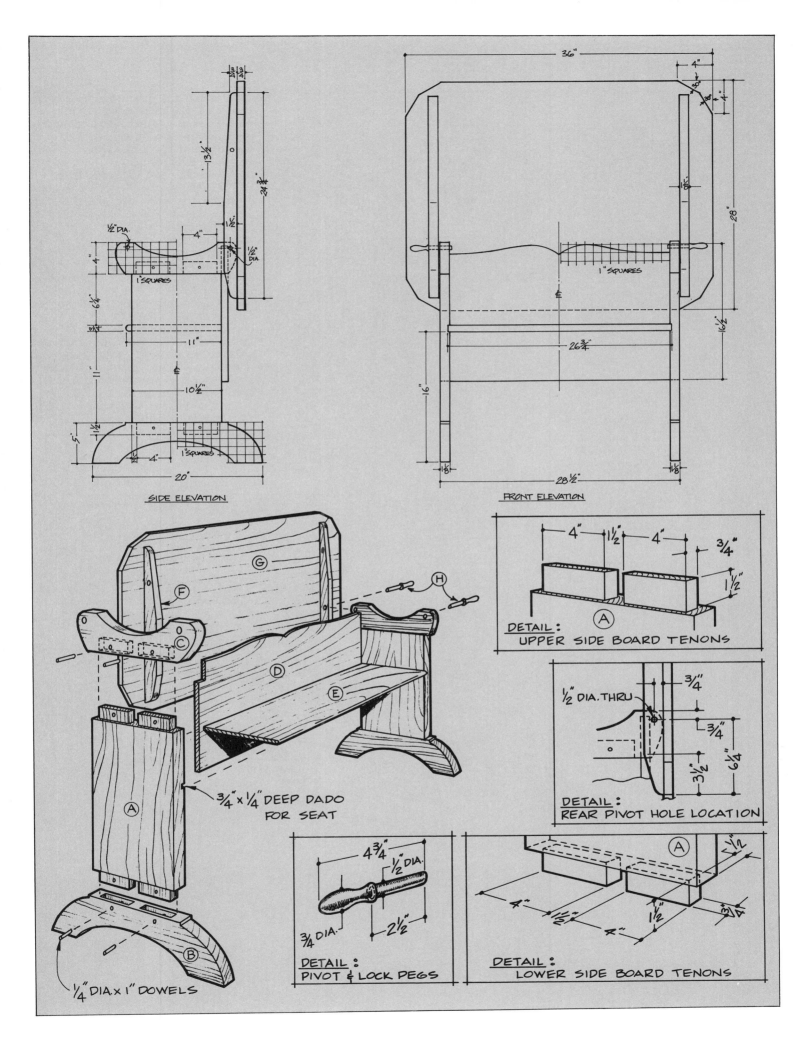

SIDE ELEVATION

FRONT ELEVATION

3/4" x 1/4" DEEP DADO FOR SEAT

1/4" DIA. x 1" DOWELS

DETAIL:
UPPER SIDE BOARD TENONS
Ⓐ

DETAIL:
REAR PIVOT HOLE LOCATION
1/2" DIA. THRU

DETAIL:
PIVOT & LOCK PEGS

DETAIL:
LOWER SIDE BOARD TENONS
Ⓐ

18th Cent. Sleigh Seat

Although not an exact reproduction, the overall design of this piece is based on a colonial original. Ours is used to display house plants in front of a sunny window, but it will also make a nice bench for a hall or den.

If you can't get 10″ wide boards it will be necessary to edge-join enough stock for the two sides and the seat. Boards cut 6 feet long will provide enough length for all three parts. For maximum glue strength, the gluing surfaces must be smooth and clean. If the edges look a bit rough or dirty, use the jointer or hand plane to clean them up. Keep knots away from the leg portion of the sides. A knot will weaken the strength of a leg.

After all parts have been cut to size and shape, give each one a thorough sanding. Assemble with glue and dowel pins as shown, using countersunk 1½ x #8 wood screws and glue to secure the aprons to the top.

Ours is finished with a coat of Minwax Special Walnut wood finish followed by two coats of Minwax Antique Oil finish.

SLEIGH SEAT - BILL OF MATERIALS		
PART	SIZE	NO. REQ'D
SIDE	¾″ x 10″ x 20″	2
APRON	¾″ x 4″ x 28½″	2
SEAT	¾″ x 10″ x 29″	1

¼″ DEEP DADO

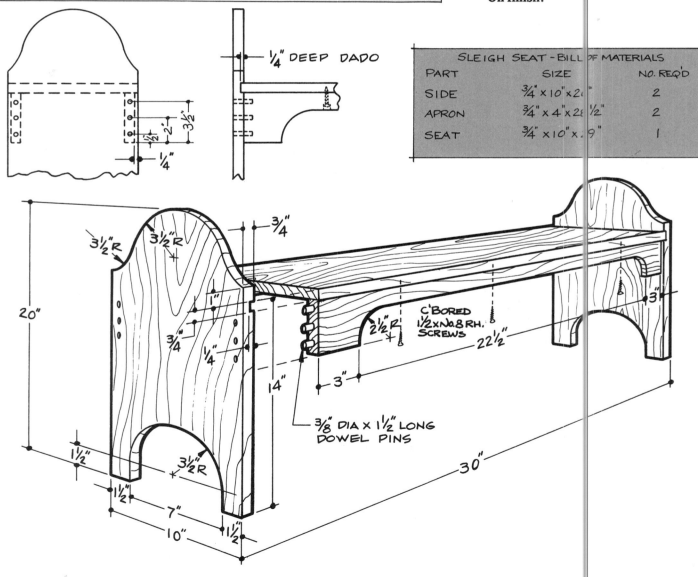

C'BORED 1½ x No.8 R.H. SCREWS

⅜″ DIA x 1½″ LONG DOWEL PINS

Child's Step Stool

Most everything in a house is sized for grown-ups, and kids soon learn that being little has some distinct disadvantages. However, here's a project that will help them out all during their growing up years. It's especially useful in the bathroom, allowing little ones to get up to the sink for brushing teeth and washing up. Sturdily constructed of ¾" pine, it features a storage area for collecting bathroom toys and other odds and ends.

Begin by edge-gluing adequate stock to take care of the two sides and the platform. Boards cut 50" long will provide enough length for all three parts. Cut the ¼" x ¾" side dado slightly less than the thickness of the mating platform. Then, when the platform is sanded, the joint should be near perfect. By the way, make sure the platform grain direction runs as shown in the drawing. Little strength will result if it runs the other way.

After cutting all remaining parts to size, give each of them a thorough sanding. Round off all corners as shown. Assemble with glue and countersunk finishing nails. If you have them, two or three pipe clamps will also be helpful here. Use two small blocks to fill in the point where the dado runs out the back.

After the glue has dried, fill all nail holes and give the entire project a final sanding. Cut and fit the pair of 2" butt hinges as shown. Ours was finished with 2 coats of yellow paint, applied according to the manufacturer's instructions.

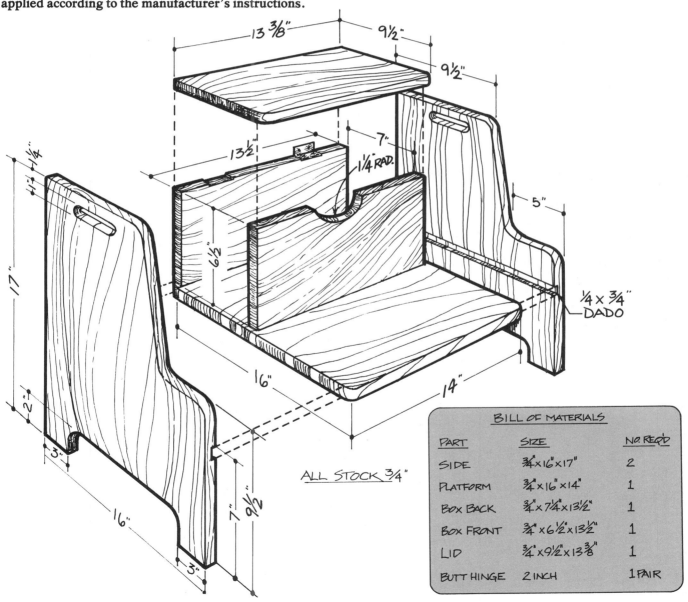

ALL STOCK ¾"

BILL OF MATERIALS		
PART	SIZE	NO. REQ'D
SIDE	¾" x 16" x 17"	2
PLATFORM	¾" x 16" x 14"	1
BOX BACK	¾" x 7¼" x 13½"	1
BOX FRONT	¾" x 6½" x 13½"	1
LID	¾" x 9½" x 13⅜"	1
BUTT HINGE	2 INCH	1 PAIR

Flying Duck

This amusing wind-animated duck is an old favorite and quite easy to build. The body and wings can be cut from exterior grade plywood or even pine but ¾" cedar is best. A length of beveled cedar clapboard when planed to 3/16" thickness is ideal for the wings.

The angled wing blocks can be slotted with a handsaw, and the wings which slant in opposite directions are epoxied into the slots. A 2¼" length of ½" dia. dowel is drilled through to take headless 3/16 x 2" bolts which serve as axles. The wing blocks are drilled for a loose fit over the axles and secured with nuts and washers as shown.

A length of brass tubing is epoxied into a hole drilled in the underside of the body. This slips loosely over a pivot rod and enables the duck to swing into the wind.

Paint the duck with exterior enamels. The eyes are white upholstery tacks with a dab of black enamel.

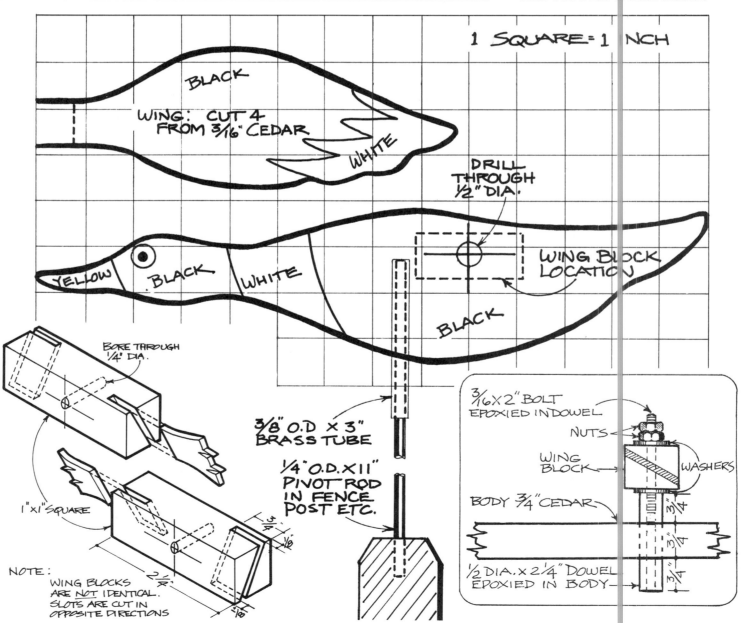

1 SQUARE = 1 INCH

BLACK

WING: CUT 4 FROM 3/16" CEDAR

WHITE

DRILL THROUGH ½" DIA.

WING BLOCK LOCATION

YELLOW BLACK WHITE

BLACK

BORE THROUGH ¼" DIA.

3/8" O.D × 3" BRASS TUBE

¼" O.D. × 11" PIVOT ROD IN FENCE POST ETC.

1" × 1" SQUARE

2½"

NOTE:
WING BLOCKS ARE NOT IDENTICAL. SLOTS ARE CUT IN OPPOSITE DIRECTIONS

3/16 × 2" BOLT EPOXIED IN DOWEL

NUTS

WING BLOCK

WASHERS

BODY ¾" CEDAR

½ DIA. × 2¼" DOWEL EPOXIED IN BODY

Trouser Hanger

A few hours in the shop is all it takes to make this nifty multiple trouser hanger...and we guarantee that you'll end up making more than one. It makes a great gift and one that should sell very well.

For durability use a hardwood such as maple or cherry. The pattern for the curved upper bar is enlarged on tracing paper and transferred to a length of ¾ x 5½ x 16″ stock. Run the ends of the board over a ¼″ dado cutter to cut the slots for the upright tenons, then bandsaw the piece to shape.

Cut uprights from ¾ x 1¼″ stock and cut dadoes in one piece for the ¼″ pivot arms as shown in the detail. Cut four pivot arms to fit snugly in the dadoes and round off one end of each.

The four trouser bars are ¾″ square, notched to fit over the pivot arms. These notches should be quite snug to prevent drooping when the bars are swung out. Round ends of bars and insert pivot arms in the bar slots so both pieces can be drilled through for the pivot pins.

Center drill the other ends of arms for ⅜″ dowel pins, glued in place, which slip into routed slots in the upright and support the bars in the closed position.

Fasten bars to pivot arms and insert pins. Use a headless wire brad to drive through the side of each arm and through the pivot pin. Force a headless brad into this hole to lock the pivot pin in place.

Glue pivot arms in place and glue and clamp the tenoned joints. A heavy wire hook is forced through a hole in the upper bar and bent over to keep the hook from pulling out. A bit of epoxy in the hole will keep the hook pointing in the right direction. As an alternate, a large screw eye can be used.

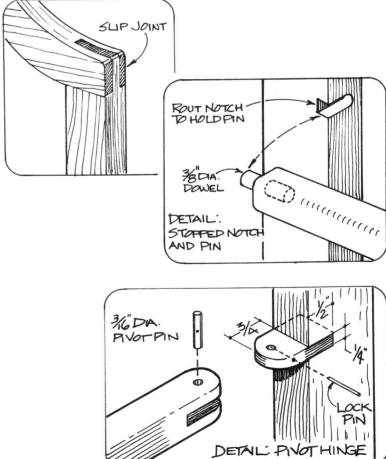

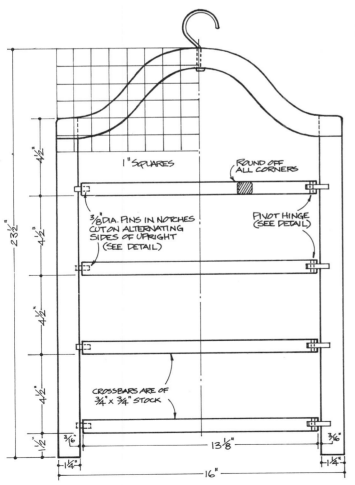

SLIP JOINT

ROUT NOTCH TO HOLD PIN

⅜″ DIA. DOWEL

DETAIL: STOPPED NOTCH AND PIN

3/16″ DIA. PIVOT PIN

LOCK PIN

DETAIL: PIVOT HINGE

1″ SQUARES

ROUND OFF ALL CORNERS

⅜″ DIA. PINS IN NOTCHES CUT ON ALTERNATING SIDES OF UPRIGHT (SEE DETAIL)

PIVOT HINGE (SEE DETAIL)

CROSSBARS ARE OF ¾″ x ¾″ STOCK

23½″

4½″

4½″

4½″

4½″

½″

3/16″

13⅛″

3/16″

1¼″

1¼″

16″

½″

¾

½

¼

Folding Sun Seat

Here's a comfortable way to relax and enjoy the warm sun this summer. It's an attractive and unusual sun seat that will easily fold up and become portable. To provide strength, ¾" ash is used for the frames and sides. To minimize weight, pre-woven (machine made) cane is used for the seat and back. If you take it to the pool or beach though, use a towel to protect it from wet bathing suits. If you don't, the wet cane may stretch out of shape and lose strength.

The two sides (A) can be made first. Referring to the Bill of Materials, cut to overall length and width, then mark the location of the ¼" deep by ¾" wide stopped dado. The dado can be cut using the dado head cutter, or by making repeated passes with a regular sawblade. Stop the cuts just short of the end of the dado, then clean up the remaining material with a sharp chisel. Now the front to back taper can be cut using a saber saw, band saw, or table saw tapering jig.

The seat frame can be made next. Cut the front and back (E) and sides (F) to length and width. The tenons on each end of parts E can be made with the dado head or by repeated passes with the sawblade. The open mortise on each end of parts F can best be made with a tenon jig. Apply glue (an aliphatic resin is a good choice) to all mortise and tenon joints, then firmly clamp the entire frame unit. Allow to dry overnight.

The spline groove can now be cut. Remove any excess glue squeeze out, then sand the top frame surface until smooth. The spline groove is made using a router equipped with a router guide and contour finger, and a 3/16" dia. straight bit. Set the bit for a ¼" depth of cut and set the contour finger for a cut ½" from the inside edge (see spline groove detail). With the contour finger firmly in contact with the inside edge, start the router and lower the bit into the frame. Begin the cut along a straight length of frame and move the router in a counterclockwise direction. As the contour finger contacts a corner, use the corner as a pivot point and swing the bit in a smooth radius. When the bit has swung 90 degrees continue the cut along a straight length. Proceed in this manner until all four sides and all four corners have been cut to form one continuous groove. Now, four ⅜" diameter x ¾" long dowel pins can be added

at each corner as shown. Complete preliminary work on the frame by using a file to shape a slight relief angle (see spline groove detail) on the inside of all four frame pieces. The back frame (parts B, C & D) is constructed in basically the same manner.

To simplify the caning process we selected pre-woven cane. A variety of weaves are available, but we chose the type designated as "fine — open ½ inch." It is sold by the running foot in several standard widths. Four feet of the 18" width is more than enough material to build this project. You will also need to order about 12 feet of #8 reed spline. Our cane was purchased from Connecticut Cane & Reed Company, P.O. Box 762, Manchester, CT 06040. Another mail-order source for pre-woven cane is The Woodworkers' Store, 21801 Industrial Boulevard, Rogers, MN 55374.

Before starting to apply the cane you'll need to make about 12 wood wedges. Cut wedges 1" wide x 1½" long and tapered from ¼" thick to ⅛" thick. These are used to press the cane into the groove and temporarily hold it in place as it is stretched on the frame. Cut the cane so that it overlaps the groove by at least ¾" on all four sides. The spline should be cut for about a 1" overlap. To make the cane and spline pliable, allow to soak 1 hour in warm water. After soaking, remove and drip dry for a few minutes before using. With the shiny side up, align the cane on the frame making sure the strands are parallel with the grooves. Now, starting with the middle of the groove furthest away from you, use a wedge to push the cane into the groove, leaving the wedge in place. Using another wedge, continue the process of pushing the cane along the length of the groove, always working from the middle toward a corner. Removing excess strands that are parallel to the groove will make it easier to work the remaining cane. Three wedges on this side should be satisfactory. Now pull the cane toward the opposite side and repeat the process. The side frame grooves can then be treated in the same manner. After all the cane has been pushed to the bottom of the groove, including corners, use a sharp chisel to cut the excess strands at a point just below the outside edge of the groove (see detail).

Apply liquid hide glue to the groove and insert the spline, tapping in place with a block of wood. Remove wedges as you go along. At the point where the spline overlaps, use a chisel to cut a miter joint. Any excess glue should be wiped off. Allow the cane about 48 hours to dry. As it dries, the cane will shrink and tighten considerably.

The project is assembled as shown in the drawing. After a thorough sanding, Watco Danish Oil was added as a final finish.

Part	Description	Size	Req'd
A	Side	¾ x 5⅝ x 22	2
B	Back Frame Sides	¾ x 1½ x 21	2
C	Back Frame Top	¾ x 1½ x 15⅞	1
D	Back Frame Bottom	¾ x 1½ x 15⅞	1
E	Seat Frame Ft. & Back	¾ x 1½ x 16½	2
F	Seat Frame Sides	¾ x 1½ x 18	2
G	Dowel Stretcher	¾ dia. x 17½	2
H	Brass Rod	5/16 dia. x 17	1
I	Pre-Woven Cane	Fine Open ½"	

Sun Seat - Bill of Materials
(All Dimensions Actual)

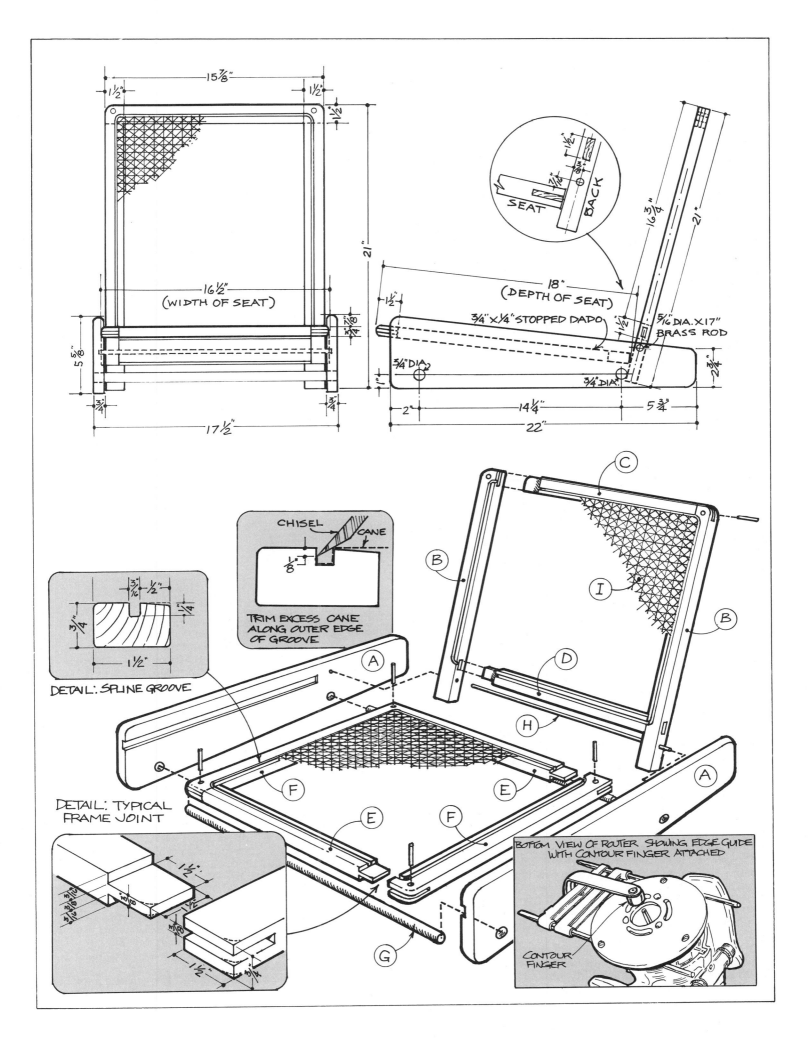

15 7/8"
1 1/2"
1 1/2"
1 1/2"
21"
16 1/2"
(WIDTH OF SEAT)
5 7/8"
3 3/4"
5 5/8"
3/4"
3/4"
17 1/2"

SEAT
BACK
1/2"
3/8"
3 1/4"
16 3/4"
21"
18"
(DEPTH OF SEAT)
1 1/2"
1/2"
5/16" DIA. X 17" BRASS ROD
3/4" X 1/4" STOPPED DADO
3/4" DIA.
3/4" DIA.
2 3/4"
1"
2"
14 1/4"
5 3/4"
22"

CHISEL
CANE
1/8"
TRIM EXCESS CANE ALONG OUTER EDGE OF GROOVE

3/16"
1/2"
1/4"
3/4"
1 1/2"
DETAIL: SPLINE GROOVE

C
B
I
B
A
D
H
E
F
E
F
G
A

DETAIL: TYPICAL FRAME JOINT
1 1/2"
3/8"
3/16"
3/16"
1 1/2"
1 1/2"
3/4"

BOTTOM VIEW OF ROUTER SHOWING EDGE GUIDE WITH CONTOUR FINGER ATTACHED
CONTOUR FINGER

Ship's Wheel Table

Furnishings and accessories with a nautical flavor have always been popular, even in areas far from the sea. This salty little table with its ship's wheel top is sure to generate a lot of favorable comment. It looks great alongside an easy chair.

Building an authentic ship's wheel is a rather tricky and time-consuming project. In this case though, it's not necessary to build a wheel as it can be mail-ordered, ready-made and completely finished for a reasonable price.

The wheel on the table shown was ordered from Prestons, 102 Main St., Greenport, NY 11944. It's listed as catalog no. 780-A (30″ overall diameter). It would be difficult to build such a wheel, including the brass hub, for less than that price.

Our wheel appears to be made of a type of mahogany, stained a golden brown to resemble teak. We chose to make the table base of maple which was stained to match the wheel. The table top of ¼″ plate glass was cut and the edges were ground by a local glass shop.

Since we cannot guarantee that the wheel you order will be dimensioned exactly as ours, it's advisable to secure your wheel first before shaping the table legs and stretchers.

The three legs are turned first from either solid or glued up 1¾″ square x 20″ long stock. Unless you've got a good eye, it's usually best to prepare a full-size hardboard template of the turning profile to use for marking off and shaping the various elements of the turning. This will insure that all legs are identical. The legs are belt sanded between centers at slow speed and it's also convenient to stain and apply the finish while rotating the leg by hand.

If you lack a lathe, an alternate leg is shown which is also in a traditional style and quite attractive. Stopped chamfers are cut along the corners between the squares and the feet are carved to a taper.

After completing the legs, prepare a plywood or cardboard pattern of the wheel showing the inside and outside diameters of the flat rim to which the legs will be joined. Draw leg locations on the pattern and lay out the leg stretcher assembly. Note that the centers of the leg posts are 120 degrees apart and the squared leg tops are inset about 3/16″ from the outer edge of the flat rim.

The curved portion of the anchor shaped stretcher assembly can be cut from a 5/4 (1⅛″ actual) x 6 x 17½″ board. Use tracing paper to transfer the shape of the curved piece from the pattern to your stock.

Cut the curved piece with bandsaw or sabersaw and leave the ends a bit longer than required so that they can be trimmed for an exact fit against the lower square portions of the legs. Also cut the straight stretcher using the pattern as a guide for length.

Note that the holes for the ⅜″ dia. dowel tenons are drilled square to the legs and stretcher ends. Locate dowel centers on a diagonal in the stretcher ends and drive small brads into the center points, clipping the heads off so that about 1/16″ of the brad protrudes.

Center one end of the curved stretcher on a leg square 2⅞″ up from the bottom of the foot and press the parts firmly together. The brad points will punch corresponding dowel center marks in the leg. Repeat this procedure for the other stretcher joints.

Use a doweling jig to drill the dowel holes in stretchers and legs. The combined depth of both holes should be about ⅛″ longer than the dowel lengths to allow space for trapped glue.

Cut dowels to length and groove them to permit trapped air to escape. The dowels should be sized so that they can be easily tapped into the holes with a mallet. Fit up the leg-stretcher assembly without glue to check the fit of the joints.

Before gluing the assembly, prepare a clamping jig from scrap stock as shown in the detail. Use a thin stick to place glue in dowel holes and on stretcher ends, and join two legs with curved stretcher. Two light-duty bar clamps are then used with the clamping jig to draw joints together. Wipe all squeezed out glue from the joints and allow this assembly to dry.

In the meantime, drill through the straight stretcher for a ⅝″ dia. cross-piece. This is glued in place and tipped with wooden balls drilled out to fit on the ends.

The end of the straight stretcher will have to be shaped with a rasp and sandpaper to conform to the slight curve of the other stretcher. Join the straight stretcher to the remaining leg; then join this assembly to the other leg-stretcher assembly, using a bar clamp to hold everything together until dry.

The flat rim on our wheel had a very slight convex shape so it was necessary to file a slight corresponding concavity on the top of each leg post to achieve a nice fit of the legs to the wheel. After this, it was a simple matter to drill the legs and the wheel for the ¾″ dia. x 1½″ dowel pins that hold the base to the top. Again, clipped brads were used to locate dowel centers.

Finally, six small rubber buttons are fastened to the topside of each wheel spoke on the square shoulder just inside the wheel rim. These buttons (which can also be of felt) should be high enough to keep the glass top just clear of the central wheel hub.

The glass, which should be cut to a diameter of about 1/16″ less than the inside of the wheel will protrude about ⅛″ above the rim when resting on the buttons.

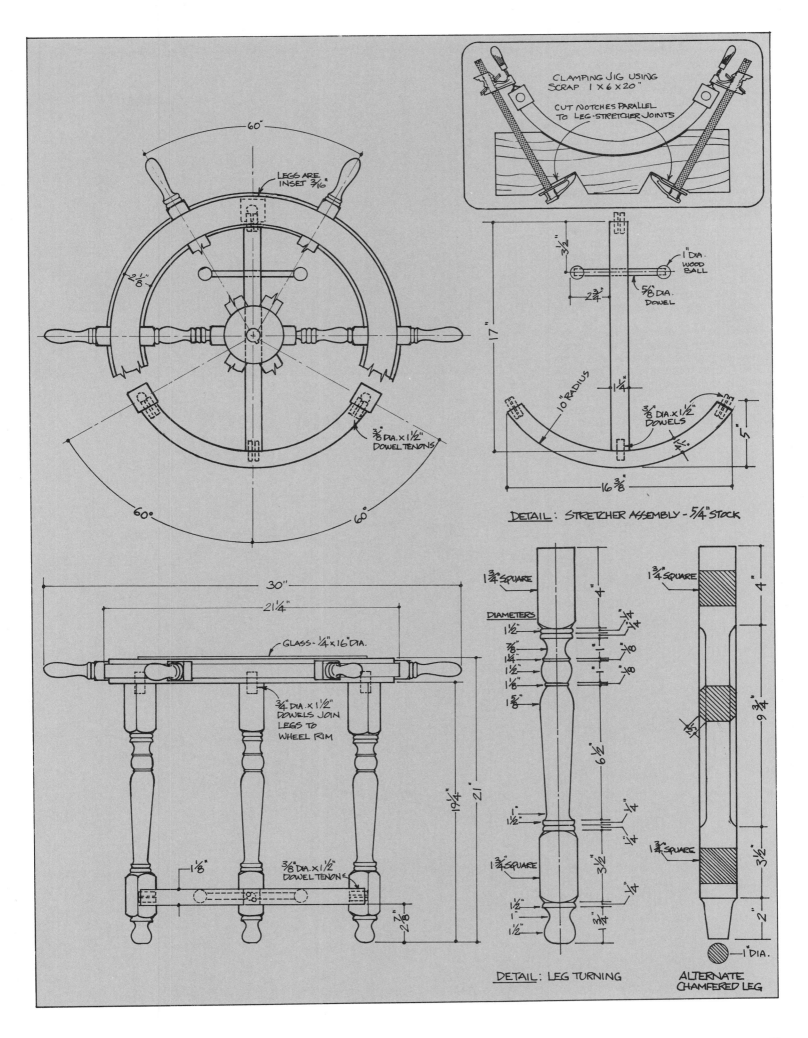

60°

LEGS ARE
INSET 3/16"

2 1/8"

3/8" DIA. x 1 1/2"
DOWEL TENONS

60°

60°

CLAMPING JIG USING
SCRAP 1 x 6 x 20"

CUT NOTCHES PARALLEL
TO LEG·STRETCHER JOINTS

3 1/2"

1" DIA.
WOOD
BALL

2 3/4"

5/8" DIA.
DOWEL

17"

10" RADIUS

3/8" DIA. x 1 1/2"
DOWELS

1 1/4"

5"

4 1/2"

16 3/8"

DETAIL: STRETCHER ASSEMBLY - 5/4" STOCK

30"

21 1/4"

GLASS - 1/4" x 16" DIA.

3/4" DIA. x 1 1/2"
DOWELS JOIN
LEGS TO
WHEEL RIM

19 1/4"

21"

1 1/8"

3/8" DIA. x 1 1/2"
DOWEL TENONS

2 7/8"

1 3/4" SQUARE

DIAMETERS
1 1/2"
7/8"
1 1/4"
1 1/2"
1 1/8"
1 5/8"

4"
1/4"
1/4"
1/16"
1/16"

6 1/2"

1"
1 1/2"

3 1/2"

1 3/4" SQUARE

1/4"
1/4"

1/2"
1"
1 1/2"

3/4"

DETAIL: LEG TURNING

1 1/4" SQUARE

4"

9 3/4"

1 1/2"

1 3/4" SQUARE

3 1/2"

2"

1" DIA.

ALTERNATE
CHAMFERED LEG

63

Designed to hold three coffee mugs, this good-looking rack is a useful accessory for either a boat or a recreational vehicle. Make it of ⅜" mahogany or teak to match a boat interior or use ⅜" plywood enameled to suit the decor of a camper van.

Our rack was sized for an average set of mugs having a major diameter of 3 inches, but if you prefer larger mugs, the size of the compartments and the width of the handle slots can be altered to suit.

Since no nails or screws are used in the joinery, it's important that all parts are cut square and the rabbet and dado joints fit perfectly. Dadoes should be cut on the snug side to allow for sanding. If the rack is to be used on a boat use a water-resistant glue. Use extra care in sanding all parts and rounding off corners.

If you've got enough clamps, the entire unit can be clamped up at once; otherwise join back, bottom and parts D and C first, then later add the ends A and B. Finish with penetrating oil, enamel or urethane varnish.

It's a very nice way to say "thank you" for a week-end invitation on board.

Mug Rack

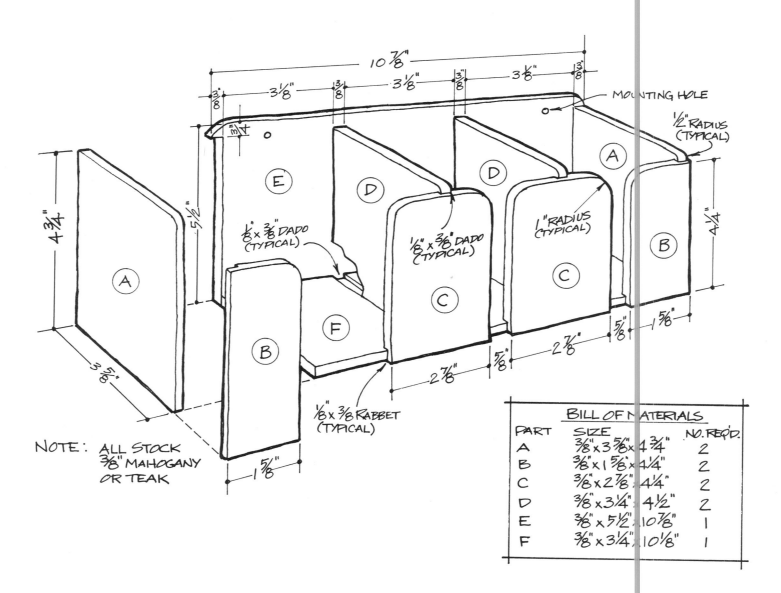

NOTE: ALL STOCK ⅜" MAHOGANY OR TEAK

BILL OF MATERIALS		
PART	SIZE	NO. REQ'D.
A	⅜" x 3⅝" x 4¾"	2
B	⅜" x 1⅝" x 4¼"	2
C	⅜" x 2⅞" x 4¼"	2
D	⅜" x 3¼" x 4½"	2
E	⅜" x 5½" x 10⅞"	1
F	⅜" x 3¼" x 10⅛"	1

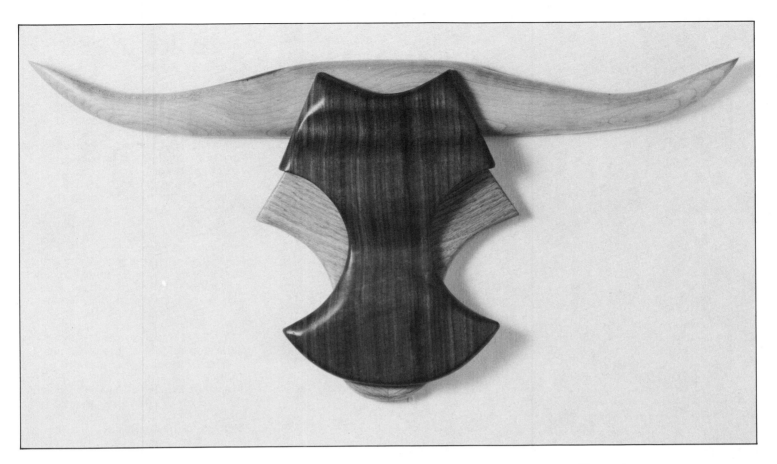

Longhorn Steer
by Ted J. Pagels

Made from oak, walnut, and maple, this most unique wall plaque will make a handsome addition to your family room, den, or perhaps over the bar.

Basically, the project consists of four parts — a maple horn, a walnut face, and two oak back section halves. All stock is 1″ nominal thickness (actual 13/16″).

Cut the maple horn to overall length and width, then use a saber or band saw to cut the front profile shown. Shape the cross-sectional profile using a rasp and/or a Surform tool. Further smooth with a file and sandpaper.

Referring to the sketch, cut the walnut face to the front profile shown. Use the saber and band saws to make the cut. Again use the rasp and Surform tool to shape the cross-sectional profile. Sand smooth.

Stock for the oak back section half is cut with the grain at 45 degrees. Cut both halves, then edge join with glue. When dry, cut to the front profile shown. Sand smooth.

Use wood screws to attach the horn and back to the face. Give the entire piece a very complete sanding, as good smooth surfaces are most important with a project like this. Finish with two coats of polyurethane followed by a rub down with 0000 steel wool. A light coat of lemon oil completes the piece.

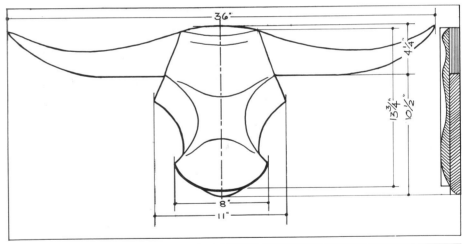

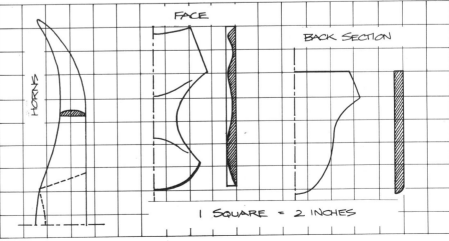

FACE

BACK SECTION

HORNS

1 SQUARE = 2 INCHES

65

Bike Rack

Made from standard 2 x 4 construction lumber and dowel stock, this sturdy rack will hold as many as eight bicycles. It's designed to fit most any size bike, from the 26″ 10-speeds to the variety of smaller kid's models.

Two pieces 8 feet long will provide all the 2 x 4 stock that's needed. From each length cut two 28″ pieces (for the frame) and one 39″ piece (for the base). Try to pick out lengths that have a minimum of warp.

The seven frame dowels are 1″ dia. and cut to 28″ lengths. The two base dowels are 1¼″ dia. birch dowel stock (available from Woodworks, 4013-A Clay Ave., Fort Worth, TX 76117) and cut to 28½″ lengths. Again, look for stock that's reasonably straight.

A rabbet is cut on both ends of the frame top and bottom and 1″ dia. by ¾″ deep dowel holes are drilled as shown. Also drill 1¼″ dia. x ¾″ deep dowel holes in the 39″ long base ends.

If the rack is to be kept outdoors, use a water resistant glue such as Weldwood Plastic Resin. Assemble the frame first. Apply glue, then clamp firmly with pipe clamps and allow to dry. The base, including the two 1¼″ dia. dowels, is added next. For a permanent joint, apply glue and clamp securely. If you expect to move someday, and would like to be able to disassemble the rack, a pair of lag screws on each end will do the job nicely. Final sand, then finish with paint or varnish as desired.

BILL OF MATERIALS		
PART	SIZE (INCHES)	QUANTITY
A	1½ x 3½ x 39	2
B	1½ x 3½ x 28	2
C	1½ x 3½ x 28	2
D	1″ DIA. x 28 DOWEL	7
E	1¼″ DIA. x 28½″ DOWEL	2

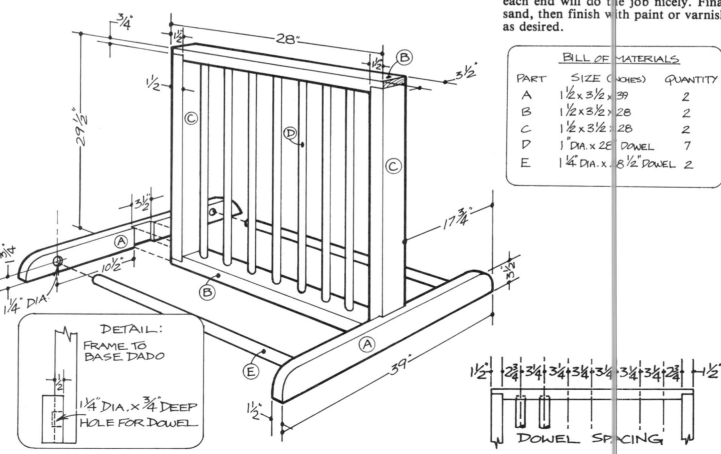

DETAIL:
FRAME TO BASE DADO

1¼″ DIA. x ¾″ DEEP HOLE FOR DOWEL

DOWEL SPACING

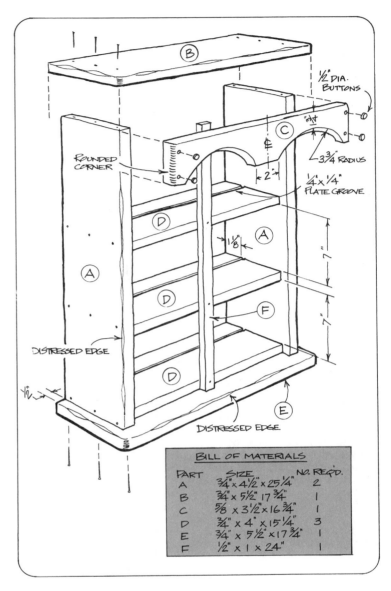

	BILL OF MATERIALS	
PART	SIZE	NO. REQ'D.
A	3/4" x 4 1/2" x 25 1/4"	2
B	3/4" x 5 1/2" 17 3/4"	1
C	5/8 x 3 1/2" x 16 3/4"	1
D	3/4" x 4" x 15 1/4"	3
E	3/4" x 5 1/2" x 17 3/4"	1
F	1/2" x 1 x 24"	1

Curio Shelves

If care is used in construction and finishing, this simple piece will look very attractive. It can be completed in a few hours by a novice woodworker using only hand tools. Units of this type can be mass-produced easily and are always popular gift items.

Ordinary knotty pine of 3/4" thickness (actual) is used for all parts, although parts C and F will have to be planed down. If you use a handsaw, cut the parts slightly wide and plane the edges to the finished width. Remember to sand all parts before assembly and be sure to wipe all glue drips off with a damp rag.

Start by cutting sides A and the three shelves D to size. The plate grooves in the shelves are cut by clamping two straight strips to the shelves with just enough space between to run a handsaw blade. The saw is used to start a straight groove, then the strips are moved a very slight distance to start another groove. A 1/4" chisel or gouge is then used to clean up and finish the groove to an equal depth.

Cut top B and bottom E to size. Coat ends of A with a thin layer of glue and allow to dry. Then spread on another layer and nail top and bottom to sides using 1 1/2" finish nails. The shelves should be inserted when nailing to keep the sides evenly spaced. The top and bottom are nailed flush with back edges of sides with an equal 1/2" overhang at the ends.

Mark locations of shelves and nail them in place making sure they are level and flush with the back edges of sides. Part C is then cut to size and planed down to 5/8" thickness. Lay out and make the circular cut-outs using a coping or saber saw.

Clamp part C to the edges of sides and butt tightly against the overhanging top. The center divider F is then cut and planed to 1/2" thickness. This is nailed to the center edge of each shelf and glued and clamped to the back of C. Bore holes in C to take decorative buttons or pieces of dowel to simulate pegs.

A half-round cabinet file is used to distress the outer edges of the unit as shown. Sand all surfaces again with 220 grit paper playing particular attention to smoothing the distressed edges. Stain unit with an oil type stain such as Minwax Early American. Apply stain with a disposable foam brush and use a rag to wipe and spread the stain evenly.

After at least 24 hours, apply two coats of satin finish urethane varnish. When the last coat is dry rub down all surfaces with 4/0 steel wool until an even soft luster is obtained, then polish with a soft cloth.

Miniature Empire Chest

by Thomas A. Gardner

This lovely miniature chest came from an old family estate. Its style, construction, aged patina and old repairs all seem to indicate that it was made during the Empire Period, 1800-1825. It is a choice antique piece. Some call these small chests "salesman samples", but it's just as logical to say they were made for little girls who wanted to play house. Both claims are probably valid.

Most parts of the original chest are made from cherry. The pine drawer fronts are veneered with crotch mahogany. Some trim and the drawer pulls are of rosewood. To simplify construction, we've designed ours to use solid stock for all parts. However drawer fronts can be veneered if you prefer. Just keep in mind that it's usually a difficult job to veneer reverse curves such as found on the upper drawer front (T), especially with crotch veneer.

First, the front posts (A) and rear posts (B) are made. The front posts are shorter than the rear, but cut all four the same length. This will prevent any error later when "pairing" the two sides for assembly. The grooves and rabbets in all four posts are identical.

Posts (A) and (B) are joined together by a panel assembly, consisting of two side rails (F) and a side panel (I). The grooves in (F) are for the side panels (I) and splines (G). Cut and glue the splines to the rails, thus forming tenons to fit into the post grooves. Assemble (F), (I) and the posts for a trial fitting. Check for squareness. If right, glue and clamp and again check with the try square. The panels must be free to move so don't glue them in place. Parts (M) serve as both runner and drawer guides. They are fitted and glued into the rabbets of the front and back posts as shown. After the glue has set, reinforce with 1" brads.

The drawer rails (K) can now be made. Cut a tenon in each end to fit into the ⅛" grooves of the posts. The ⅛" back panel (H) is cut from glued up strips of resawed pine, or ⅛" plywood may be substituted. For a trial fitting, assemble the rails and back with the sides. Check for squareness. If right, glue, clamp and again check for squareness. Part (J) is made with a tenon at each end to fit the grooves in the pilaster block (C). Assemble, then glue and clamp to the front posts.

Use ½" squares to make a pattern for the pilasters (D). Trace onto the work, then cut out on band or jig saw. Glue and clamp to the front posts after sanding. Note that the pilasters (D) are narrower than the posts in order to keep the drawers from binding on them. The feet (E) are also prepared from a pattern made from ½" squares. Cut out and smooth, then glue to the bottom of the posts. After the glue has set, 1" brads are driven into the posts for reinforcement.

Construction of the top completes the carcase. It is resawn to ⅜" from thicker stock. To make the resawing easier, cut it from two narrower widths, gluing up later. This will require some planing and sanding. A 1" brad into each corner post will hold the top securely. The original has square nails.

The upper drawer is made next. Although the front (T) can be made from flat stock, the curved profile is a nice detail and provides a distinctive look. The concave portion of that profile can best be formed by making a coving cut using the table or radial arm saw. After the concave shape is formed, the convex portion can be cut to rough shape with a hand plane. Finish shaping with a curved cabinet scraper and sandpaper, then cut to finish length. The lock is optional.

The middle and lower drawers are identical. Cut all parts to size using the bill of materials as a guide. Make a trial fitting of the front, sides, and back. If all looks okay, glue together, check for squareness, and insert into chest for fit. After the glue has set, fit the bottom and again check. Use brads to fasten to the bottom of the back.

The proper preparation of the wood surfaces is the secret to a top grade varnish finish. First, sand all surface parts before assembly, then give a final sanding and steelwooling after the assembly. Before applying the varnish (and between coats) dust the piece with a tack cloth. Thoroughly sand the first coat with #220 or #340 and steel wool #0000. For any additional coats sand lightly between with #600 wet or dry. Then steelwool and wax. However, for the final coat it is recomended to wait 48 hours for its treatment. The varnish will be harder and the finish nicer.

Bill of Materials-All Dimensions Actual

Part	Description	Size	No. Req'd	Part	Description	Size	No. Req'd
A	Front Post	13/16 x 1¼ x 10¾	2	M	Drawer Guides	¾ x ¾ x 5	6
B	Rear Post	13/16 x 1¼ x 12⅝	2	N	Top	⅜ x 7 x 13	1
C	Pilaster Block	13/16 x 1¼ x 4⅜	2	O	Drawer Front	½ x 2⅝ x 10	1/Dwr.
D	Pilaster	1 x 1¼ x 6⅜	2	P	Drawer Sides	¼ x 2⅝ x 5¼	2/Dwr.
E	Foot	1 x 1⅞ x 3¾	2	Q	Drawer Back	⅛ x 2⅜ x 9¾	1/Dwr.
F	Side Rail	⅜ x 2 x 4⅜	4	R	Drawer Bottom	⅛ x 9¾ x 4⅞	1/Dwr.
G	Spline	⅛ x ½ x 1 13/16	8	S	Drawer Pull	See Detail	2/Dwr.
H	Back Panel	⅛ x 10¼ x 10⅜	1	T	Drawer Front	13/16 x 3½ x 10	1
I	Side Panel	⅛ x 4⅜ x 7	2	U	Drawer Side	¼ x 3⅛ x 5¾	2
J	Upper Front Rail	½ x ⅞ x 10¼ (inc. tenons)	1	V	Drawer Back	⅛ x 2⅞ x 9¾	1
K	Drawer Rail	½ x ⅜ x 10¼ (inc. tenons)	2	W	Drawer Bottom	⅛ x 9¾ x 5⅛	1
L	Lower Front Rail	½ x ¾ x 10¼ (inc. tenons)	1				

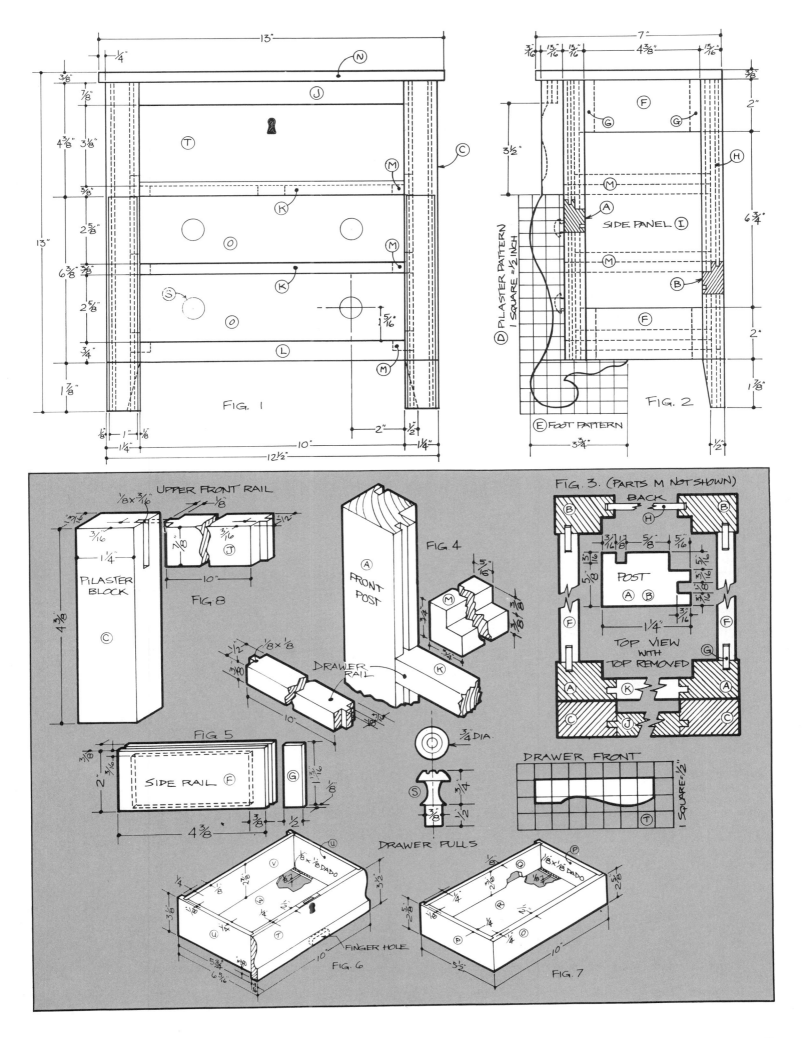

FIG. 1

FIG. 2

D PILASTER PATTERN
1 SQUARE = 1/2 INCH

E FOOT PATTERN

SIDE PANEL I

UPPER FRONT RAIL

PILASTER BLOCK
C

FIG. 8

J

FIG. 4

FRONT POST
A

DRAWER RAIL

K

M

FIG. 5

SIDE RAIL F

G

3/4 DIA.

S

DRAWER PULLS

FIG. 3. (PARTS M NOT SHOWN)

BACK

H

POST
A B

TOP VIEW
WITH
TOP REMOVED

DRAWER FRONT

T

1 SQUARE = 1/2"

FINGER HOLE

FIG. 6

FIG. 7

69

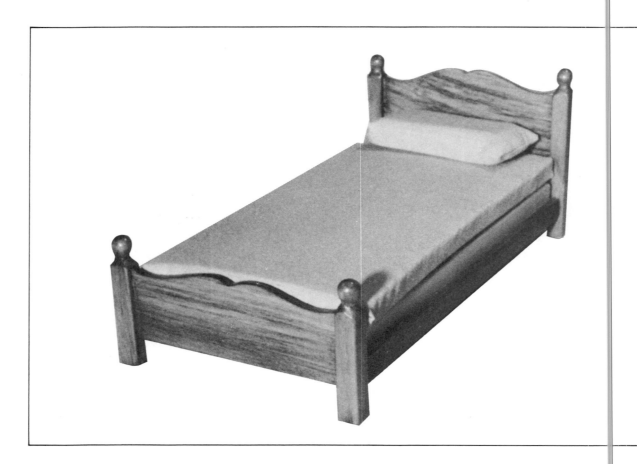

Doll House Bed
by Richard W. Koch

This bed in miniature will fit in any doll house bedroom and be enjoyed by children from 6 to 96 years. It is a collectible item and is ideal for sale to craft and gift shops.

The bed is built from white pine, cut down on a table saw to ⅛" thick. This is not difficult, but be sure to use a push stick to run the pieces through the saw. Remember, these are unusually small pieces, so take great care and keep fingers away from the blade. If you don't want to cut your own lumber, it can be obtained from most any hobby or craft shop. There are many types of woods available in larger craft shops. However, don't use balsa wood — it's too soft and won't take a good finish.

Start construction by cutting the piece for the headboard (A) from ⅛" stock. Make the width of the board 2⅜" (⅛" larger than finished size to allow for cutting the headboard design) and the finish length 3¼". You may want to make more than one bed, so cut as many of these pieces as desired. Also, at this point, make a paper pattern of the headboard (see headboard pattern). For mass production, or for making only one, place a piece of ¼" wide double-faced carpet tape at the top and bottom of the board. Working accurately, stick the pattern on the tape making sure to line it up with the bottom edge and sides of the headboard. If more than one bed is being made, stick all the headboards together with the doubleback tape and cut them all at one time. The footboard (C) is made in the same way as the headboard (see footboard pattern). (Note: if the pieces are not separated soon after cutting, you may have some difficulty separating the pieces and removing the tape.)

Head and footboard tenons are made by lining up the notches with a steel straightedge and lightly scoring the wood with a razor blade or a #11 X-Acto knife blade, not more than 1/32" deep across the grain. The end cut with the grain is done by laying the knife 1/32" in and pressing down until the waste material comes loose. It may be necessary to go over the crossgrain cut again to make the waste come off.

The construction of the posts (B & D) will require hand-carving of the knobs. Draw two lines all the way around the end of the post horizontally, one at ¼" and the other at 5/16" from the end. With the knife, notch the corners from the 5/16" line toward the end at approximately 45 degrees and about 1/16" deep. Keep notching around the post until it is semi-round, and do the same at the top of the post. Finish rounding with sandpaper.

The mortising in the post is accomplished by the use of the Dremel Moto-Tool cutter #198 (which is ¼" diameter by 1/16" thick). This cutter will make the 1/16" wide by 1/16" deep mortise. Be sure to make one left and one right-hand post for both the headboard and footboard (see post details).

The rails (E) are made from ⅜" square stock, 6-5/16" long (see section A-A). The tenons are cut on both ends as shown in detail B.

Now that all the parts have been cut and finish-sanded, assembly can proceed. Because these parts are so small, it is best to stain all parts before assembly. If this is not done, the glue will overrun the joints, and those areas with glue on them will not absorb the stain, leaving white spots. After the stain is dry, start assembly with the headboard. Glue the headboard (A) to posts (B). Next, the footboard (C) is glued to posts (D). Finally the rails, (E) are glued to the headboard and footboard. Square up the bed assembly and let dry.

The wooden boxspring (F) can now be fitted to the assembled bed. Measure the distance between the two rails and the head and footboard, then cut the boxspring to fit. The top edges of the boxspring should be rounded to remove sharp edges.

The final finish consists of two coats of polyurethane followed by a rub down with 0000 steel wool.

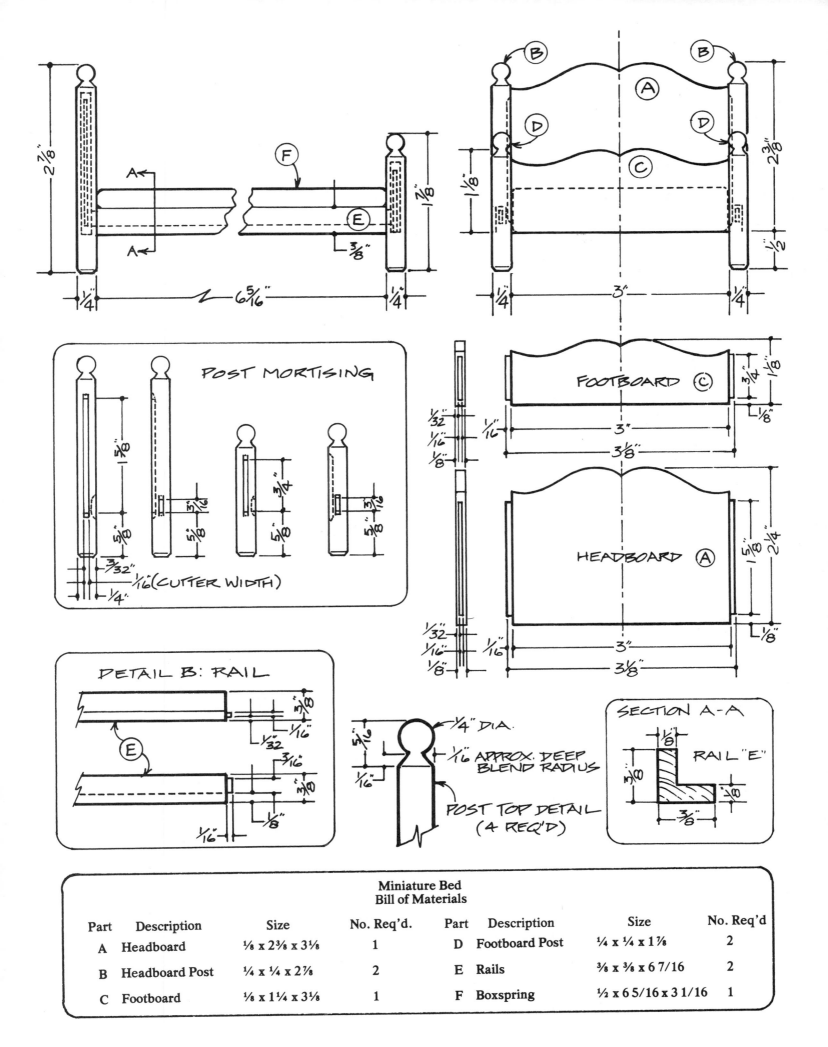

F

A — — A

A
A

B   B
A
D   D
C

FOOTBOARD C

POST MORTISING

1/16 (CUTTER WIDTH)

HEADBOARD A

DETAIL B: RAIL

E

1/4" DIA.

1/16 APPROX. DEEP
BLEND RADIUS

POST TOP DETAIL
(4 REQ'D)

SECTION A-A

RAIL "E"

Miniature Bed
Bill of Materials

Part	Description	Size	No. Req'd.	Part	Description	Size	No. Req'd
A	Headboard	⅛ x 2⅜ x 3⅛	1	D	Footboard Post	¼ x ¼ x 1⅞	2
B	Headboard Post	¼ x ¼ x 2⅞	2	E	Rails	⅜ x ⅜ x 6 7/16	2
C	Footboard	⅛ x 1¼ x 3⅛	1	F	Boxspring	½ x 6 5/16 x 3 1/16	1

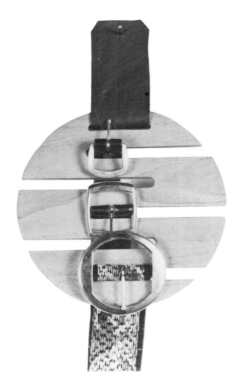

Here's a convenient way to hold as many as eight of your favorite belts. Slide them into the slots and they hang neatly in place. Made from ⅜" mahogany, it can be hung from the back of a closet door with a finishing nail through the leather hanging strap.

You'll probably have to plane down ¾" or ½" stock to get the ⅜" thickness. After planing, sand smooth, then use a compass to lay out the 7½" diameter. Also, at this time, lay out and mark the location of the slots.

Use a saber or band saw to cut the circle to shape, making sure to cut on the waste side of the line. Carefully sand the edge to remove all rough surfaces. To cut the belt slots, drill five ⅜" dia. holes as shown, then use the saber or band saw to remove the rest of the slot. The leather strap slot is made by drilling two ¼" dia. holes, then removing the waste with a saber saw.

Use a file and sandpaper to clean up the slots. Give surfaces a final sanding before applying Watco Danish Oil as a final finish.

Belt Rack

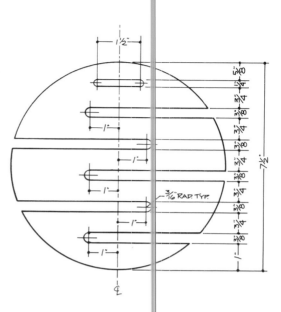

Rocker Footrest

by Henry Diamond

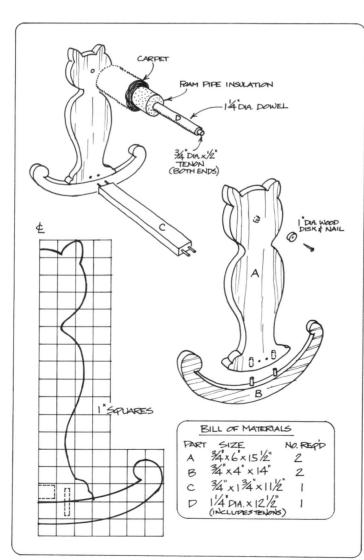

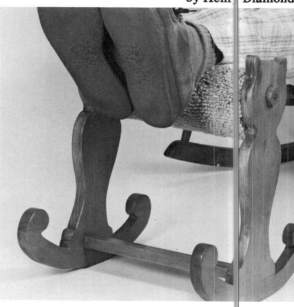

What better way to enjoy the comfort of your rocker than to be able to put your feet up as you rock.

The rockers (B) can be made first. Cut to overall length and width, then lay out and mark the curved profile. Cut to shape with a saber or band saw.

Make the two ends (A) next. Cut to dimensions shown on the bill of materials, allowing a little extra for length. Lay out the curved profile shown on the grid pattern. Mark the bottom curve using the rocker (B) as a template.

The stretcher (C) and dowel (D) are next. For the dowel use "closet pole," carried by most lumberyards. A length of foam insulation serves as a cushion. This is covered by a length of carpet which is wrapped and sewn in place.

Sand all parts, then assemble as shown. Use glue and dowels for strength. To cover the dowel tenon hole, a ¼" thick x 1" diameter wood disk is nailed into the tenon.

CARPET
FOAM PIPE INSULATION
1¼" DIA. DOWEL
¾" DIA x ½" TENON (BOTH ENDS)
1" DIA. WOOD DISK & NAIL
A
B
C
℄
1" SQUARES

BILL OF MATERIALS		
PART	SIZE	NO. REQ'D
A	¾"x 6"x 15½"	2
B	¾"x 4"x 14"	2
C	¾"x 1¾"x 11½"	1
D	1¼" DIA. x 12½" (INCLUDES TENONS)	1

Multipurpose Cabinet

by Paul Levine

The most reliable construction for cabinets of this type makes use of plywood, which is much more stable than solid wood. Using plywood is also a lot easier than forming wide surfaces from a lot of edge-joined narrow boards.

In addition to plywood, I often use plastic laminates in contemporary style cabinet work. The ease with which laminated surfaces can be cleaned plus the relatively low cost of the material makes it ideal for cabinet construction.

Given these realities, I wanted to develop a practical design that would also emphasize the beauty of natural wood. By using plywood construction for the carcase, covering it with a laminate, and then adding a distinctive solid wood front and edgings, I feel I've achieved a compromise which combines practical materials with the appeal of solid wood.

I made two of these cabinets to serve as nightstands flanking a bed, but they will also serve nicely as end or lamp tables in a contemporary setting. Since I wanted wood to dominate the design, wormy chestnut with its distinctive color, grain and worm holes was chosen for the doorframes, herringbone panel, front trim and edging strips. Almost any fine cabinet wood can be substituted, however.

Birch plywood of ¾ in. thickness was used for the box sides (A), bottom (B), and top (C), while ¼ in. birch plywood was used for the back (D). The drawings show how the five parts of the box are joined. After the box was glued up, the top and sides were covered with ¹⁄₁₆ in. plastic laminate (P) using contact cement and plenty of pressure with a rubber roller to achieve a good bond. I used a deep rust-brown laminate which harmonizes with the chestnut.

The four corners of the box were then rabbeted with a router to take the square edging strips (E) which break up the plastic surfaces and help keep the chestnut as a dominant material. I used a router with a ⅜ in. carbide straight bit and an edge-guide to cut the rabbet, taking care to move the

router from right to left to prevent chipping of the laminate. After the first pass you can then run the router from left to right to clean up. The wood edging strips are cut ⁵⁄₁₆ in. square and glued into the rabbets, then carefully planed flush and rounded off.

The face frame (parts I and J), which is cut from ¾ in. stock, mitered and then butt joined, is sized to slightly overhang the outside edges of the box. This slight overhang is later planed flush with the laminate. Mount the face frame by pre-drilling and counterboring the four members for screws. First fasten the bottom piece with glue and screws, keeping its top edge flush with the inside of the box bottom. Then hold the next piece of frame along an adjacent edge and use a sharp pencil to mark the screw holes on the box edge. A small drill bit is then used to bore the pilot holes very slightly closer to the piece already fastened. This method will help draw the pieces tightly together at the corners when the screws are driven in. Do the other adjacent edge, using this same technique and the top piece last. In order to pull the top piece miter joints tight, bore the screw holes slightly toward the inside of the cabinet.

To bring the face frame flush with the laminated surface, use a sharp plane to shave the frame while resting the plane flat on the plastic. When setting the plane iron, bury the corner of the iron that will rest on the plastic. This will prevent gouging.

Don't wipe off glue that has squeezed out of the joints while fastening. This will drive glue into the face of the frame and inhibit the finish. Instead, let the squeeze out form beads and dry. The beads will be easy to scrape or plane off later.

The cabinet base (parts G and H) can be made up of ordinary ¾ in. pine, the corners being joined with splined miters. The base can be painted flat black or covered with

(continued on next page)

the black plastic trim sold especially for kitchen counter bases. I do not feel that it's necessary to screw the base to the box; a good glue bond should be sufficient.

The doorframe, parts K and L, is joined with mortises and tenons. A ⅜ by ⅜ in. rabbet is routed around the frame inside after assembly to hold the door panel (M). The panel can be handled in a wide variety of ways. The method I chose was to make up an oversize panel of chestnut boards planed to ⅜ in. thickness and lap joined at the sides and ends. This permits the direct glue-joining of both halves of a herringbone pattern without splines. The glued up panel is weighted to keep it flat and, when dry, is cut to 14⅞ in. square, allowing ⅛ in. all around for expansion in the door-frame.

The panel is held in place on the back of the door with four battens or retainers (N) which are simply butted and screwed in place. These retainers should be cut and located after the hinges have been temporarily mounted. The door is hinged to glued-in hinge blocks (Q) inside the case which bring the hinges out flush with the face frame. The concealed European style hinges (O) are full-overlay, self-closing, and fully adjustable after installation. These hinges are available from The Woodworkers' Store, (see source index) and through other mail-order firms that carry cabinetmaker's supplies. Instructions for mounting are usually included with the hinges.

The batten (N) adjacent to the hinges will have to be located and notched to provide clearance for the hinge arms when the door is closed. Also, the door frame must be mortised with a Forstner bit, as shown in the hinge detail, to take the hinge cups.

To form the door pull, rout the back of the door frame starting 2½ in. from the top with a ½ in. cove bit. This cut can be made to suit or 3½ in. long as shown. Next, round the face of the doorframe with a ¼ in. quarter rounding bit. Run the bit all around the frame except where the cove cut was made.

Set the router against the frame edge near where the pull is to be, and mark where the router base lies when the bit guide bearing is against the side of the frame. Clamp a straightedge ³⁄₁₆ in. away from this mark and rout the part of the frame face in line with the cove on the back.

The final step is the screw mounting of ¼ in. by 1 in. mitered back trim strips (F) around the sides and top back of the cabinet. These add to the design and cover the exposed dadoes. They are also handy for clamping on a nice adjustable reading lamp. The cabinet (and much of my other work) is finished with several coats of Watco Danish Oil.

	Bill of Materials	(all dimensions actual)	
Part	Description	Size	No. Req'd.
A	Side	¾ × 16⅞ × 21	2
B	Bottom	¾ × 16⅞ × 20	1
C	Top	¾ × 16⅞ × 20	1
D	Back	¼ × 20 × 19¼	1
E	Edging Strip	⁵⁄₁₆ × ⁵⁄₁₆ × 16⅞	4
F	Back Trim	¼ × 1 × 21	3
G	Base Side	¾ × 3¼ × 17	2
H	Base End	¾ × 3¼ × 13	2
I	Face Frame Rail	¾ × 1½ × 21	2
J	Face Frame Stile	¾ × 1½ × 21	2
K	Doorframe Rail	¾ × 2½ × 16¼*	2
L	Doorframe Stile	¾ × 2½ × 19¼	2
M	Door Panel	⅜ × 14⅞ × 14⅞	1
N	Battens	½ × 1¼ × as req'd.	4
O	Hinges	full overlay**	1 pair
P	Laminate	¹⁄₁₆ × 16⅞ × 21***	3
Q	Hinge Blocks	¾ × 1¼ × 3	2

*Includes 1 in. long tenons.

**Available from: Woodcraft Supply Corp., (see source index) order part no. 13M21-XM.

***Wilson Art part no. D-60-6.

Cabinet base consists of four pieces of pine with ends mitered and grooved for splines.

The completed box and base assembly ready to be covered with plastic laminate.

After laminate is applied, the four corners are routed for the strips which are glued in place and rounded off.

Rear view of door showing battens (N) holding panel. Note notches in batten for hinge arm.

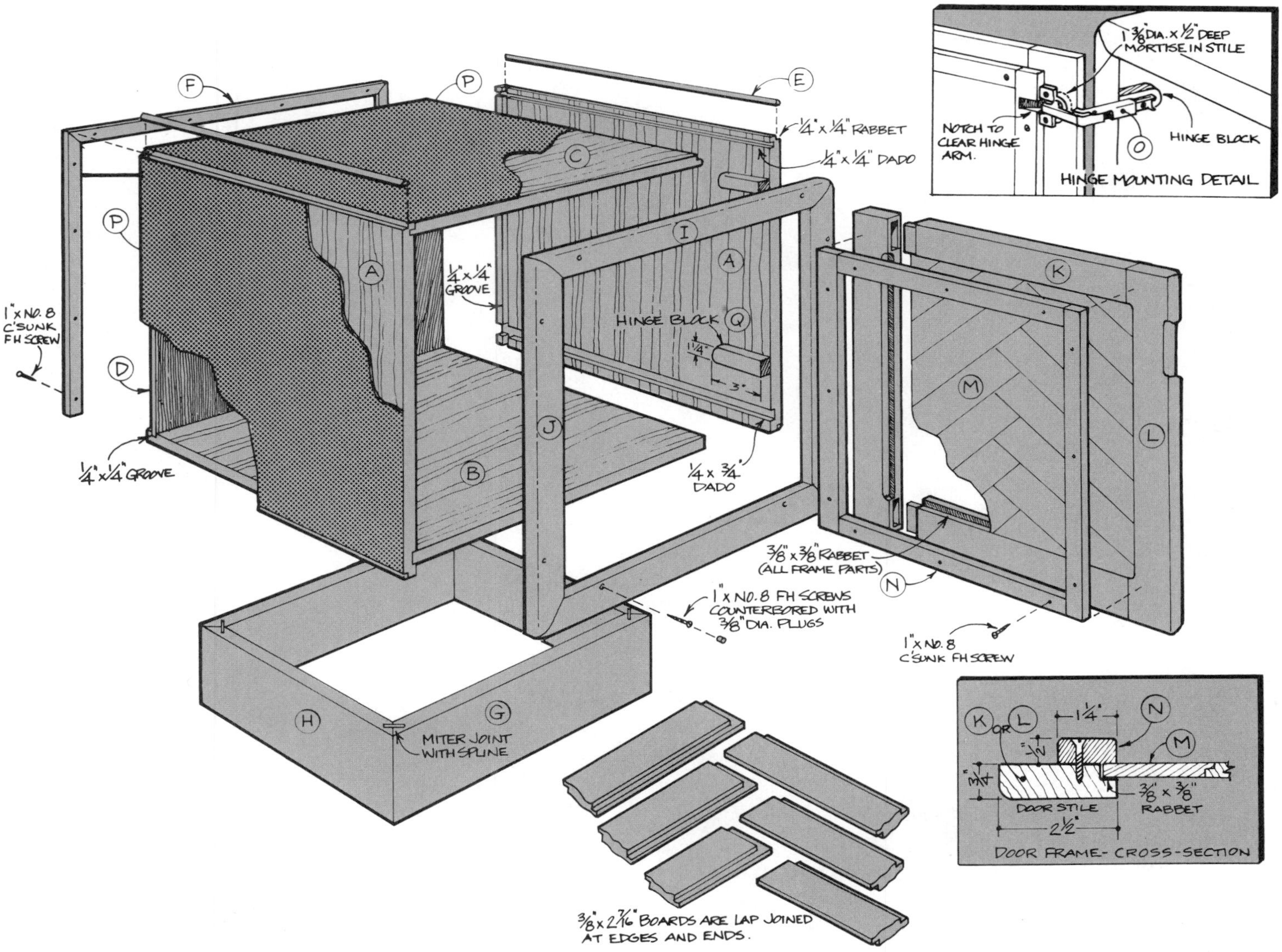
F
P
E
1/4" x 1/4" RABBET
1/4" x 1/4" DADO
C
P
A
I
A
K
1/4" x 1/4" GROOVE
1" x No. 8 C'SUNK FH SCREW
HINGE BLOCK Q
1/4"
3"
D
J
M
L
1/4" x 1/4" GROOVE
B
1/4 x 3/4 DADO
3/8" x 3/8" RABBET (ALL FRAME PARTS)
N
1" x No. 8 FH SCREWS COUNTERBORED WITH 3/8" DIA. PLUGS
1" x No. 8 C'SUNK FH SCREW
H
G
MITER JOINT WITH SPLINE
3/8 x 2 7/16" BOARDS ARE LAP JOINED AT EDGES AND ENDS.
1 3/8" DIA. x 1/2" DEEP MORTISE IN STILE
NOTCH TO CLEAR HINGE ARM.
O
HINGE BLOCK
HINGE MOUNTING DETAIL
K OR L
1 1/4"
N
M
3/4"
3/8" x 3/8" RABBET
DOOR STILE
2 1/2"
DOOR FRAME - CROSS-SECTION

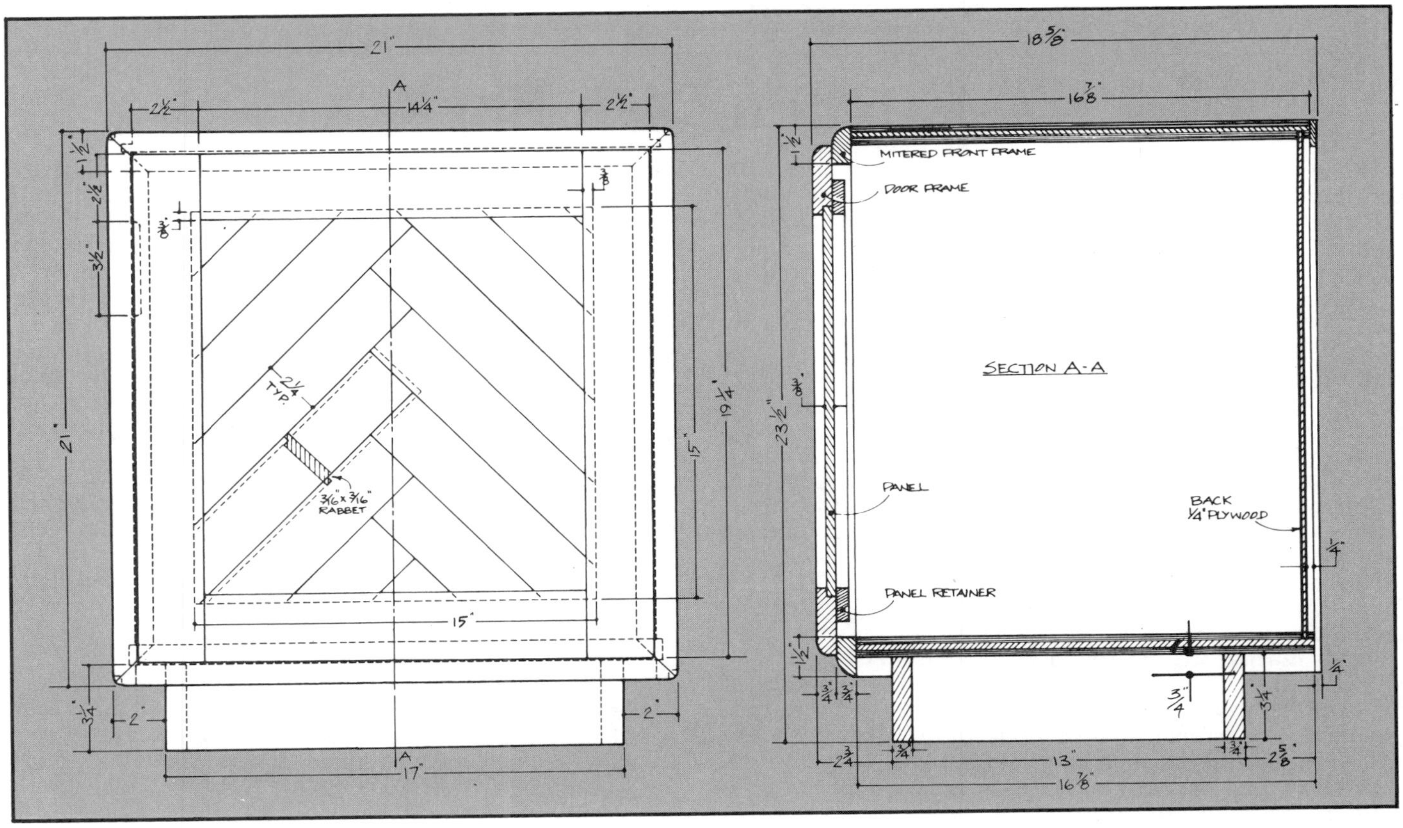
21"
A
2 1/2"
14 1/4"
2 1/2"
2 1/2"
3 1/2"
2 1/4 TYP.
3/16" x 3/16" RABBET
21"
19 1/4"
15"
15"
3/4"
2"
2"
A
17"
18 5/8"
16 7/8"
MITERED FRONT FRAME
DOOR FRAME
SECTION A-A
23 1/2"
PANEL
BACK 1/4" PLYWOOD
PANEL RETAINER
1/4"
3/4
3/4
2 3/4
13"
2 5/8"
16 7/8"

Kitchen Dish Rack

The dish rack is generally considered a purely utilitarian kitchen utensil - one that's just not expected to ever look like much. However, we think ours is an exception. Made from white ash, this rack is not only very attractive, it also folds flat so that it can be hung neatly on the kitchen wall.

The slats are made first. Begin by cutting two pieces of 1″ ash (13/16″ actual) stock to 1½″ wide by 38½″ long. Set the table saw rip fence for a ½″ wide cut and adjust the saw blade height to 13/16″. Now feed the stock, on edge, through the saw blade. (Note: be sure to use a pushstick and keep hands away from the blade.) This will produce a cut slightly more than halfway through the 1½″ wide stock. Next, flip the stock over and repeat the cut. This operation, called resawing, reduces the thickness of the stock from ¾″ to ½″. Now this ½″ thick x 1½″ wide stock can be ripped to ⅜″ widths, then cut to 7½″ lengths. This method of cutting will result in 30 slats (4 extra), each measuring ⅜″ x ½″ x 7½″. Also, at this time, cut the cup rack base (¾ x 1 x 17⅜) and back (2 pcs. ¼ x ⅜ x 17⅜).

Begin making the horizontal frame members by cutting ¾″ (actual) stock to 4½″ wide x 20″ long. At the middle of the board length (10″ from each end), mark the location of the center dado. Then, working out toward the ends, continue to mark the location of the remaining dadoes (6 on each side). This layout method assures that there will be room for the frame ends later on.

Now the dado head can be used to cut the thirteen, ⅜″ wide x ⅛″ deep dadoes across the 4½″ board width. Make several test cuts on scrap stock to make sure the slats fit snugly. If necessary, make adjustments in the dado width. When all 13 cuts have been made, the board can be ripped into 4 pieces, each 1″ wide. These pieces are longer than needed, but will be trimmed to fit when assembled.

Cut the four frame ends to size (¾ x 1 x 15), then cut the cup rack dadoes on the two short rack legs. Now lay out the location of the ⅜″ pivot pin hole. With each frame end pair edge-to-edge, drill the hole through both pieces. (Make sure the hole is square).

The slats can now be glued in place. Since the dish rack will have constant exposure to water, it's most important to use a glue that has good water resistance. Weldwood Plastic Resin is a good choice. Clamp firmly.

Assemble all other parts as shown. Always use water resistant glue and dowel pins where shown. The pivot pins are glued only to the long rack frame ends, leaving the short frame free to pivot.

Thoroughly sand all surfaces. A belt sander is useful here, especially on end grain surfaces. Slightly round all edges. No finish is necessary, since white ash is very suitable for applications that require regular washing and scrubbing.

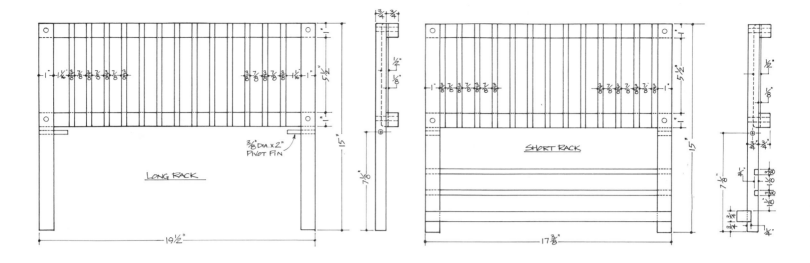

LONG RACK

3/8" DIA. x 2"
PIVOT PIN

19½"

SHORT RACK

17⅜"

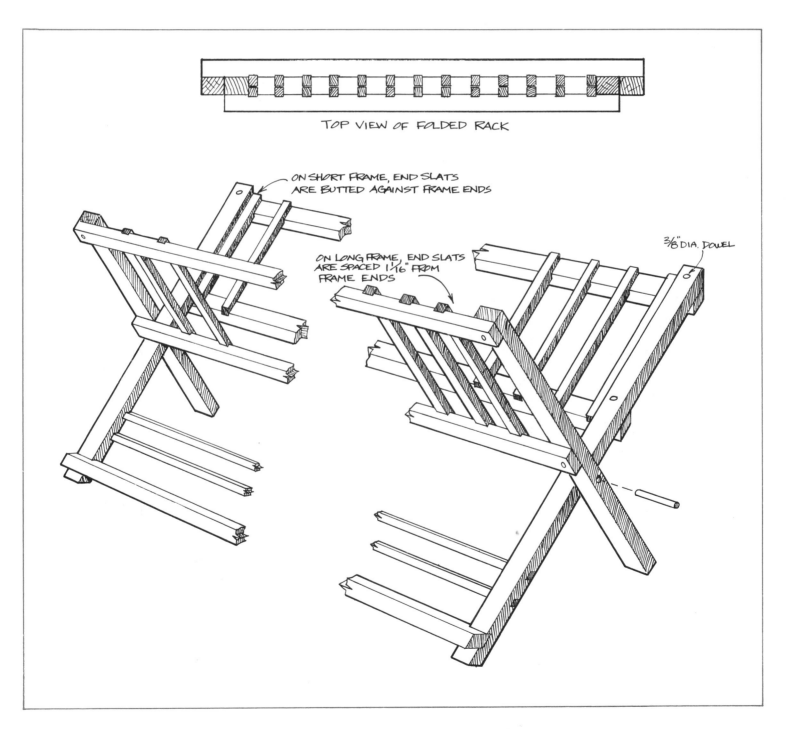

TOP VIEW OF FOLDED RACK

ON SHORT FRAME, END SLATS
ARE BUTTED AGAINST FRAME ENDS

ON LONG FRAME, END SLATS
ARE SPACED 1¹⁄₁₆" FROM
FRAME ENDS

3/8" DIA. DOWEL

Early American Wall Shelf

Wall shelves are always popular with our readers and this one should be no exception — especially if you enjoy the flavor of Early American.

Begin construction by cutting the two sides to length and width. Lay out and mark the location of the ¾" wide x ¼" dadoes, then use the dado head to cut out. This operation can also be done by making repeated passes with the saw blade. Now, referring to the grid pattern, lay out the profile shown, then cut out with the saber or band saw.

The back is made up of tongue-and-groove pine boards. First lay out the back stock, allowing ⅛" space between the boards, clamp temporarily on a flat surface, transfer the illustrated grid and cut to shape (top & bottom). Later, the back boards will be screwed as shown to the shelf backs, maintaining the ⅛" spacing to allow for wood movement.

Next, cut the three shelves and drawer dividers to size. Give all parts a complete sanding, then assemble with glue and finishing nails. Now add the back. The three drawers are then made as per the bill of materials and drawer detail shown. Note the sides and back are ½" stock. A ⅜" x ¾" x 1" drawer stop block is glued to the drawer support shelf. Center it just behind the drawer front.

Use a file to give all edges a good rounding before final sanding. Some well chosen distress marks will add a lot of old charm to new pine. Finish by staining with two coats of Minwax Early American stain followed by two coats of Minwax Antique Oil Finish.

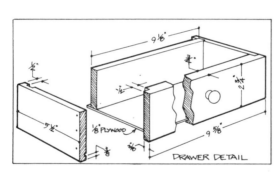

DRAWER DETAIL

Bill of Materials (Dimensions in Inches)		No. Req'd.
Side	¾ x 7 x 19⅜	2
Upper Shelf	¾ x 4½ x 31	1
Lower Shelf	¾ x 6¼ x 31	1
Drawer Support	¾ x 6¼ x 31	1
Drawer Divider	¾ x 2¾ x 6¼	2
Back	¾ x 22⅜ x 30½	1
Drawer Front	¾ x 2¾ x 9⅜	3
Drawer Side	½ x 2¾ x 5½	6
Drawer Back	½ x 2¼ x 9⅛	3
Drawer Bottom	⅛ x 5⅜ x 9⅛	3

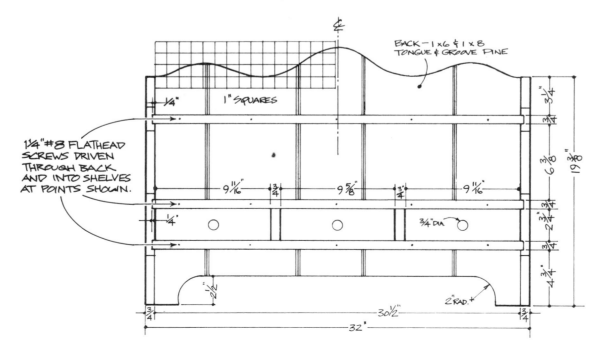

BACK—1x6 & 1x8 TONGUE & GROOVE PINE

1" SQUARES

1¼" #8 FLATHEAD SCREWS DRIVEN THROUGH BACK AND INTO SHELVES AT POINTS SHOWN.

¾" DIA

2" RAD.

30½"

32"

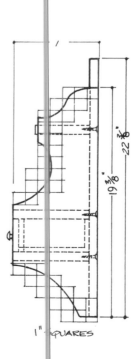

1" SQUARES

Deacon's Wall Shelf

Resembling an old-fashioned Deacon's bench, this attractive wall unit will add a bit of charm to most any room.

Begin by cutting the sides (A) to length and width. Lay out and mark the location of the ¼" deep dado and lower rabbet, then make the cut with a dado head cutter, or make repeated passes using the table or radial arm saw. Cut the rabbet and dado slightly narrower than the mating parts (E & F). Then, when parts E and F are sanded, the fit will be just right. The back notches can be cut using the same method. Next, using the grid pattern shown, lay out, mark, and cut the curved profile.

Parts E and F can now be cut to size. Note each one has a ¼" deep dado to take part G. Cut part G so that its end grain goes into the dadoes rather than showing in front.

After parts B and C are cut to size, lay out and mark the location of the sixteen dowels. Use a ⅜" dia. bit to drill each hole to a depth of ⅜". If you have one, use a countersink bit to apply a slight (1/16") chamfer to each hole. It's a small detail, but one that shows that care and concern went into the piece.

Sand all parts thoroughly, then assemble using glue and finishing nails. Since the shelf is fairly heavy and is hung from part B, be sure to glue each dowel for added strength. Assemble the drawers as shown. A ¼" by 1" notch is cut in the bottom of part K to permit the drawer to fit over part H.

Our shelf is finished with one coat of Deft Pumpkin wood stain followed by two coats of Deftco (Deft) Danish Oil Finish. Two angled holes drilled through part B and into part A permit the shelf to be hung on a pair of finishing nails.

Bill of Materials
(All Dimensions Actual)

Part	Description	Size	No. Req'd
A	Side	¾ x 7¼ x 11	2
B	Upper Back	¾ x 3 x 24½	1
C	Lower Back	¾ x 4 x 24½	1
D	Dowel	⅜ dia. x 5¾	16
E	Bottom	¾ x 6½ x 23½	1
F	Shelf	¾ x 6½ x 23½	1
G	Divider	¾ x 6½ x 2½	1
H	Drawer Stop	¼ x ¾ x 1	2
I	Drawer Front	¾ x 2 x 11⅛	2
J	Drawer Side	½ x 2 x 5⅝	4
K	Drawer Back	½ x 2 x 10⅝	2
L	Drawer Bottom	¼ x 4-15/16 x 10-9/16	2

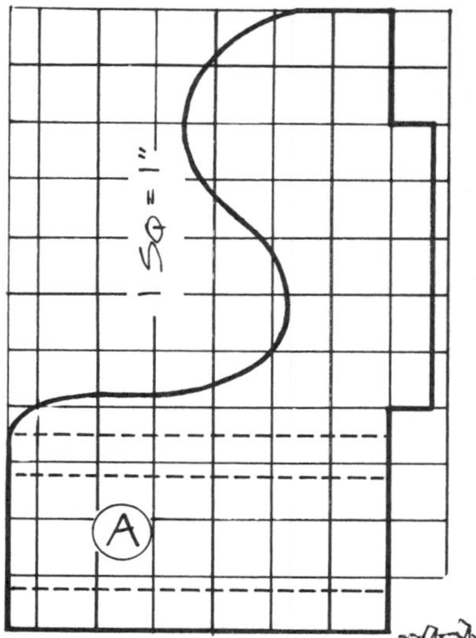

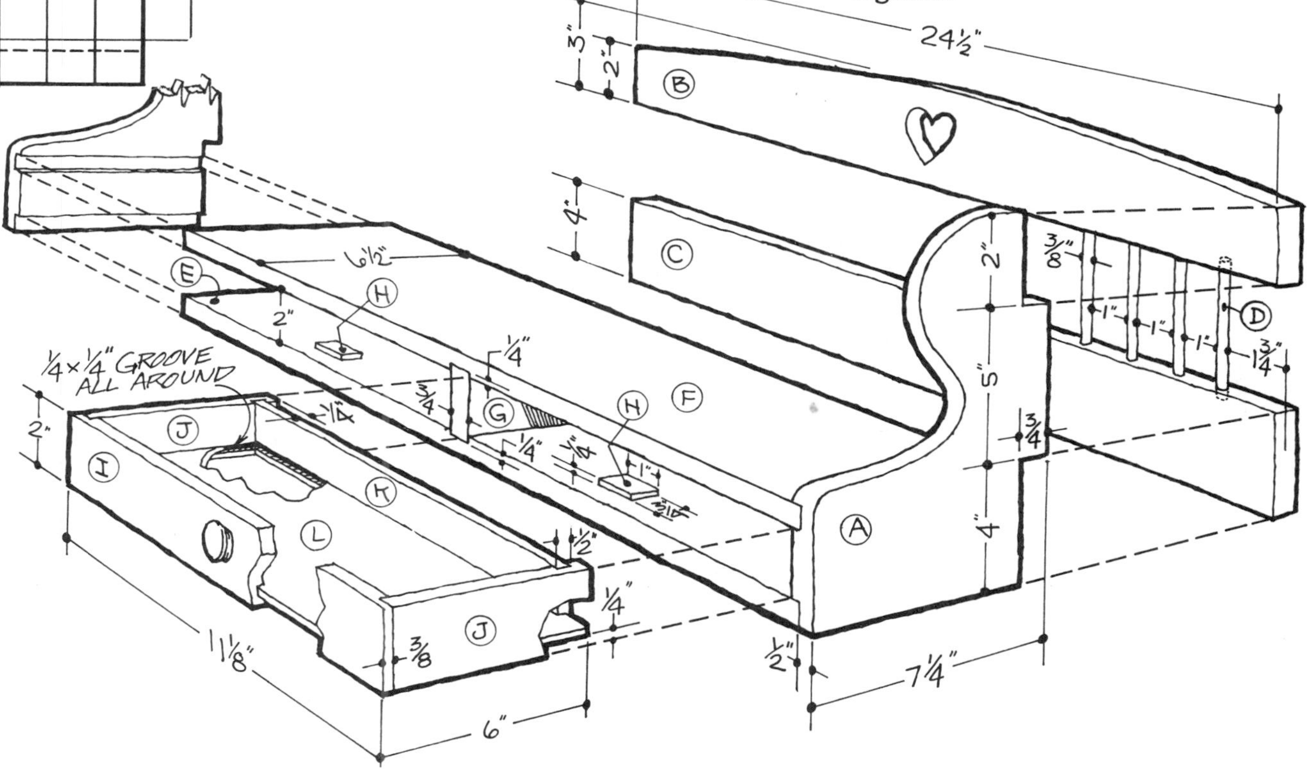

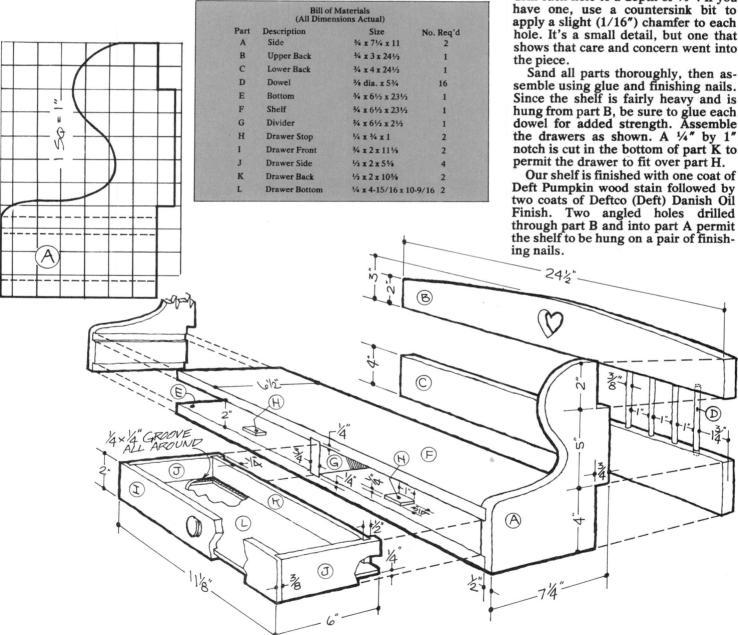

18th Cent. Rudder Table

Space was at a premium in most early American homes, which perhaps explains why tables like this were so popular during that period. With the leaves folded down, the table took up little room when not in use. We think that feature was a good one, and that it can still be enjoyed today — especially for anyone with a small house or apartment.

Ours is made from #2 common pine. The construction techniques are fairly straightforward and should not present any unusual difficulty.

Make the two sides (A) first. Standard 1 x 12 stock will provide enough width, or if necessary you can edge-join narrower stock. Cut to the length and width shown in the bill of materials, then lay out the location of the ⅜" thick x 2" wide x 1" long double tenons.

To make the tenons, equip the table saw with a dado head cutter and set it for a 3/16" depth of cut. With the stock held securely against the miter gauge, make a 3/16" x 1" rabbet cut on one end. Turn the stock over and repeat the cut. If you don't have a dado head, you can accomplish the same cut making repeated passes with a regular table saw blade. Since the stock is 2 feet long, you'll have a lot more control if you attach about an 18" length of scrap stock to the miter gauge. Make sure the scrap stock is straight. Now use a back saw to establish the 2" tenon width, then remove the remaining material with a sharp chisel.

The dado head cutter can also be used to cut the ⅜" x 2" notch for part C and the ⅜" x 6" notch for part D. Next, the 3½" high x 6" wide drawer opening can be located and marked on the stock. Drill one or two starting holes, then cut out with the saber saw. Note the drawer opening is located 1½" from the top and 1-1/16" from each side. Now transfer the grid pattern from the drawing and cut the profile to shape with the saber saw.

Cut the feet (B) to length and width, then lay out the location of the ⅜" x 2" x 1" mortises. It's a good idea to make the mortise a little deeper than 1" to allow for any excess glue. Use a ⅜" dia. drill bit to remove most of the stock, then use a chisel to square the corners and clean up waste stock. Transfer the grid pattern and cut to shape with the saber saw.

The stretchers (C) and aprons (D) can now be cut to length and width. Size the width for a good fit in the side (A) notches. The ⅜" x ¾" rabbets can be cut with the dado head on the table saw. Note that the stretcher (C) has a ⅜" dia. x ½" deep hole drilled to take the rudder (part E) tenon. Locate the hole halfway (14⅜") across the length and right in the center of the ¾" thickness.

Cut the rudder (E) to length and width. A ⅜" dia. x ¾" deep hole is drilled at a point ⅝" in from the side edge. Two holes are required, one at the top and one at the bottom. These holes must be located exactly in the center of the ¾" thickness in order for the rudder to operate properly. Now, transfer the grid pattern and cut to shape. Note that the rudder also has a slight notch with rounded corners. This is to insure that the rudder will clear the apron (D).

The top (H) can be made from standard 1" x 12" stock which measures 11¼" wide. Select stock that's flat and free of large knots or other imperfections. The ⅜" dia. x ½" deep hole for the rudder tenon is drilled on the underside of H. Locate the hole halfway across the length and ½" in from the edge. If you think the drill bit point might break through the other side, make the hole just ⅜" deep and shorten the rudder tenon to fit. The leaves (I) can also be made from standard 1" x 12" stock. Cut these parts slightly longer than necessary, then butt together and scribe a 33¾" dia. circle. Cut out with the saber saw.

Before assembly, give all parts a complete sanding. Take extra care with the curved edges so they look clean and smooth. Cut ⅜" dia. x 1¼" long dowel stock and glue in place for the rudder tenons. Assemble parts A and B using glue and clamps. When dry, parts C and D can be joined to the leg, again using glue and clamps.

Parts F and G can then be cut, sanded, and glued together (see Detail), then joined to fit the apron (D).

Attach the four hinges, then assemble the top to the base using the four fastening blocks (see Detail part J). Changes in moisture content will cause the top to change in width, therefore the blocks require elongated holes which allow free movement of the top. If this free movement is not permitted, stresses will build that could cause the top to crack. When installing, it's not necessary to overtighten the screw - just enough so the top contacts part D. The two drawers (K) are made as shown.

Our table was finished with two coats of Deft Pumpkin wood stain followed by two coats of Deftco (Deft) Danish Oil finish.

Bill of Materials (All Dimensions Actual)		
Part	Size	No. Req'd
A	¾ x 11 x 24 (inc. tenons)	2
B	1½ x 2 x 19	2
C	¾ x 2 x 28¾	2
D	¾ x 6 x 28¾	2
E	¾ x 11¼ x 20½	2
F	¾ x 1½ x 27¼	2
G	¹¹⁄₁₆ x ¾ x 27¼	2
H	¾ x 11¼ x 33½	1
I	¾ x 11¼ x 33½	2
J	¾ x 1 x 2½	4
K	See Drawing	2

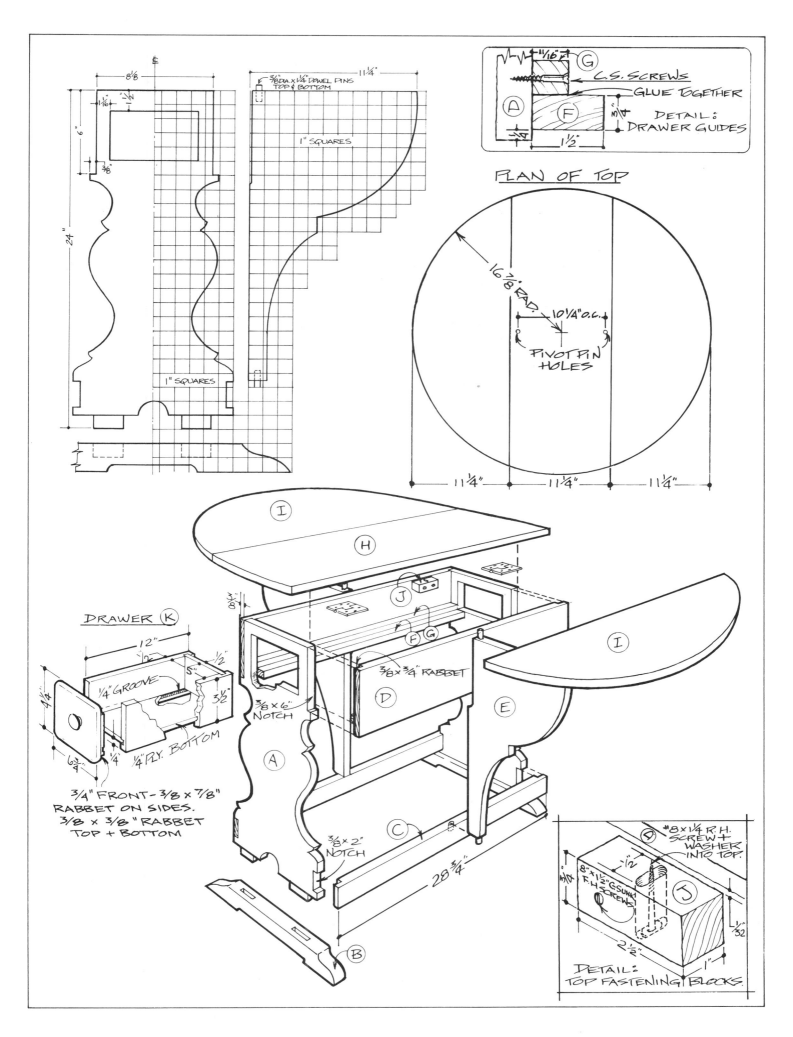

1" SQUARES

3/16" DIA. x 1/4" DOWEL PINS
TOP & BOTTOM

1" SQUARES

DETAIL: DRAWER GUIDES

C.S. SCREWS
GLUE TOGETHER

PLAN OF TOP

16 7/8" RAD.

10 1/4" O.C.

PIVOT PIN HOLES

11 1/4"   11 1/4"   11 1/4"

DRAWER K

12"
1/4" GROOVE
5"
1/2"
1/4"
4 1/2"
3 1/2"
6 3/4"
1/4" PLY. BOTTOM

3/4" FRONT - 3/8 x 7/8"
RABBET ON SIDES.
3/8 x 3/8" RABBET
TOP + BOTTOM

3/8 x 3/4" RABBET

3/8 x 6" NOTCH

3/8 x 2" NOTCH

28 3/4"

DETAIL: TOP FASTENING BLOCKS.

#8 x 1/4" R.H.
SCREW + WASHER
INTO TOP.

8" x 1 1/2" C'SUNK
F.H. SCREWS

2 1/2"
1"
1/32"

by Sam Allen

Musical Jewelry Box

Laminating curved shapes is an interesting aspect of woodworking. It can make seemingly impossible projects easy. This jewelry box is an example. The lid would be difficult to produce without using laminating techniques. If you haven't tried laminating before, this is a good starter project because the laminating form is simple to build and the project is small enough that ordinary clamps can be used to exert pressure on the form. Using the form, a number of sheets of veneer are glued together and clamped to the desired curve. When the glue dries, the laminated sheets will remain nicely curved. There are several ways to construct a laminating form. One way is to glue up several pieces of thick pine to make a block 4½" x 8" x 12" (Fig. 1). Lay out the 2¾" and 3" radii on the end of the block and cut on the smaller radius with a band saw. On the female half of the form make a second cut along the 3" radius line. The ¼" of waste allows for the thickness of the veneers that make up the lid.

Cutting this block requires a band saw with a large depth-of-cut capacity. If you do not have access to such a machine, another method is to turn a 5½" dia. x 11¼" cylinder on the lathe using a block of glued-up pine. This will be the form over which the veneer will be bent. A section of 6" dia. galvanized stovepipe is cut to 17½" wide x 12½" long and fitted with clamping cleats secured with screws and washers (Fig. 2). The second photo shows how this flexible steel is bent around the form, pressure being applied with C-clamps.

If you can't buy veneers locally, they are available by mail from Albert Constantine and Son, 2050 Eastchester Rd., Bronx, NY 10401. Veneers can range in thickness from 1/40" to 1/28". The lid lamination is ¼" thick and consists of an outer walnut veneer with decorative inlay, a core of cheaper veneers and an inner veneer, also of walnut. The core consists of any grade B veneer. Poplar crossbanding is excellent for the core as it is low in cost, flexible, and comes in sheets 12" wide. The number of laminates in the lid will

vary depending on the thickness of the veneers you obtain, but you should try for a final thickness of ¼ inch.

The outside or face veneer, which is inlaid, is applied later, after the core veneers and inside face have been laminated. Cut the pieces of veneer 10" wide x 12¼" long, a bit larger than finish size of the lid to allow for trimming later. Use liquid hide glue; it comes ready-to-use in a bottle, and allows for longer setup. Apply it evenly to both surfaces of each laminate. A 2" paint roller is an easy way to spread the glue evenly.

Whichever type of form you use, be sure to cover both surfaces with wax paper to prevent the veneer from sticking to the form. Use a piece of scrap veneer the same thickness as the face veneer to act as a spacer to compensate for the face veneer to be added later. Clamp the two halves of the wood form together with large handscrews, or if you use the wood plug and stovepipe form, clamp together with C-clamps. After the glue is dry, remove the lid from the form and cut its ends square and trim to finish size.

Next, the ends of the lid (C) are cut on the band saw for a good fit in the lamination. The ends are then used as templates to cut the curved ¼" x 1" wide decorative strips (D) which are glued to the ends.

The ends are glued to the lid lamination by clamping in place either of the forms previously used. When dry, file and sand the tops of the ends until they are perfectly flush with the lid. Fill any voids that are present as any irregularities in the tops of the lid will telegraph through to the face veneer.

I used a commercially made inlay (Constantine #1W9), but you could make your own. The inlay I used comes in a piece of walnut veneer 8" x 12" which is a little too narrow to cover the entire lid so it's necessary to joint and tape a 2" wide strip of matching walnut veneer to the edge that will be near the backside of the lid.

Coat the top of the lid and side of the inlaid sheet that doesn't have paper or tape on it with glue. Remove the veneer spacer from the form and place the inlay and lid into the wood mold. The male half of the mold will no longer fit because of the ends glued to the lid, so simply place a board across the ends to clamp the lid into the form. The alternate cylinder and sheet metal form can be used without modification for the final lamination though care will have to be taken to make sure that the face veneer comes into good contact with the top of the curved trim pieces D. The face veneer could have been installed at the same time the lid was being laminated but by doing it in this sequence, the joints between the ends and the lid are completely hidden, as shown in Detail A. After removing the completed lid from the form, scrape off the paper and tape that covers the inlay and jointed edges and sand the inlay smooth.

The box is constructed of ¼" walnut as shown in Figs. 3 and 4. The box bottom and music box case are made of resawed aromatic red cedar. The easiest way to attach the decorative strips to the box front and back is to use the jig shown in Fig. 5. Lay the strips (F pieces are ¾" wide, E pieces are 1" wide) face down on the jig so they butt together, and apply yellow glue; then clamp a side (A) down on top of the jig. The removable rabbeted strips on the jig provide the proper spacing to form the corner joint. After the glue is dry, these strips must be unscrewed to release the assembly.

Assemble the box and add ¼" x 1" wide decorative strips to the box ends so they cover the corner joints, as shown in Detail B. Once all the decorative strips are on, use a router with a ⅜" cove bit and pilot to cove all the outside corners and around the outside curve of the lid. Set the depth so the cutter comes within 1/16" of the edge of the front strips F, as shown in Detail B.

The inside edges of the frame are coved also but not as deeply as the outside corners. To do this it is necessary to grind ⅛" off the length of the pilot as shown in Detail A; otherwise the pilot will butt against the box ends and prevent the cutter wings from contacting the wood. It would be wise to practice these cuts on scrap, taking very light cuts.

Low cost music box movements are available from Constantine. The exact mounting position may vary according to the type of movement you buy. The winding key is recessed in the box bottom by boring a 1½" dia. hole part way through with a spade or auger bit. The movement comes with a trip wire that stops the air-vane governor on the movement. This wire is usually too short to reach the lid of the box and must be extended. Drill a 1/16" dia. hole in the box end as shown in Detail C. The hole position will depend on the location of the trip wire of your movement. Next drill a ⅜" dia. hole part way through the end to intersect with the 1/16" hole. Enlarge the top of the 1/16" hole to accept a ball point pen spring under slight compression. Now snake a piece of stiff wire through the hole, install the spring and bend a loop in the end of the wire to keep the spring in place. The other end of the wire is linked with the trip wire as shown.

The jewelry box tray is an optional feature and automatically lifts out of the box as the lid is raised. Two 3/16" thick walnut arms make this possible. They are recessed into the side of the tray and pivot on brass wood screws (see Figs. 6 and 7). A brass screw also connects the tray to the lid and allows the tray to pivot. Small felt washers are placed between the lid and tray to allow clearance and prevent damage to the finish.

The placement of the pivot points must be exact or the tray will bind or not be level in its raised position. Measurements for the pivot are given from the hinge edge of the box to eliminate any error that might occur because of variation in wood thickness. If you change any of the dimensions of the box, you will have to determine new pivot points by building a mock up of one side of the box from scrap.

The ring holder (M) in the center of the tray is just a slotted block. A ⅛" slot will fit most rings but you can make some of them larger for wider rings. Cover the block with felt, pushing the felt down into each slot. A bit of glue at the bottom of the slot will hold the felt in place. The entire tray can be covered with felt (except for the routed ends) or the wood can be left exposed.

Any clear finish will work on this project. I used Danish

(continued on next page)

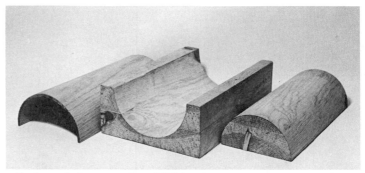

Left to right: completed lid lamination, female mold, male mold.

Alternate form makes use of stove pipe clamped around cylinder with glued veneer in between. Clamping cleats are screwed to stove pipe.

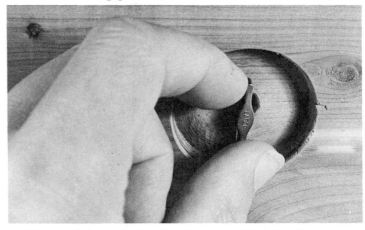

The music box winding key is recessed into box bottom.

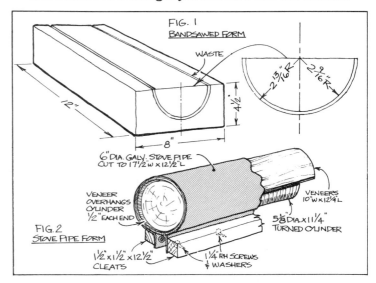

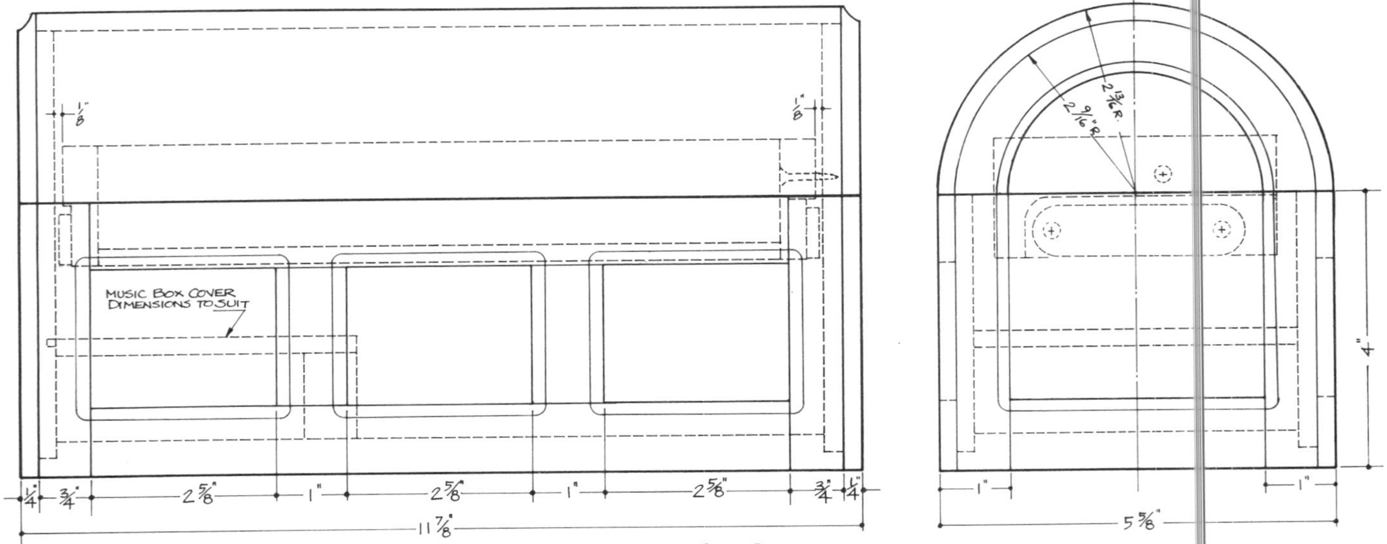
1/8"
1/8"
MUSIC BOX COVER DIMENSIONS TO SUIT
1/4"
3/4"
2 5/8"
1"
2 5/8"
1"
2 5/8"
3/4"
1/4"
11 7/8"
2 13/16" R
2 9/16" R
4"
1"
1"
5 5/8"

FIG. 3

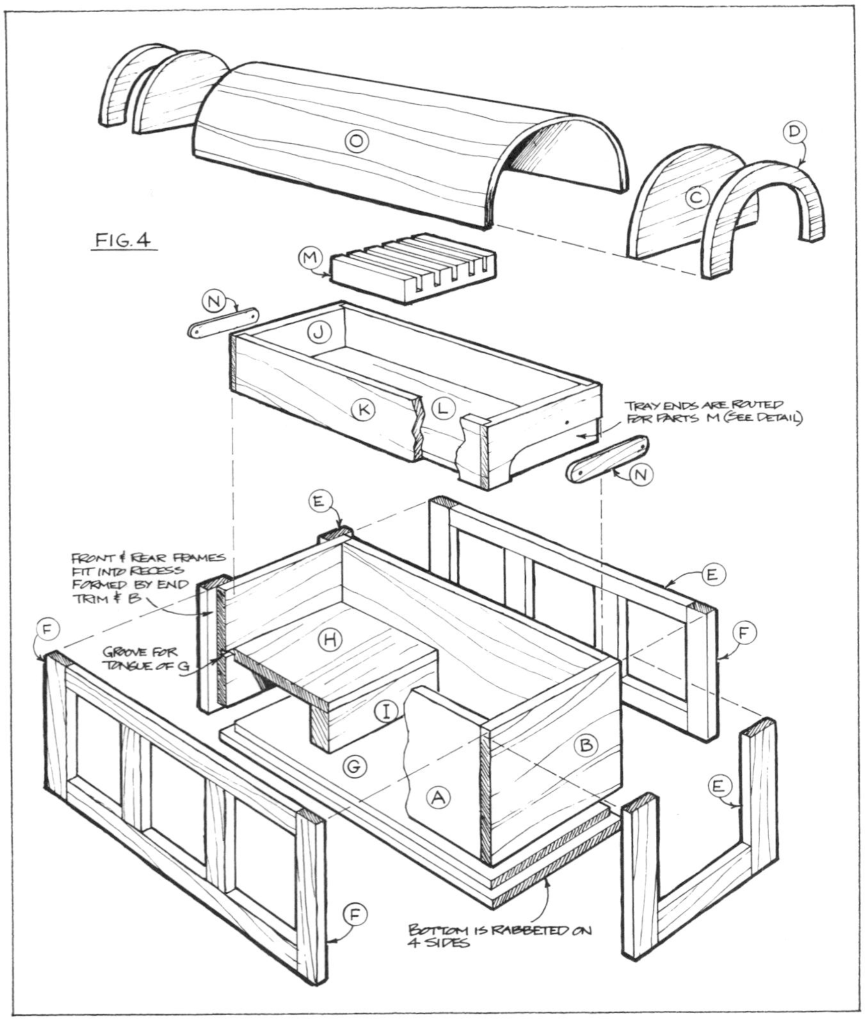
FIG. 4
O
D
C
M
N
J
K
L
TRAY ENDS ARE ROUTED FOR PARTS M (SEE DETAIL)
N
E
FRONT & REAR FRAMES FIT INTO RECESS FORMED BY END TRIM & B
E
F
H
F
GROOVE FOR TONGUE OF G
I
B
G
A
E
F
BOTTOM IS RABBETED ON 4 SIDES

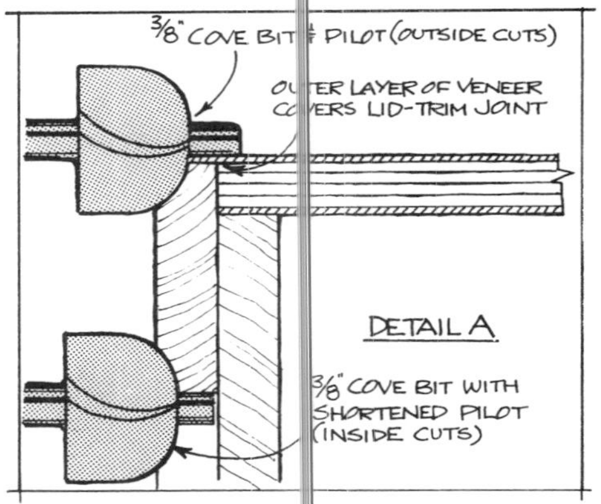
3/8" COVE BIT PILOT (OUTSIDE CUTS)
OUTER LAYER OF VENEER COVERS LID-TRIM JOINT
DETAIL A
3/8" COVE BIT WITH SHORTENED PILOT (INSIDE CUTS)

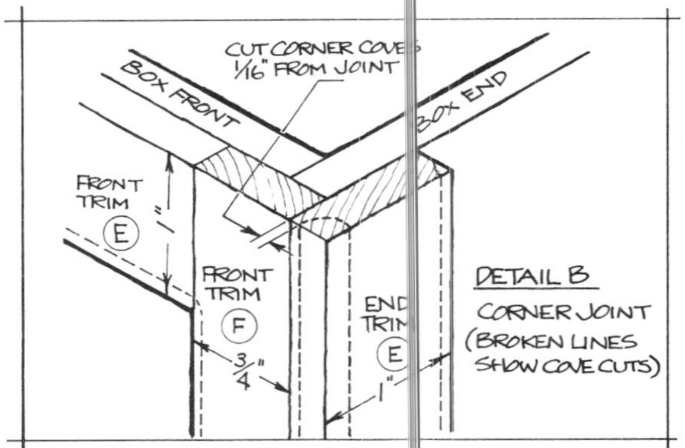
CUT CORNER COVES 1/16" FROM JOINT
BOX FRONT
BOX END
FRONT TRIM
E
1"
FRONT TRIM
F
3/4"
END TRIM
E
1"
DETAIL B
CORNER JOINT
(BROKEN LINES SHOW COVE CUTS)

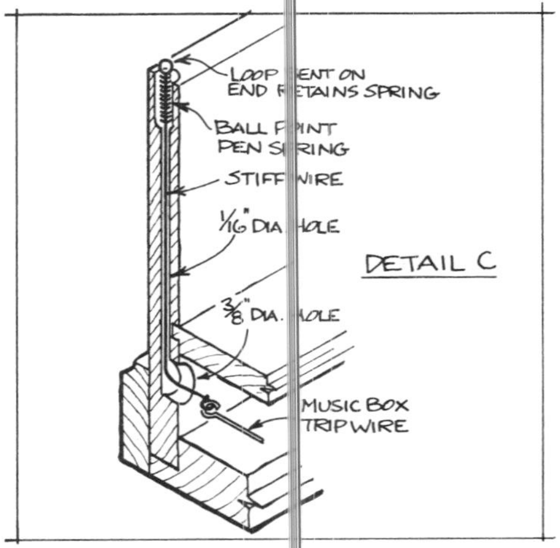
LOOP BENT ON END RETAINS SPRING
BALL POINT PEN SPRING
STIFF WIRE
1/16" DIA. HOLE
DETAIL C
3/8" DIA. HOLE
MUSIC BOX TRIP WIRE

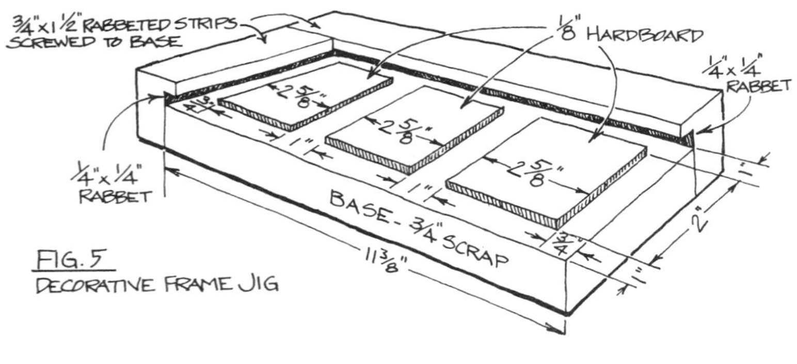
3/4" x 1 1/2" RABBETED STRIPS SCREWED TO BASE
1/8" HARDBOARD
1/4" x 1/4" RABBET
1/4" x 1/4" RABBET
2 5/8"
2 5/8"
2 5/8"
1"
1"
3/4"
3/4"
BASE - 3/4" SCRAP
11 3/8"
2"
1"
1"

FIG. 5
DECORATIVE FRAME JIG

Oil. Don't use stain as it will obscure the inlay. Mask the cedar bottom and any area to be covered with felt and leave them unfinished. Cover mating edges of the box and lid with felt. This gives a nice finished look, makes the lid close quietly and hides the joints. Also, cover the bottom of the box with felt to protect the finish of the surface the box will sit on.

The felt is applied with white glue spread very thin. If the glue is too heavy it will soak through the felt and ruin its appearance. Cut the felt larger than needed and trim to size with a razor knife after the glue has dried.

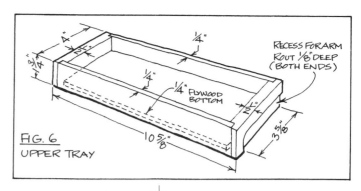

FIG. 6
UPPER TRAY

Bill of Materials (All Dimensions Actual)			
Part	Description	Size	No. Req'd.
A	Front & Back	¼ x 3¾ x 10⅞	2
B	Box Ends	¼ x 3¾ x 5⅛	2
C	Lid Ends	¼ x 2⁹⁄₁₆ x 5⅛	2
D	Lid Strip	¼ x 2¹³⁄₁₆ x 5⅝	2
E & F	Stripping	¼ x ¾, ¼ x 1	As Req'd.
G	Bottom	½ x 5⅛ x 11⅜	1
H	Cover	¼ x (to fit) x 4⅜	1
I	End Block	½ x (to fit) x 4⅜	1
J	Tray Ends	½ x 1¾ x 4	2
K	Tray Front & Back	¼ x 1¾ x 10⅛	2
L	Tray Bottom	⅛ x 3¾ x 10⅛	1
M	Ring Holder	¾ x 3 x 3½	1
N	Tray Arms	³⁄₁₆ x ¾ x 3	2
O	Lid Laminations	Veneer	As Req'd.

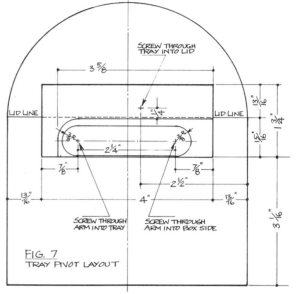

FIG. 7
TRAY PIVOT LAYOUT

Colonial Candlestick

An attractive pair of wooden candlesticks always makes a nice gift item. Colonial homes depended on them for precious table light, especially on cold winter evenings. While not the necessity they once were, we still enjoy them today for the warmth and charm they add to the family dining table. We made ours from maple (stained), but birch, walnut, and cherry can also be used.

To minimize waste, the candlestick is made in two parts. Part A is a spindle turning and part B is a faceplate turning.

Make part A from a 2″ square turning block. Start with a length of about 9″. Rough out the stock to a 2″ diameter cylinder, then cut to the profile shown. Thoroughly sand all surfaces before removing from the lathe. The top should be slightly dished-in to collect candle drippings. To make the tapered candle hole, grind or file the edges of a ⅞″ spade bit so that it tapers to ¾″ at the end. Use this bit to drill a 1″ deep hole.

After faceplate turning, part B can be joined to part A with a 1½ x #8 woodscrew, countersunk ¼″. Final sand all surfaces, then stain if desired. We used a walnut stain on our maple set. Two coats of Watco Danish Oil completes the project.

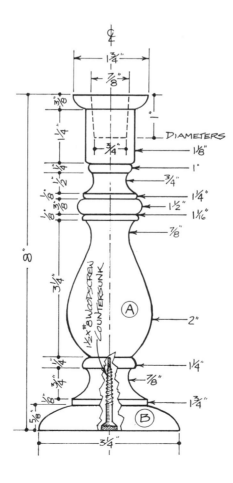

Sewing
Cabinet

With
Tambour Doors

by Thomas A. Gardner

This charming antique sewing cabinet has been a family posession for years. When it was made, or where, is not known. Most of the parts are walnut, but readers will find that just about any wood species, even pine, is acceptable. To avoid trouble, it's absolutely necessary to work accurately and follow the construction details with care.

Begin with part F, cutting it to overall length and width. Lay out and mark the ⅛" deep x 5/16" wide x 3⅛" long groove, then cut out using a router and a straight bit. The cove is cut with a ¼" cove bit.

Part D can now be cut to length and width. This part also has ⅛" deep x 5/16" wide by 3⅛" long grooves cut in the underside. In order for the base to be square, these grooves must be exactly in line with those in part F. As shown in the front elevation view, these grooves are located ⅜" in from each end. The ¼" cove bit cuts the front and side coves.

An easy-to-make template is used to cut the tambour grooves for part D. To make the template, cut ¾" plywood to the shape of the inner oval on the detail of the tambour groove cut (see drawing). Note that it measures 2¾" wide x 6⅝" long with a 1⅜" radius on each end. Carefully locate the template on part D, then secure with two short wood screws. The ⅛" deep groove is cut using a drill press and 3/16" round bottom router bit. The material in back is cut away to permit the insertion of the tambour doors after the body is assembled. Part D also has a groove to accept part C. Locate these ⅜" in from the side as shown. Use a router with a

⅛" straight bit to make the cut.

The next step is marking out and cutting the tambour groove in part B so that it is exactly over the groove in part D. Perhaps the best way to do this is to place B & D back-to-back, tambour groove side up. Now transfer the groove locations from D to B. Again use the template to cut the groove. Part B also has ⅛" x ⅛" x 1¾" grooves for part C. Be sure these line up exactly with the mating grooves in part D. A ⅛" x ⅛" x 7⅜" stopped rabbet can now be cut in the back edge to accept the back (H). Complete B by cutting the 2⅛" radius and routing the cove with the ¼" cove bit.

Part E has a ⅛" x ⅛" rabbet for the back (H) and ⅛" x ¼" notches are made on both front corners. Part C has a ⅛" x 3/16" rabbet for the back. A 1-11/16 radial cut allows room for the tambours. It's also rabbeted and notched to fit parts B & D. Part A can now be made as shown in the drawing.

Parts A, B, C, D, E, & F are now assembled. Sand thoroughly, then start by joining D, E, & F. First, dry assemble for fitting and squareness. If o.k., apply glue and clamp, again checking for squareness. Part A is attached to B using ¾" x #6 wood screws. Parts B and C can now be joined to D.

The tambour strips are cut and shaped as shown. Canvas, denim, or any other tough, flexible material can be used for the backing. Cut it so it will be ⅜" from the top and bottom. To apply the backing, place the tambour strips face down tightly against one another. Square the strips. Now, using thin strips of wood, fashion a frame

tightly around all four sides and secure with brads. This frame acts to keep the strips in place while applying glue and backing. Coat the tambours with glue and apply backing, keeping it smooth and even. After the glue has set, break the joint between the tambours. Round the upper and lower corners of the leading and rear tambours.

The tambours are now installed from the back of the cabinet. Some sanding will generally correct any irregularities. When adjusted, apply a coat of wax to the tambour ends, then attach the back (H).

Cut the thread holder (parts I) as shown. The spindle (J) is turned and attached off-center in the ½" holes. The holes for the thread holders are drilled using a #4 finishing nail with the head removed. Now drill 14 holes for the thread holder (8 in the upper, 6 in the lower, evenly spaced). Number 4 finishing nails, shortened to 1", are set in each hole from the bottom. The wood screw acts as a fulcrum for turning the thread holder out of the cabinet.

The pin cushion holder is prepared as shown. The interior is either routed or chiseled out by hand. Attach it with either a screw or with glue. The cushion can be made out of sponge rubber covered with fabric. It is glued in place. The assembly is attached to the cabinet with a round headed screw and a washer under the lower level---for smoother movement. Test for performance. Make any necessary adjustments. It will be a time saver if all parts of the thread holder are sanded, varnished and waxed before assembling.

The drawer is of simple construction. The front is walnut, the other parts are of pine. The bottom, ⅛" plywood, is inserted into ⅛" x ⅛" grooves cut in all four sides, as shown.

Finish with 2 or 3 coats of satin polyurethane, rubbing down the final coat with 0000 grade steel wool. A good grade of furniture wax completes the project.

Bill of Materials - Sewing Cabinet (All Dimensions Actual)		
Size	Part	No. Req'd
A	¼ x ¾ x 8	1
B	7/16 x 4 x 8½	1
C	⅜ x 2 x 5⅛	2
D	7/16 x 4½ x 8½	1
E	5/16 x 4¼ x 2¼	2
F	¾ x 4¼ x 8⅜	1
G	⅛ x 5 x 5¼	16
H	⅛ x 7¼ x 8-5/16	1
I	(See Detail)	2
J	(See Detail)	1
K	(See Detail)	1
L	⅜ x 2 x 7¼	1
M	¼ x 2 x 3⅛	2
N	¼ x 2 x 6¼	1
O	¼ x 3¼ x 6¼	1

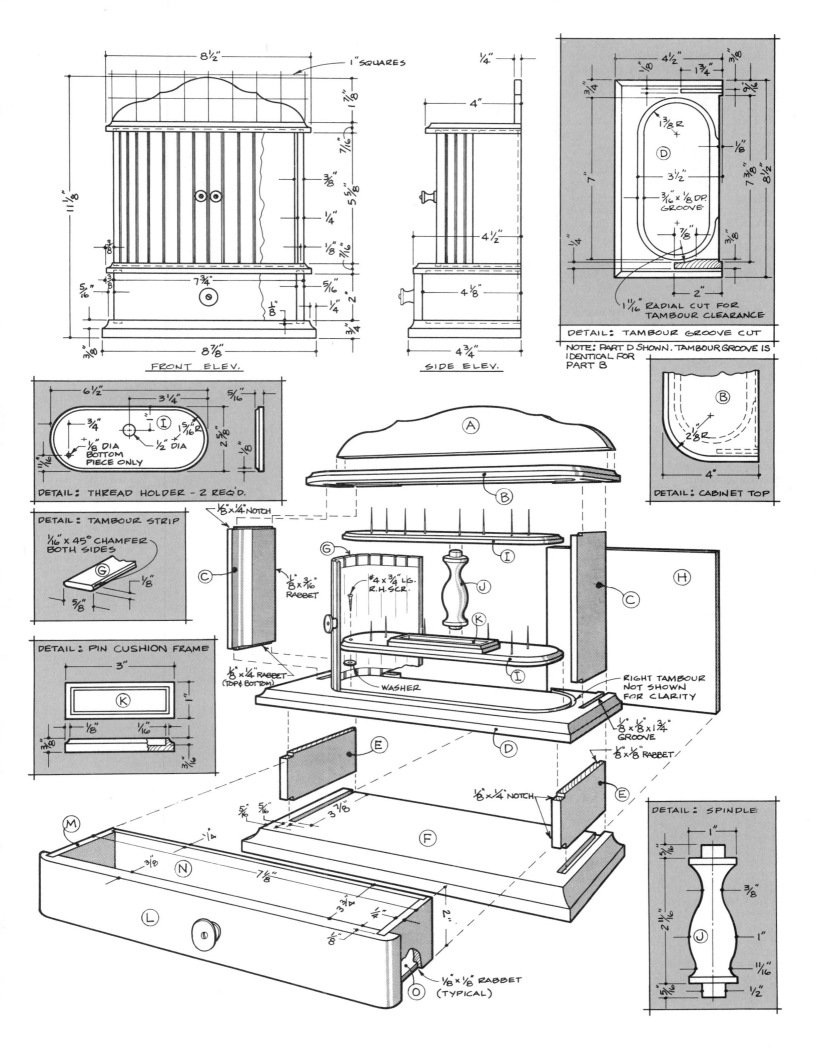

This well-proportioned little table features drop-leaf sides and nicely detailed leg and stretcher turnings. It can be made from a variety of cabinet hardwoods including cherry, maple, birch, walnut, and mahogany. Since pine and other softwoods do not lend themselves to detailed turnings (they tend to tear), it's best not to use them for this project.

Start by gluing-up stock as needed for the top (H) and leaves (I). To minimize any tendency to warp, it's best to use two or three boards for each part, making sure to alternate the direction of the annular rings. Clamp firmly, then set aside to dry.

Make the legs (A) next, referring to the detailed drawing for all dimensions. Note that the leg has a 1″ dia. by 1¼″ deep mortise in the square center section to accept the stretcher (C) tenon. It's a good idea to make this hole slightly deep to allow for any excess glue. Also, at this time, drill and countersink for a 1½ x #10 wood screw that will reinforce the joint. Locate the screw hole so that it will be centered on the tenon.

The stretcher (C) is made next, again referring to the drawing for all dimensions. Note that both ends have a 1″ dia. by 1¼″ long tenon. These tenons should be sized for a good fit in the leg mortises.

Cut the two feet (B) to overall length and width, then lay out the location of the ⅜″ wide x 1½″ long x 1¼″ deep mortise. Use a ⅜″ dia. drill bit to remove most of the material, then square the corners and clean-up with a sharp chisel. Transfer the profile from the grid pattern to the stock before cutting out with a band or saber saw.

The front and back aprons (D) and the side aprons (E) have mitered corners. Before making these miters, check your table or radial arm saw to be sure it's cutting at exactly 45 degrees. If not, make adjustments before starting.

Make the four fastening blocks (G) as shown. Changes in moisture content will cause the top to change in width, therefore the blocks have elongation holes which allow free movement of the top. If this free movement is not permitted, stresses will build that might cause the top to crack.

The rule (drop-leaf) joint can now be cut on the top (H) and leaves (I). This can be done on a shaper using a matched set of ½″ drop-leaf bead and cove cutters, or with a router using a ½″ rounding-over bit and ½″ cove bit.

Two pairs of brass table (drop-leaf) hinges are required (available from Woodcraft Supply, 41 Atlantic Ave., Woburn, MA 01888, p/n 16R42-PH). Note that one-half the diameter of the hinge barrel is mortised in the underside of the top. Also, the center of the barrel must be in line with the shoulder of the rule joint. To get a feel for cutting this joint and locating the hinge, it's a good idea to make a

18th Cent. Tavern Table
by Robert A. McCoy

practice joint on some short lengths of scrap pine.

A router equipped with a ¼″ beading bit is used to apply the decorative bead to the top and leaves. When cutting, use care at the point where the leaves meet the top, as this area may tend to split. To minimize this problem, use a small wedge of wood to fill the space between the two parts.

Final sand all parts, then dry assemble the legs, feet, stretcher, and aprons. If the assembly is satisfactory, the feet can be glued and clamped to the legs. When dry, the remaining base parts can be assembled, clamped and checked for squareness.

The finish is a matter of personal choice. The table can be stained, or if an open-grain wood is used, the reader may choose to start with a wood filler to fill-in the pores. Be sure to carefully follow manufacturer's directions with all finishing products. Final finish using 3 or 4 coats polyurethane varnish, with overnight drying between each coat. A light sanding with fine sandpaper is required after each coat has dried. Rub down the last coat with 0000 grade steel wool followed by a good wax polish.

To attach the top, place it upside down on clean papers or a pad to protect the finish. Center the base on the top, then fasten using 1¼″ x #8 round head wood screws and washers. Remember the top must be free to move

so don't overtighten the screws.

Two 6″ table drop-leaf supports are required (available from The Woodworkers' Store, 21801 Industrial Blvd., Rogers, MN 55374, p/n D4510). The dimensions shown are based on The Woodworkers' Store hinge. These dimensions are critical and must be carefully adhered to if the hinge is to work properly. Hinge dimensions from other suppliers may vary somewhat, so check before installing.

18th Cent. Tavern Table
Bill of Materials
(All Dimensions Actual)

Part	Description	Size	No. Req'd
A	Leg	2 x 2 x 25½	2
B	Foot	2 x 2¼ x 11	2
C	Stretcher	2 x 2 x 21½ (Inc. tenons)	1
D	Ft. & Back Apron	¾ x 3⅛ x 20½	2
E	Side Apron	¾ x 3⅛ x 7	2
F	Glue Block	¾ x ¾ x 3⅛	4
G	Fastening Blocks	¾ x 1 x 2½	4
H	Top	¾ x 10 x 26	1
I	Leaf	¾ x 8 x 26	2

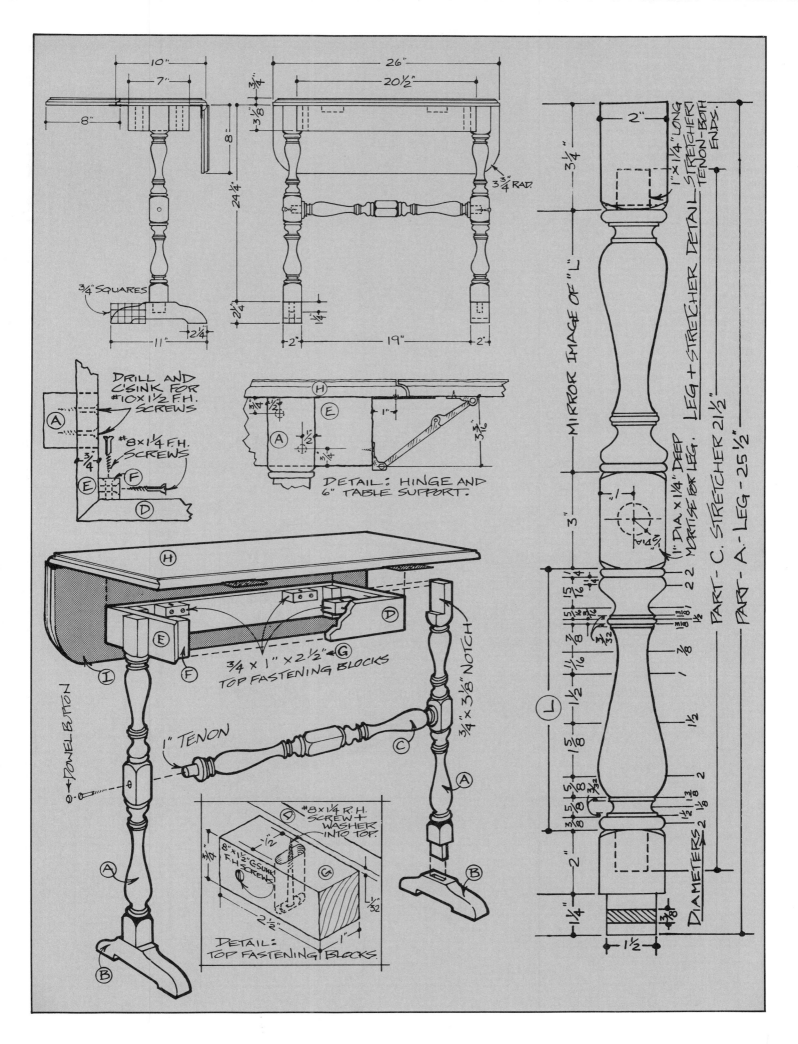

10"
7"
8"
26"
20½"
¾"
3/8"
24½"
8"
3¾ RAD.
¾" SQUARES
2¼"
11"
2½"
¼"
2"
19"
2"

DRILL AND C'SINK FOR #10 x 1½ F.H. SCREWS
Ⓐ
#8 x 1¼ F.H. SCREWS
¾"
Ⓔ Ⓕ
Ⓓ

Ⓗ
¾"
½"
Ⓔ
Ⓐ
½"
¾"
1"
3 3/16"
DETAIL: HINGE AND 6" TABLE SUPPORT.

Ⓗ
Ⓓ
Ⓔ
Ⓕ
Ⓘ
¾ x 1" x 2½" TOP FASTENING BLOCKS
Ⓖ
¾ x 3/8" NOTCH
Ⓐ

PANEL BUTTON
1" TENON
Ⓒ
Ⓐ
Ⓑ

#8 x 1¼ R.H. SCREW + WASHER INTO TOP.
¾"
½"
8" x 1½" C'SUNK F.H. SCREWS
Ⓐ
Ⓖ
1/32"
2½"
1"
DETAIL: TOP FASTENING BLOCKS.
Ⓑ

2"
3¾"
MIRROR IMAGE OF "L"
1" x 1¼" LONG STRETCHER TENON—BOTH ENDS.
1" DIA. x 1¼" DEEP MORTISE FOR LEG.
22
3"
LEG + STRETCHER DETAIL
1"
14 9/16
Ⓛ
15 15/16
5 5/16
7 1/8
3 3/32
7/8
½
1 1/16
1
1½
1 15/16 8/16
5 5/16
1 2 1/8 3
1½ 2
2"
3 5/16 8/16
3 3/32
1¼"
3/8
1½

PART-C. STRETCHER 21½"
PART-A-LEG—25½"
DIAMETERS 2 2½ 1½ 2

89

Little people are sure to enjoy this friendly fellow whose mouth opens and closes as he rolls along. Since they can be pretty tough on toys though, it's best to use a hardwood here, preferably maple or birch.

Start by cutting 2″ nominal (1¾″ actual) stock to 5″ wide x 10″ long. Transfer the hippo's profile to the stock, then locate and drill the 9/16″ center hole and 7/16″ wheel holes. Next, use a band saw to cut out the hippo profile. Also cut out part G and the area of scrap stock, following the saw cuts shown. The 11/16″ slot is cut in the front leg with a back or dovetail saw. Make two cuts to establish the width, then remove scrap with a sharp chisel.

Cut the remaining parts, then assemble as shown. Be sure that part C is firmly glued to part E. When dry, sand thoroughly, removing all sharp edges. No final finish is added.

Editor's Note: Our thanks to Cherry Tree Toys for providing us with the plans for this project. Cherry Tree Toys is a company supplying plans for wooden toys and hardwood toy wheels and parts. For their catalog, send $1.00 to: Cherry Tree Toys, P.O. Box 369, Belmont, OH 43718.

Toy Hippo

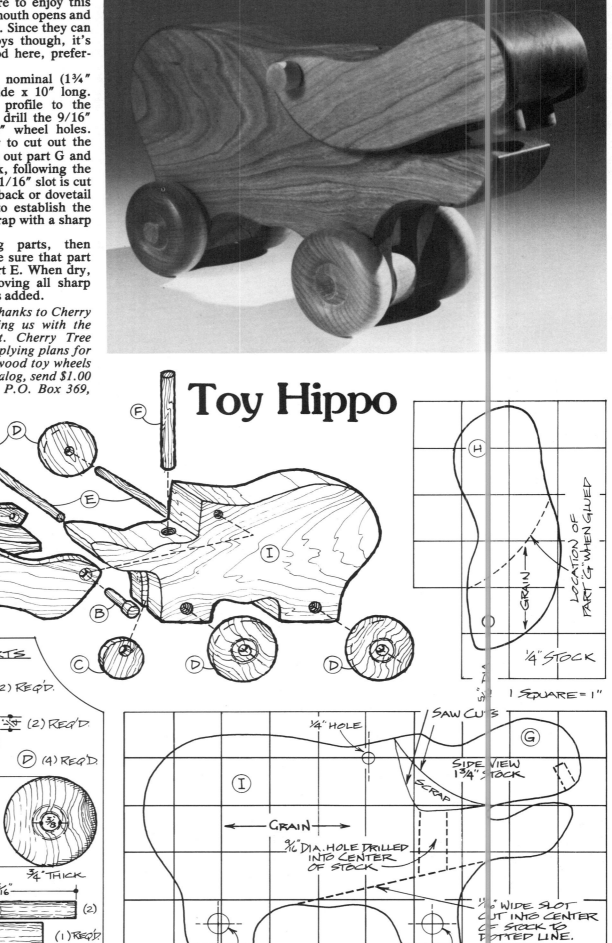

About eight years ago I obtained an old icebox, one that was a basket case by the time I got it home. After restoring and using it for magazine storage I decided to build one myself. I chose to make mine out of oak, since that's what most of the originals were made of.

To simplify construction, I joined the frame members using dowel pins, although more advanced woodworkers may want to consider the mortise and haunched tenon, a more permanent form of construction.

Make the front frame first (parts A, B, C, D, and E). Select good flat stock. Cut parts to dimensions shown in the bill of materials. These cuts must be square so check your saw before starting. Drill dowel holes as shown. If available, a doweling jig will be helpful for this step. Assemble the five front frame parts with glue, then clamp securely with bar or pipe clamps. Check for squareness and make adjustments if necessary. Allow to dry overnight.

The two side frames, consisting of parts F, G, H, and I, can be made next. Drill dowel holes as shown. The upper part H has a ¼" x ¼" groove cut along its lower edge while the center part H has the same groove cut on both edges. Part I has the groove on its upper edge. Either a table saw or router can be used to cut these grooves. Parts F and G also have a ¼" x ¼" groove; however, the groove must be stopped short of the ends or else it will show. The stopped groove is best made with the router. In addition, part G has a ¼" x ¼" rabbet (see blind doweling detail) for the back. This rabbet is stopped 1" short of the bottom. Note that dadoes are required in parts F & G, and that the dado location (for the shelves) on the left frame differs from the right frame.

Begin making the end panel (J) by cutting ½" stock to 10½" wide by 12" long. Edge-join stock if wide enough material is not available. The tapered edge can be cut on the table saw, radial-arm saw, or with a panel raising cutter on the shaper. Thoroughly sand the completed panel.

Assemble the end frame as shown. Do not glue the panel in place. It must be free to expand and contract in the frame. As with the front frame, make sure all parts are square before setting aside to dry.

The ¼" back (K) can be made from common fir plywood or you may want to consider oak plywood. Chances are your local lumberyard won't stock oak plywood, but it usually can be ordered. You'll need one-half sheet (4 foot by 4 foot). It's not cheap, but it does do a lot for the interior appearance.

Changes in moisture content will cause the top (Q) to change in width, therefore the rear rail (O) and the mounting block (P) have elongated holes which allow free movement of the top. If this free movement is not permitted, stress will build which could cause the top to crack.

The bottom (L), divider (M) and shelves (N) are also made from ¾" plywood. Like the back, it can be fir, but

Old-Time Icebox by Richard Wonderlich

oak would look considerably better. To keep the plywood laminations from showing on the front edge, I glued ⅛" thick oak strips to parts L and N. These strips are ripped from ¾" thick oak solid stock.

The left and right doors are made in the same manner as the frame. When locating the dowel holes, make sure you don't get too close to the edges or they will show when the door lip is added. Note that the outer edge has a ¼" radius and a ⅜" x ⅜" rabbet all around to form the door lip. Check doors for a good fit in the front frame.

The icebox is assembled as shown in the exploded view. Solid brass icebox

hardware can be ordered from: Constantine's, 2050 Eastchester Rd., Bronx, NY 10461. Order part no. 1B1 for the hinges (6 required), part no. 1B2 for the right hand latches (2 required), part no. 1B3 for the left hand latch (1 required), and part no. 1B7 for the Baldwin nameplate (1 required). Note: Hardware as specified is traditional solid brass design; Victorian style ornamental design shown in photo not available.

Choosing a final finish will depend to a great extent upon the type of wood used for the icebox, as well as individual taste. No matter how you decide to finish this project though, it should be done with patience and care.

Bill of Materials
(All Dimensions Actual)

Part	Description	Size	No. Req'd	Part	Description	Size	No. Req'd
A	Front Top Rail	¾ x 2½ x 26	1	N	Shelf	¾ x 14⅞ x 15⅜	3
B	Front Side Stile	¾ x 3 x 36	2	O	Rear Rail	¾ x 2¾ x 30½	1
C	Center Stile	¾ x 2½ x 26½	1	P	Mounting Block	¾ x ¾ x 2½	6
D	Center Rail	¾ x 2½ x 11¾	1	Q	Top	¾ x 16¾ x 33½	1
E	Front Bottom Rail	¾ x 2½ x 26	1	R	Backing	¾ x 3½ x 29	1
F	Front End Stile	¾ x 2¼ x 36	2	S	False Pan Front	¾ x 4 x 26	1
G	Rear End Stile	¾ x 3 x 36	2	T	Foot	¾ x 2¾ x 6	2
H	End Rail	¾ x 2½ x 10	4	U	Left Door Stile	¾ x 2½ x 27¼	2
I	Lower End Rail	¾ x 7 x 10	2	V	Left Door Rail	¾ x 2½ x 7½	2
J	End Panel	½ x 10½ x 12	4	W	Left Door Panel	½ x 8 x 22¾	1
K	Back	¼ x 31 x 35	1	X	Right Door Stile	¾ x 2½ x 12¾	2/Door
L	Bottom	¾ x 14⅞ x 31	1	Y	Right Door Rail	¾ x 2½ x 7½	2/Door
M	Divider	¾ x 15 x 29	1	Z	Right Door Panel	½ x 8 x 8¼	1/Door

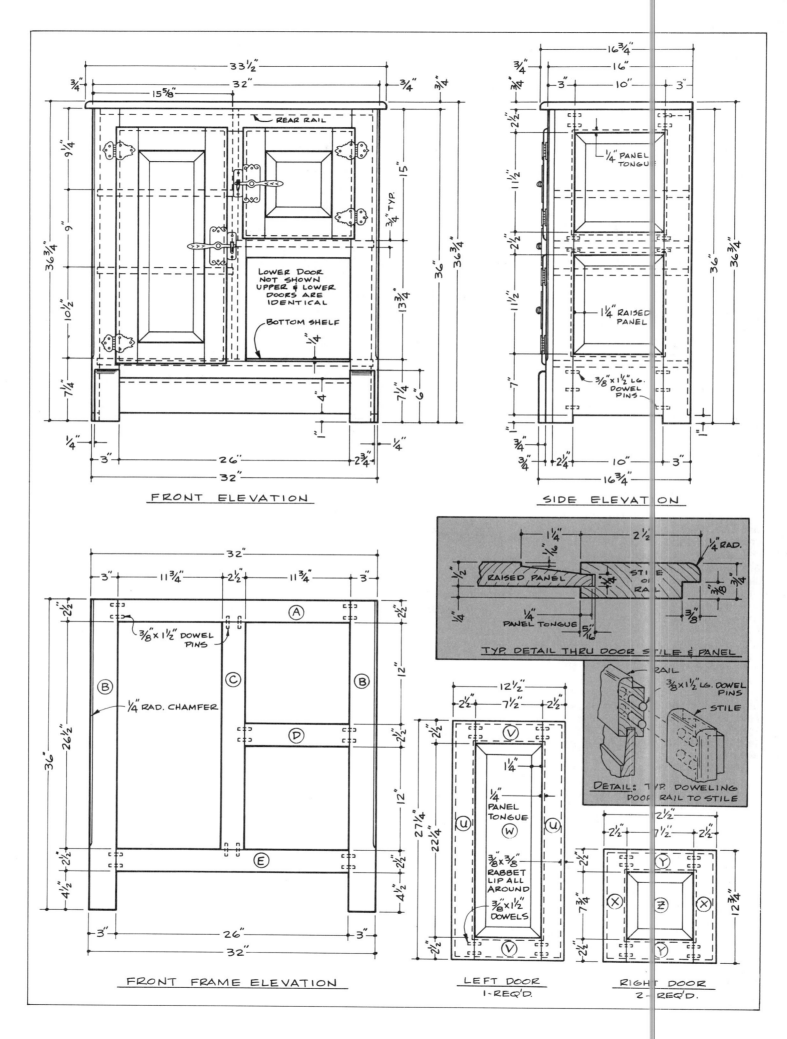

FRONT ELEVATION

SIDE ELEVATION

REAR RAIL

LOWER DOOR NOT SHOWN UPPER & LOWER DOORS ARE IDENTICAL

BOTTOM SHELF

1/4" PANEL TONGUE

1 1/4" RAISED PANEL

3/8" × 1 1/2" LG. DOWEL PINS

FRONT FRAME ELEVATION

3/8" × 1 1/2" DOWEL PINS

1/4" RAD. CHAMFER

A B C D E

TYP. DETAIL THRU DOOR STILE & PANEL

RAISED PANEL

STILE OR RAIL

1/4 RAD.

PANEL TONGUE

DETAIL: TYP. DOWELING DOOR RAIL TO STILE

RAIL

3/8" × 1 1/2" LG. DOWEL PINS

STILE

LEFT DOOR
1-REQ'D.

1/4" PANEL TONGUE

3/8" × 3/8" RABBET LIP ALL AROUND

3/8" × 1 1/2" DOWELS

V U W

RIGHT DOOR
2-REQ'D.

X Y Z

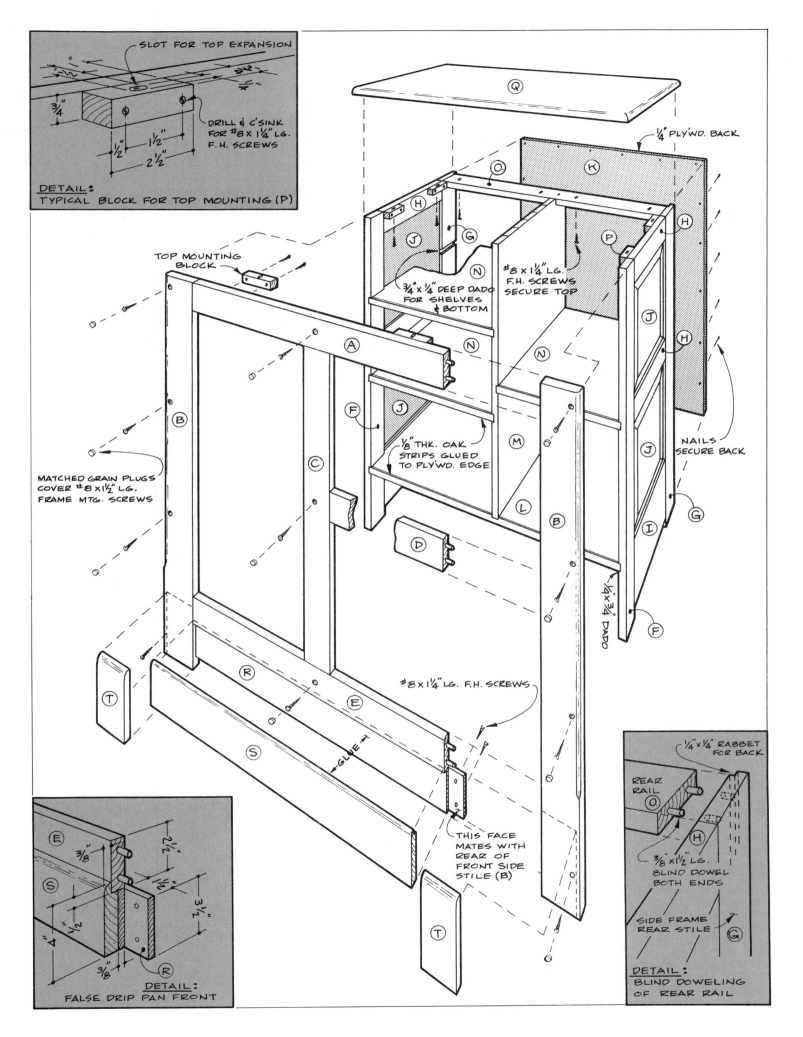

SLOT FOR TOP EXPANSION

DRILL & C'SINK FOR #8 X 1¼" LG. F.H. SCREWS

¾"
½" 1½"
2½"

DETAIL:
TYPICAL BLOCK FOR TOP MOUNTING (P)

TOP MOUNTING BLOCK

MATCHED GRAIN PLUGS COVER #8 X 1½" LG. FRAME MTG. SCREWS

¼" PLY'WD. BACK

¾" X ¼" DEEP DADO FOR SHELVES & BOTTOM

#8 X 1¼" LG. F.H. SCREWS SECURE TOP

⅛" THK. OAK STRIPS GLUED TO PLY'WD. EDGE

NAILS SECURE BACK

¼" X ¾" DADO

#8 X 1¼" LG. F.H. SCREWS

THIS FACE MATES WITH REAR OF FRONT SIDE STILE (B)

GLUE

¼" X ¼" RABBET FOR BACK

REAR RAIL

⅜" X 1½" LG. BLIND DOWEL BOTH ENDS

SIDE FRAME REAR STILE

DETAIL:
BLIND DOWELING OF REAR RAIL

E
3/8"
2½"
½"
3½"
4"
S
½"
3/8"
R

DETAIL:
FALSE DRIP PAN FRONT

Tile Clock by Roger E. Schroeder

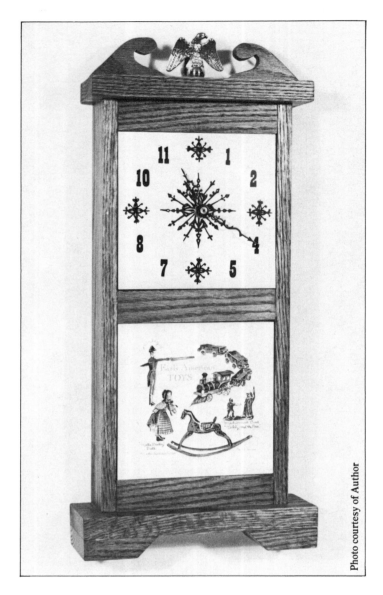

Photo courtesy of Author

Parts A, B, and C can now be glued and clamped together. Make sure parts A are square to parts B & C. Part D is cut to size and attached using countersunk 1½" x #8 flathead wood screws. These should be located where they will be covered by parts G (see drawing).

After cutting to size, part E is held to the case with ¼" diameter wood dowel pins and glue. Drill ⅜ inch diameter by ¾ inch deep holes in the bottom of parts A, and use dowel centers to mark the location of the holes in part E. Parts F are bevel cut to a 45-degree angle on one side, then added to part E with glue.

Parts G, the decorative scrolls, are cut to size from ½ inch thick stock. Transfer the profile from the detail, then cut out on the jig or saber saw. Attach to part D with ¼ inch diameter by ½ inch long dowels as shown.

The back panel, part H, is cut to size from ¼ inch plywood, as is the dial board, part I. Be sure to cut both parts square.

Give all components a complete sanding, taking care to remove planer marks. Watch for areas of excess glue squeeze-out and remove with sandpaper or a sharp chisel. If desired, round all corners to simulate years of wear. Final sand using 220 grit paper.

All hardware and clock parts (excluding the ceramic tile) are available from: Klockit, P.O. Box 629, Highway H North, Lake Geneva, WI 53147. They have a variety of quartz movements, dial faces, and hands that are suitable for this project, in addition to the hanger and the brass eagle ornament shown. A copy of their catalog is available at no charge.

The plywood back (H) is secured to the case with turnbuttons (not shown), which permit easy access to the clock interior to change batteries when necessary. These turnbuttons are also available from Klockit. The 6 inch square porcelain tile below the clockface is mounted with contact cement. Your local tile shop should have a wide variety of decorative ceramic tile to chose from.

Finish is a matter of personal choice. I used McCloskey's dark oak stain. After the stain was thoroughly dry, several coats of tung oil were applied as a final finish.

If a lighter finish is preferred, try Minwax Provincial Wood Finish. Apply two coats following the manufacturer's directions for drying time. This can be followed by two coats of polyurethane varnish. Rub down between coats and after the final coat using 0000 grade steel wool.

This attractive clock will be a fine addition to a colonial setting or nearly any room in the house, from den to nursery. It's a project that's surprisingly easy to build; in fact the work can be completed in just one afternoon.

Except for the back (H), the dial board (I), and the decorative scroll (G), all parts are made from 1" (¾" actual) pine. If possible, when choosing boards, select stock that's reasonably free of knots. Of course, other wood species are also suitable, particularly the hardwoods. Walnut results in a rich dark look while maple or birch is much lighter. Oak and mahogany are also good choices. With a project like this, there's no hard and fast rule that predetermines the particular type of wood. The choice is left to the individual woodworker. If you can't find hardwoods locally, there are a number of companies that sell domestic and imported hardwoods via mail-order (see source index).

Begin by cutting the two sides (A) to size. These can be made from a single piece of stock about 3 feet long. A ¼" x ¼" rabbet is cut on both edges. The router will make this cut, although the table or radial-arm saw can also be used.

The center rail (B) and the upper and lower rails (C) are next. These can be made from a single piece of 1¾" wide stock, about 2 feet long. Make the ¼" x ¼" rabbet cuts along both edges of the stock, then cut it into three lengths, each measuring 6⅟₁₆". For parts C, remove one of the rabbets by cutting it flush on the table saw. Then, on all three pieces, make a ¼" x ½" rabbet cut on both ends.

Bill of Materials
All Dimensions Actual

Part	Description	Size	No. Req'd
A	Side	¾ x 2⅛ x 15⅞	2
B	Center Rail	¾ x 1¾ x 6-1/16	1
C	Rail	¾ x 1½ x 6-1/16	2
D	Top	¾ x 3 x 8¼	1
E	Bottom	¾ x 3 x 9	1
F	Foot	¾ x 3 x 2¾	2
G	Scroll	See Detail	2
H	Back	¼ x 6-1/16 x 15⅞	1
I	Dial Board	¼ x 6 x 6	1
J	Movement	2¼ x 2¼	1

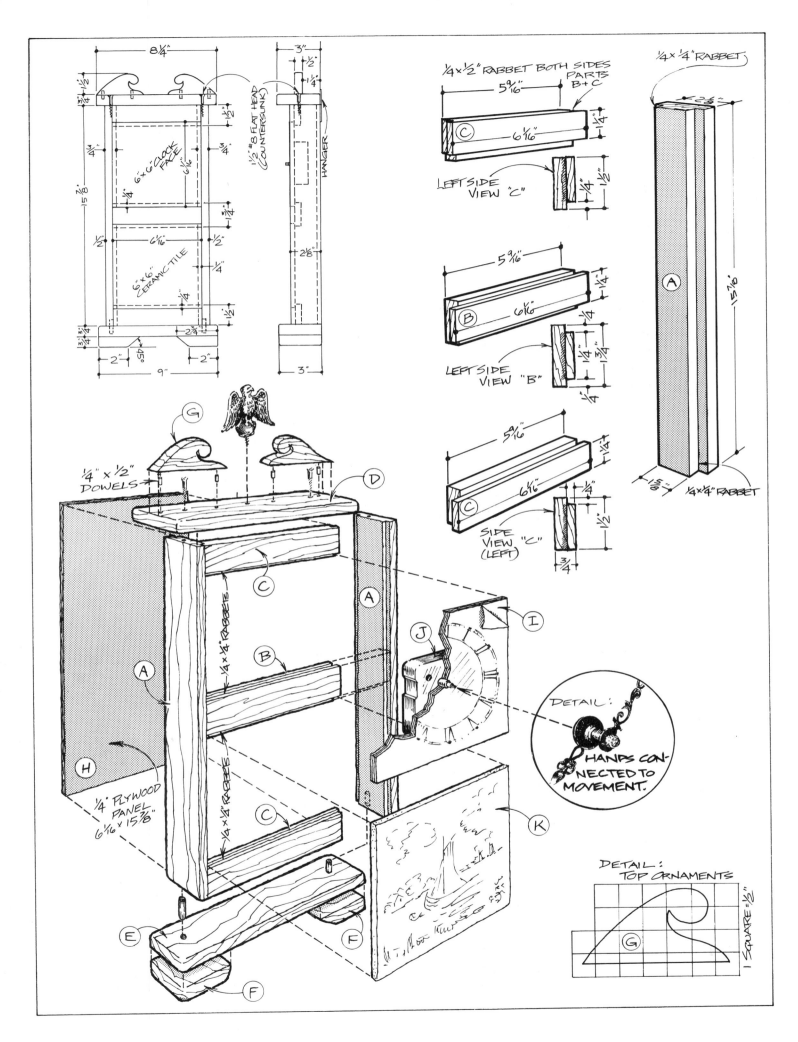

Victorian Sled

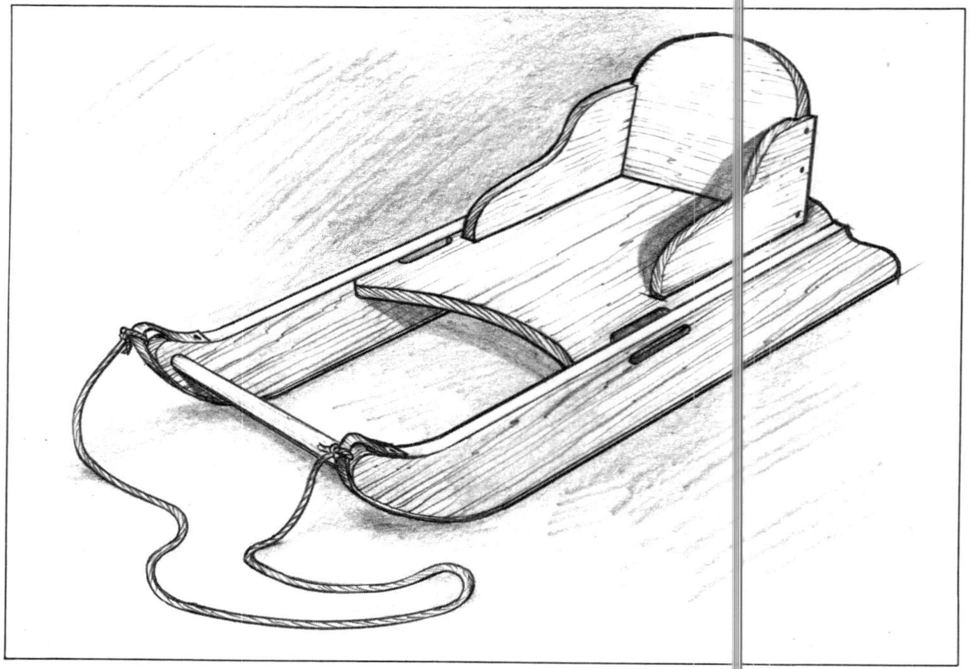

This sled from the 1880's is a bit of pure nostalgia and the perfect vehicle for a toddler's first winter snow ride. Unscrew the seat portion and bigger kids can have a lot of fun with it too, once they learn the knack of steering with body English.

Hardwood such as oak or maple should be used for the main parts. The runners (A) can be cut from 8″ wide boards, but it's less expensive to use 5½″ wide boards and simply glue and dowel on pieces of 2½″ x 6″ stock to form the horns at the front. A saber saw will do a nice job of cutting the curves. Lay out the hand slots and drill the ends with a ¾″ auger; then cut between the holes. Also bore ⅜″ deep sockets for the 1″ birch dowel.

Steel strap, available at hardware stores is bent to form a loop over each runner horn and drilled and countersunk at 4″ intervals. Fasten the steel "shoes" with ⅝″ x No. 6 flathead wood screws and trim the shoes flush with the back ends of the runners.

The bed (B) is made of two or three edge-joined ¾″ boards (or a piece of plywood). Lay out and cut the curves at each end and the notches which are centered on the runner slots. Screw the cleats (C) to the underside using 1½″ x No. 8 roundhead wood screws.

The seat parts are cut next. Note that the seat back is tilted and fits into a ¼″ rabbet in the sides. Join these parts with six 1½″ x No. 6 flathead wood screws and glue and bevel off the bottom edge of the back. Sand all parts carefully, putting a generous radius on all upper edges.

Scribe a line 1¼″ below the top edge of each runner to serve as a guide for locating the corner braces which are fastened with ¾″ x No. 6 flathead wood screws. Turn the sled upside down, add the front dowel and with pipe clamps holding the bed between the runners, screw the corner brackets to the bed. The seat is fastened centered on the bed and about 4″ from the back edge using 1½″ x No. 6 roundhead wood screws.

Many of these sleds were gaily decorated with bright colors and gold striping, but this easily wears away unless heavily coated with varnish. The sled looks fine if left natural and just given two or three coats of urethane varnish.

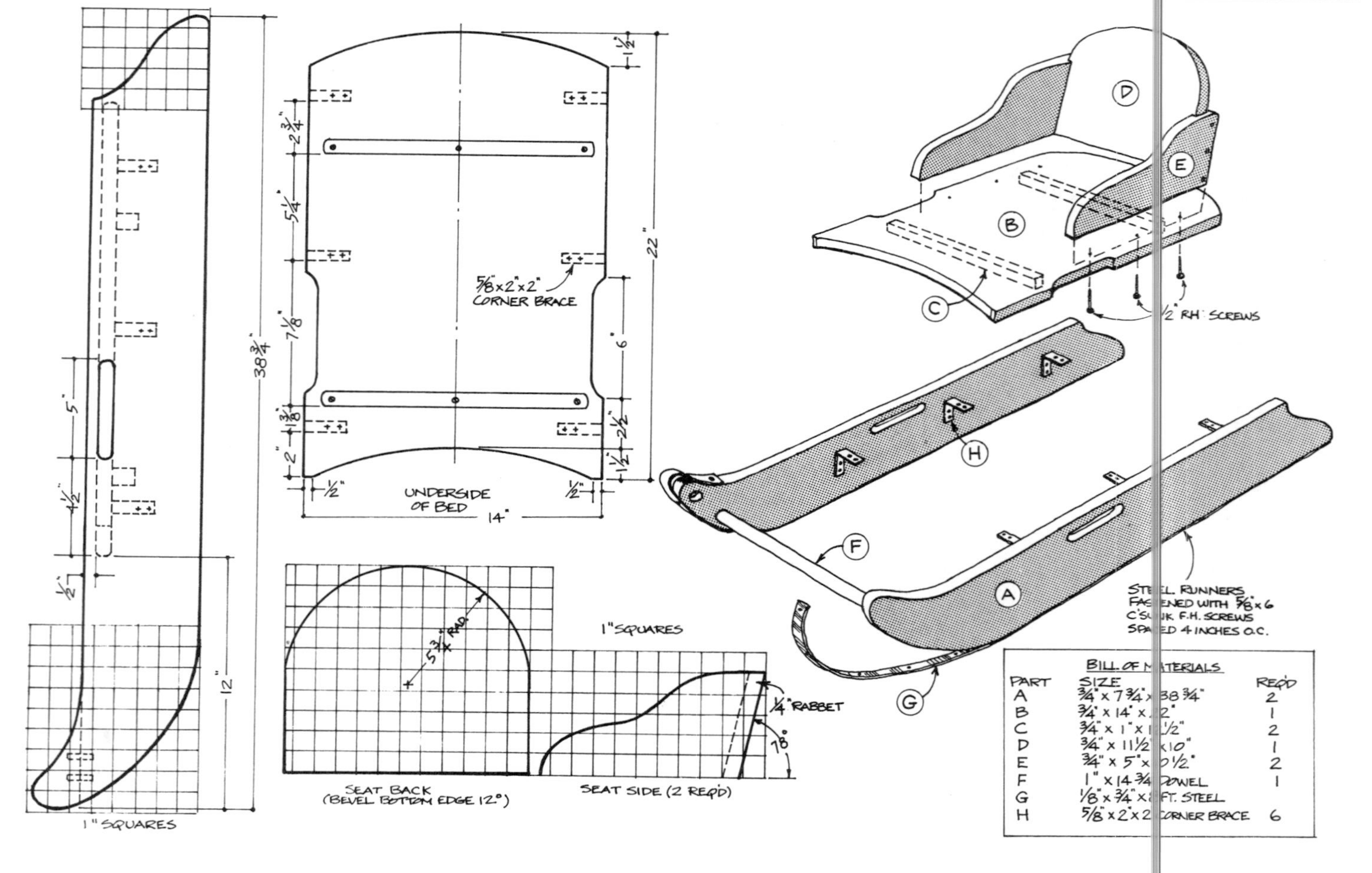

1" SQUARES
38¾"
5"
4½"
½"
12"
UNDERSIDE OF BED
14"
22"
⅝x2"x2" CORNER BRACE
3¾"
2¼"
5¼"
7⅛"
6"
1⅜"
2"
1½"
2½"
½"
5¾" RAD.
1" SQUARES
SEAT BACK (BEVEL BOTTOM EDGE 12°)
SEAT SIDE (2 REQ'D)
¼" RABBET
78°
½" RH SCREWS
STEEL RUNNERS FASTENED WITH ⅝"x6 C'SUNK F.H. SCREWS SPACED 4 INCHES O.C.
A
B
C
D
E
F
G
H

BILL OF MATERIALS

PART	SIZE	REQ'D
A	¾" x 7¾" x 38¾"	2
B	¾" x 14" x 22"	1
C	¾" x 1" x 11½"	2
D	¾" x 11½" x 10"	1
E	¾" x 5" x 10½"	2
F	1" x 14¾" DOWEL	1
G	⅛" x ¾" x 8 FT. STEEL	
H	⅝ x 2" x 2" CORNER BRACE	6

Wine Glass Holder

by Roger E. Schroeder

Although reasonably easy to make, this lathe project is an ideal gift item, and it can certainly be done with a minimum amount of scrap lumber.

The top and bottom can be made from birch plywood (as the top of this one is), pine, or even a hardwood. The four turned posts should be hardwood, however, and these were turned from 5/4 (1¹⁄₁₆ actual) maple.

The top and bottom can be done on a lathe, although a bandsaw or jig saw will also cut them to shape. A router equipped with an ogee bit was used to cut the bottom molding. The top was rounded over with a ¼″ rounding over bit.

To locate the post tenon holes, clamp together the top and bottom and drill a ½ inch diameter hole through both pieces. Back-up the bottom with scrap stock to prevent splintering. The holes on the top will be covered with ½ inch wood buttons. The four notches in the top piece are started using a ½ inch drill bit and finished on a bandsaw.

Here's a way to insure a tight fit for the post tenons: predrill holes for a small ¾ inch screw into the centers of the tenon ends. Then cut a notch along their diameter lines with a dovetail saw. Glue and clamp the assembly together and put the screws in. These will cause the tenons to separate and make a tight fit. Cover the top holes with the wood buttons.

The project was finished with a dark walnut stain followed by two coats of satin polyurethane varnish. The final step was to glue the cork disc to the bottom. Four wine glasses and a bottle of wine provide the finishing touch.

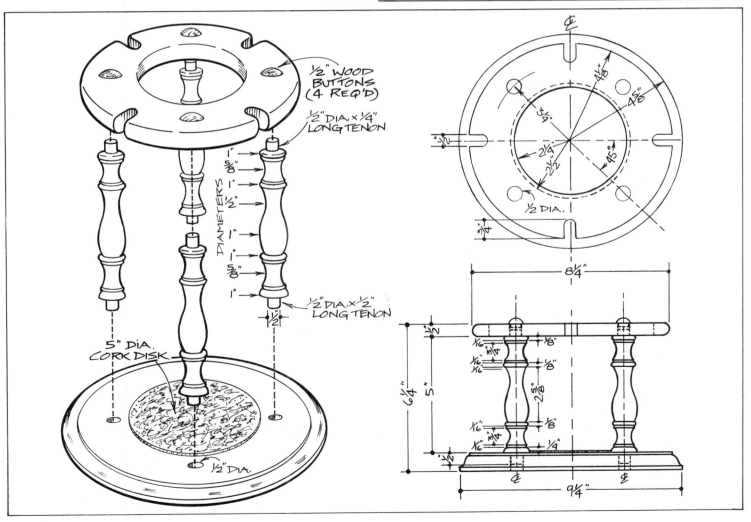

Bagel Slicer

by Victor F. Ptasznik

While this kitchen accessory will become an attractive conversation piece for the cook's guests, it's really designed to allow the user to slice bagels safely. With the ever increasing popularity of these donut shaped breads, you should also find it to be a marketable item. Cherry was used, but any other dense hardwood that's suitable for turning can be substituted. Cut your material to the exact dimensions, making sure that the grain on parts A, B, and C runs in the same direction.

The jaws, parts A & B, are made first. Cut each one from 1" stock (¾" actual) to a 5½" square. A lathe equipped with a faceplate will cut the 3½" diameter contoured face on each jaw. Note that the 3½" diameter contour is exactly in the center of the 5½" square.

To achieve a uniform shape on all three pieces and, more importantly, to precisely locate the dowels, you will need to temporarily hold together parts A, B & C for machining. One solution is to use common nails. At the centerpoint of each dowel location, accurately drill a hole just large enough to hold a two-inch long nail. Held together by these three nails, the resulting stack of wood can be cut to the bell shape with a bandsaw or jigsaw. Then remove one nail at a time and, with a drill press, drill a ½" hole using the nail hole as a guide. Insert a dowel and drill out the remaining two holes in the same manner. After removing the dowels, enlarge the holes in part B with a rasp so that it can freely slide on the dowels.

Use a router equipped with a ¼" rounding-over bit to round all edges except those on the base surface. With part B in place, glue the dowels into parts A and C. Flush sand the dowel ends.

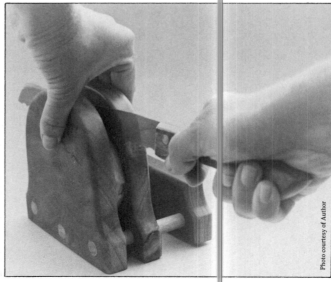

Photo courtesy of Author

Seal Push Toy

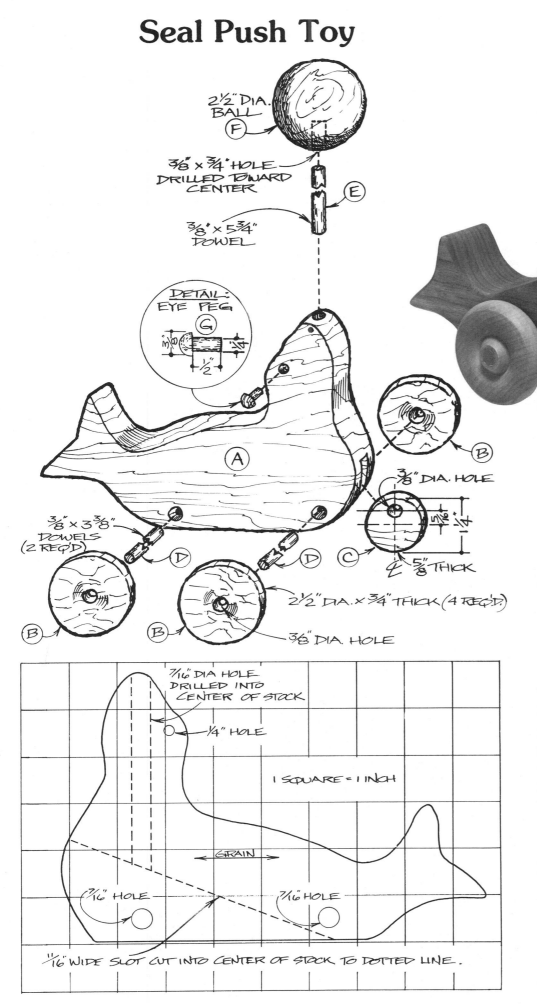

2½" DIA. BALL **F**

⅜" × ¾" HOLE DRILLED TOWARD CENTER

⅜" × 5¾" DOWEL **E**

DETAIL: EYE PEG **G**
⅜   ¼   ½

A

B

⅜" DIA. HOLE

5/16"   ¼"

C

5/8" THICK

⅜" × 3⅜" DOWELS (2 REQ'D) **D**

D

B

B

2½" DIA. × ¾" THICK (4 REQ'D)

⅜" DIA. HOLE

7/16" DIA HOLE DRILLED INTO CENTER OF STOCK

¼" HOLE

1 SQUARE = 1 INCH

← GRAIN →

7/16" HOLE

7/16" HOLE

11/16" WIDE SLOT CUT INTO CENTER OF STOCK TO DOTTED LINE.

Children seem to have a special fascination when it comes to push toys . . . and we expect this one will be no exception. As the seal is pushed along, the ball bounces up and down. The company Cherry Tree Toys provided us with the plans for this cute project. For a copy of their catalog, which lists many other toy plans plus hardwood toy wheels and parts, send $1.00 to them at P.O. Box 369, Belmont, OH 43718.

For durability, it's best to use a hardwood for this project, preferably maple or birch. Make the body (part A) first, cutting 2" stock (1¾" actual) to 6" wide by 10" long. Next, transfer the grid pattern from the drawing to the stock and lay out the location of the two 7/16" dia. axle holes and the ¼" eye hole. Cut part A to shape with a band saw. The drill press can now be used to drill the axle and eye holes, and the 7/16" dia. hole for part E. The 11/16" slot is cut with a back or dovetail saw, making two parallel cuts to establish the width, then removing scrap with a sharp chisel.

The remaining parts are made to the dimensions shown. The 2½" dia. ball can be lathe turned or purchased from Cherry Tree Toys (they also can furnish the wheels (B), the cam (C) and the eye peg (G).

Sand all parts thoroughly, taking care to remove all sharp edges. Assemble as shown. Keep in mind that part C is glued to part D. For toys, it's always best to use a glue that's nontoxic such as Elmer's Glue-All. A final finish is not added.

Antique Knife Tray

In times past, the knife tray was used as a means to store and carry the household table knives. We found this fine example of an early knife tray at the Gunn Historical Museum in Washington, Connecticut. The museum was kind enough to let us take photographs and some actual measurements.

This well-proportioned tray owes its graceful appearance to the sloping sides and ends, and the use of thin stock throughout. The divider incorporates a sensitively shaped dowel which is fastened to the top for a handle.

Referring to the drawing, make all parts as shown. Assemble with glue and finishing nails. Note that the handle bottom is planed flat before attaching with angled dowels and glue. Sand thoroughly, stain and final finish with two coats of Minwax Antique Oil Finish.

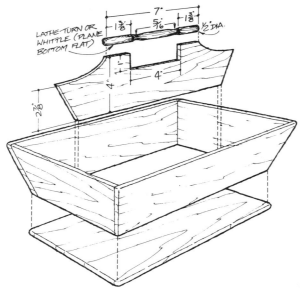

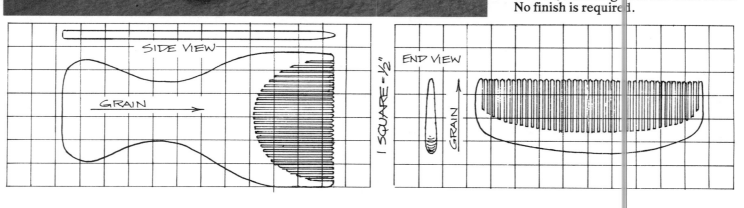

Wooden Combs

Why wooden combs? Well, for one thing, they're a lot more attractive than the usual molded plastic kind. For another, they don't generate any static electricity. We made ours from birch, but maple, beech or any other close grain hardwood will also be suitable.

There are various ways to make them, but perhaps the easiest is to start with ¼″ thick stock and transfer the shape from the grid pattern. Be sure to run the grain in the direction shown. Use the band or jig saw to cut out the profile. Plane or sand the side (or end) view taper as shown, then again use the band or jig saw to cut the individual teeth. Sand all surfaces smooth, including between each tooth. No finish is required.

Message Cube

by Sam Allen

Note pads using adding machine paper rolls are not new but they take up a lot of desk space and the paper rolls from the top down so any additions to a list must be made at the top rather than the bottom. This compact note paper dispenser overcomes these drawbacks, The plans are for a 2¼" wide roll of paper but you can change dimensions to suit other sizes.

Begin by nailing two ⅛" hardboard sides to the ¾" pine sides to form a box. Next, close the top of the box with a piece of hardboard. Leave a small gap between the back of the box and the top for the paper to pass. Round the edges of the top along the gap to help the paper slide easily.

Use contact cement to fasten two strips of 1/16" plastic laminate that form the paper guides; then cover the four sides of the box with 1/16" laminate. The top edges of all four sides should be flush with the top of the paper guides. On the front file out an exit notch between the guides and down to the hardboard top.

Cut a square of laminate to fit the cube top and lay out an opening 2¼" wide x 3½" long. Drill a ¼" hole in each corner of the opening and cut between the holes with a coping saw. Use a fine file to smooth the cut edges. Roughen the tops of the paper guides with sandpaper and cement the top to them. File the edges of the top flush with the sides. The edge that is over the exit slot should be beveled to form a tear-off blade.

The base of ¾" pine is centered on the bottom and held with two countersunk screws. Paint the base black or a color that contrasts with the laminate. To add paper, only one screw needs to be removed; the base will pivot on the other screw.

To install paper, cut a 12" strip from the roll and push it through the front slot, working it down through the slot at the back. Push about 6" inside the box, letting the rest ex-

tend out the exit slot. Use tape to connect the end inside the box to the end of the roll, then pull the other end to thread the roll paper through the guide. When the roll is almost empty, a red strip will appear on the edge of the paper. When this happens, open the cube and cut the old roll off. Tape the end of a new roll to the old paper and pull it through.

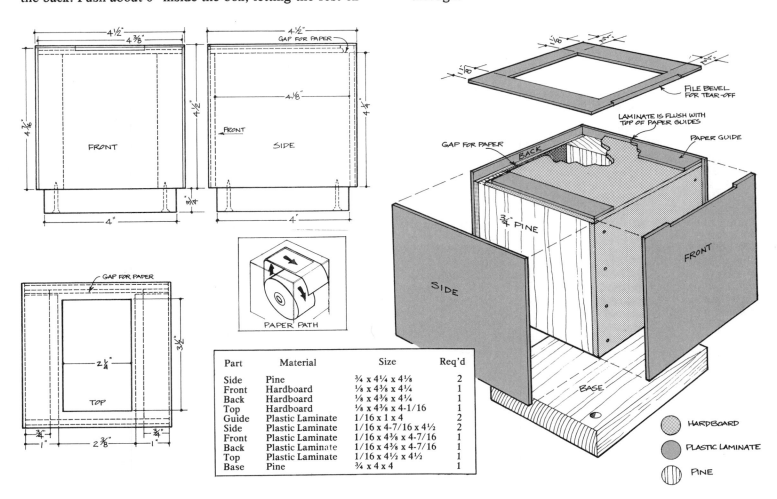

Part	Material	Size	Req'd
Side	Pine	¾ x 4¼ x 4⅛	2
Front	Hardboard	⅛ x 4⅜ x 4¼	1
Back	Hardboard	⅛ x 4⅜ x 4¼	1
Top	Hardboard	⅛ x 4⅜ x 4-1/16	1
Guide	Plastic Laminate	1/16 x 1 x 4	2
Side	Plastic Laminate	1/16 x 4-7/16 x 4½	2
Front	Plastic Laminate	1/16 x 4⅜ x 4-7/16	1
Back	Plastic Laminate	1/16 x 4⅜ x 4-7/16	1
Top	Plastic Laminate	1/16 x 4½ x 4½	1
Base	Pine	¾ x 4 x 4	1

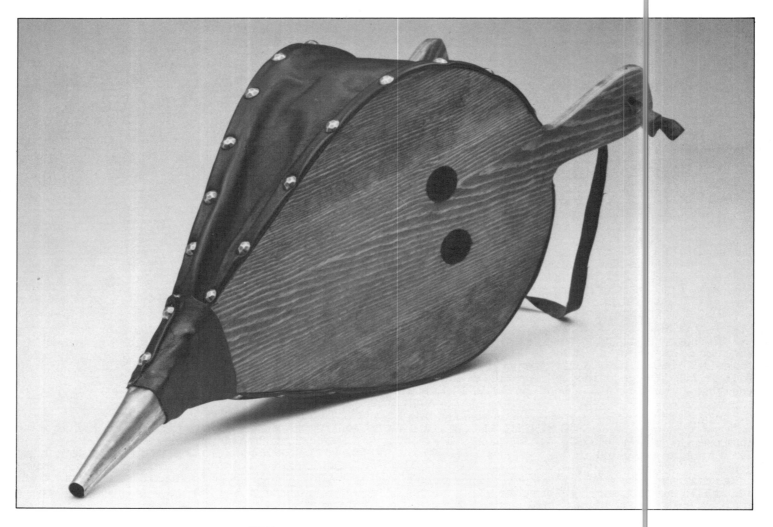

Fireplace Bellows

by Raymond Schuessler

In addition to woodworking, this old style bellows requires a little metalwork and leatherwork. None of it is very difficult though, and the whole project can be completed in just a few evenings in the workshop. The one shown is made of pine, but any good cabinet wood is suitable.

Make the wooden halves first. If ½" thick stock is not available in your area, you'll have to hand plane thicker stock. To do this, edge-join two pieces of 1" (¾" actual) thick stock by 6" (5½" actual) wide by 37" long stock. This extra length and width is good to have in case some edges splinter as you plane. If you use dowels when edge-joining, make sure you locate them where they will not show when the bellows is cut to shape. Also, planing is much easier if the grain of both boards runs in the same direction.

Clamp the edge-glued board to your bench so that you can plane without interference from your clamps. A sharp jack plane will remove most of the material. Finish up with a smooth plane.

Cut the board into two pieces, each one 9" wide by 18" long, then transfer the profile for the grid pattern and cut to shape on the band saw. Clamp both halves together and drill a ½" diameter by 3" long hole in the center of the nozzle end. Cut off 1½ inches of the tip of one board and glue and clamp this piece to the other board as shown. Also, in one board, drill two 1" dia. valve holes.

Next, make the metal tip, using copper (or brass) sheet, about .030-inch thick. We used copper flashing purchased locally. Lay out a pattern as shown and cut with metal shears. Roll the sheet into a cone, lapping the edges ⅛ inch and soldering the seam. When the solder has set, shape the large end of the cone into a square. The end of the bellows is fitted into the square end of the metal tip, the end first being shaped carefully with a carving knife to fit the square snugly, and so the metal laps the wood by ½ inch. Use epoxy to secure the metal tip to the bellows end. All the wood parts are then sanded, and finished with stain, varnish or paint. We chose to finish ours with a coat of walnut stain followed by two coats of satin polyurethane varnish. To minimize chances of warping, it is necessary to finish both sides of the boards in the same way. Allow to thoroughly dry before proceeding with assembly.

A leather "web" is cut from a 36-inch length of soft hide to the dimensions shown in the drawing. From the scrap material left from shaping the web, cut two small leather squares, 2 by 2 inches. These are the flapper valves for the air intake holes. Stretch each square tightly on the inner face of the bellows, one over each hole, and tack it in place with one carpet tack at each corner.

Attach the web, starting at the center, between the handles of the bellows. Fold the leather over ½-inch all along the edge so that a double thickness takes the ornamental brass upholsterer's tacks. The tacks are placed at 1¼-inch intervals. No tacks are necessary where the leather crosses near the handles, but the leather should be stretched tightly across this unfastened area.

Referring to the pattern, cut a piece of leather to wrap around the tip of the bellows - wide enough to cover the end of the cone and to extend up the bellows 1½ inches past the hinge. This leather piece is glued to the metal cone and ornamented with upholsterer's tacks.

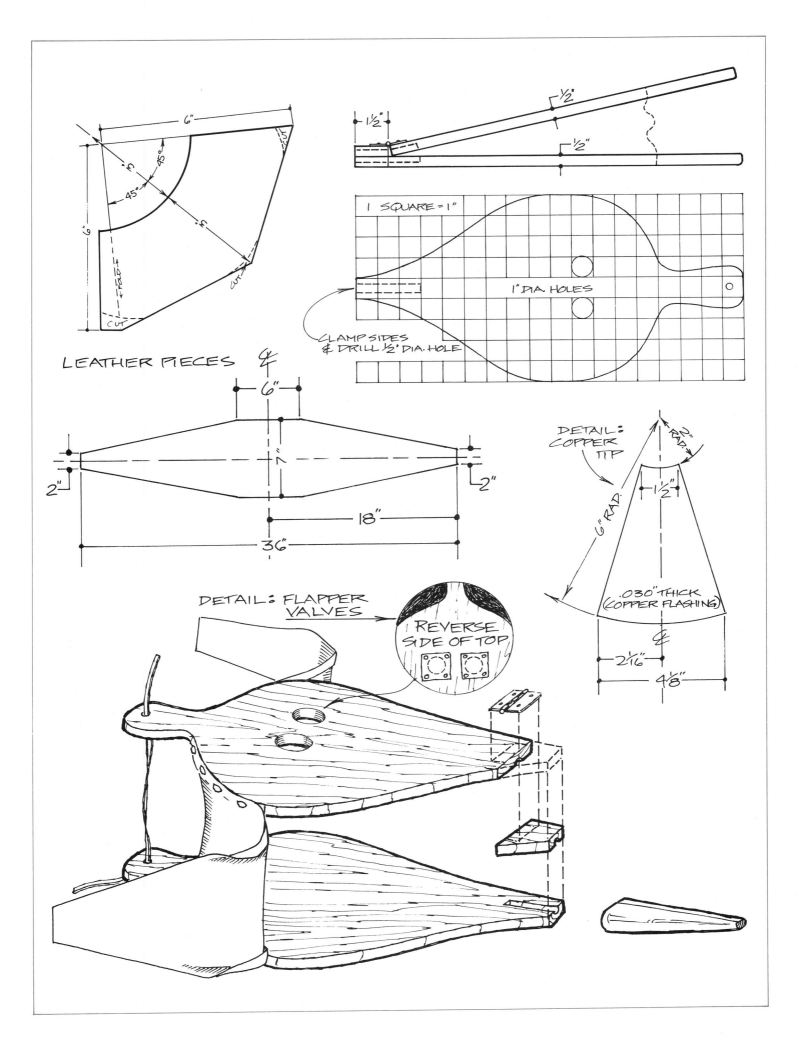

LEATHER PIECES

1 SQUARE = 1"

1" DIA HOLES

CLAMP SIDES
& DRILL ½" DIA. HOLE

6"

7"

2"   2"

18"

36"

DETAIL: FLAPPER
VALVES

REVERSE
SIDE OF TOP

DETAIL:
COPPER
TIP

6" RAD.

2" RAD.

1½"

.030" THICK
(COPPER FLASHING)

2 1/16"

4 1/8"

1½"

1½"

1½"

Incorporating a pair of hinged triangular towers, this impressive shelving system folds flat for easy moving and storage - an appealing feature for college students and those who move on a regular basis. Ours is made with 6 foot long shelves, but the towers can be moved apart to accomodate 8 foot shelves as well. The stiles and rails are made from birch solid stock, with edged birch plywood serving for the shelves. Oak, no doubt, would also look very attractive.

It's most important that the stiles (A) and rails (B) be made from flat stock. If you can't get satisfactory solid stock, you may want to consider birch plywood with edging strips for these parts.

Although the joinery is reasonably basic, there are a lot of joints to cut (and sand), so there's a fair amount of time needed to build this unit. It's a good idea to plan your building schedule accordingly.

Make the rails (part B) first. A total of 24 are required for both towers, each one cut to 2½ inches wide by 20 inches long. Check each one for straightness and flatness.

The rails are joined to the stiles with half-lap joints. Each rail will have two ⅜ inch deep by 2½ inch wide rabbets. The actual depth of the rabbet will depend on the thickness of your stock. If it measures slightly more than ¾ inch the rabbet will have to be slightly more than ⅜ inch. Accordingly, if the rail is a bit less than ¾ inch, the cut will be just under ⅜ inch. Some careful trial cuts will be very helpful.

A total of 48 rabbet cuts will have to be made so it certainly makes sense to set up your table or radial-arm saw for multiple cuts. On the table saw, use a dado head cutter and attach a stop block to the rip fence. While holding the edge of the rail against the miter gauge, butt the end of the rail against the stop block, then use the miter gauge to pass the rail over the dado cutter. Set up the stop block so the cut establishes the correct rabbet width. Two or three more passes will have to be made to clean out the remaining stock. When attaching the stop block, make sure the block is far enough in front of the dado cutter so that once the cut starts, the rail will be free and clear of the stop block. This eliminates any chance of binding which could cause kickback. To set up the radial-arm saw for cutting the rabbet, attach a stop block to the guide fence.

The stiles can be made next. A total of eight are needed for both towers, each one cut to 2½ inches wide by 72 inches long. As with the rails, be sure to check for straightness and flatness.

Each stile will have four ⅜ inch deep by 2½ inch wide dadoes and two ⅜ inch deep by 2½ inch wide rabbets. Again the actual depth will depend on the thickness of your stock (and the depth of the rail rabbet cut).

Contemporary Shelving Unit

To allow for a good snug fit for the rails, it's best to cut the stile dadoes slightly undersize. Later, when the rail edges are planed or sanded smooth, they can be adjusted for an exact fit.

A stop block can again be used to cut the stile dadoes and rabbet. The rabbet can be made on each end first, then move the rip fence to cut the dado nearest each end. Since the distance was too extreme to use our rip fence, the two inner dadoes were cut without a stop block.

After sanding the inside edges and adjusting the rails for a good fit, the frames are glued and clamped one at a time. Pipe clamps will pull the stiles together while a C-clamp or hand screw can be used to squeeze each half-lap joint. The frame should be checked for squareness before setting aside to dry overnight.

After all four frames have been assembled, a thorough sanding is necessary. Sand all joints for a smooth fit. A belt sander is most useful here. Use care to remove all cross-grain scratches.

Use the table or radial-arm saw to rip the 45-degree bevel on the front edge. Three hinges are mortised as shown to join each pair of frames.

The edging strips for the shelves are ripped from solid stock to a thickness of about ⅛". It's best to make them slightly thicker than necessary. Later they can be planed for a good fit in the frames. Also, be sure to cut the strips a little wider than the shelf thickness, then plane or sand flush with the shelf surface.

An application of Deft Danish Oil completed the project.

Bill of Materials (All Dimensions Actual)			
Part	Description	Size	No. Req'd
A	Stile	¾ x 2½ x 72	4/Tower
B	Rail	¾ x 2½ x 20	12/Tower
C	Shelf	¾ x 10¼ x 72¼*	4
D	Hinge	2½	3/Tower

*Includes edging.

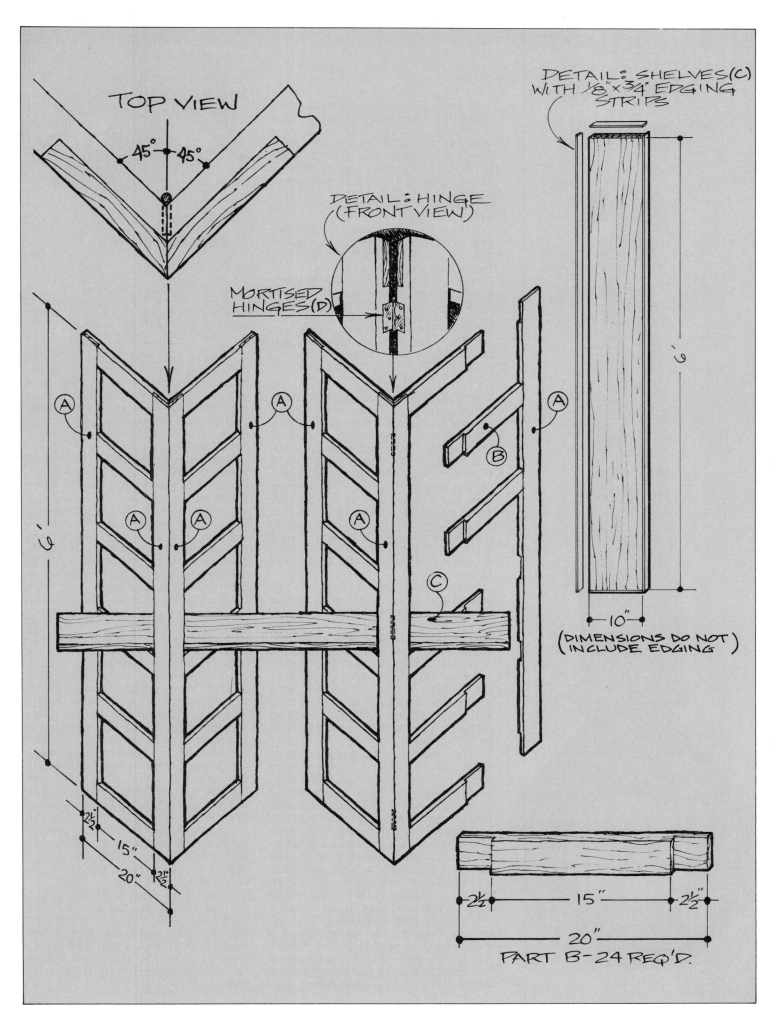

TOP VIEW

45° 45°

DETAIL: SHELVES (C)
WITH ⅛" × ¾" EDGING
STRIPS

DETAIL: HINGE
(FRONT VIEW)

MORTISED
HINGES (D)

Ⓐ Ⓐ Ⓐ Ⓐ Ⓑ Ⓒ

6'

10"

(DIMENSIONS DO NOT)
(INCLUDE EDGING)

6'

2½"
15"
20"
2½"

2½" 15" 2½"
20"

PART B-24 REQ'D.

105

Weather Station

by Sam Allen

If you enjoy carving like I do, you probably sit down occasionally with a small scrap of wood and start to carve with no potential project in mind. That's what happened with the eagle on top of this weather station. Once it was completed, I liked it so much I had to come up with a project to use it on, so I designed this weather station to go with the eagle.

Before beginning construction, it's best to buy all instruments so you can make any adjustments if the sizes vary from those shown on the plan.

A 4¼" diameter aneroid barometer is available from Mason & Sullivan, 586 Higgins Crowell Rd., West Yarmouth, Cape Cod, MA 02673. Order part no. 4011X. The hygrometer, part no. 3630G30, and the thermometer, part no. 3610G10, are available from Craft Products Co., 2200 Dean Street, St. Charles, IL 60174.

The eagle is made of walnut as is the entire weather station. Start with a carving block approximately 1" x 6" x 4". The extra length gives you something to hold on to while you're carving. Transfer the design of the eagle from the plan to the carving block and cut out the rough shape with a coping saw. The detailed carving is done with small knives and chisels. The feathers are greatly exaggerated and cut in bold relief, so they will show up from a distance. For those who don't carve, an alternate turned finial is also shown.

Next, make the molding to go around the octagon, using a molding head cutter equipped with an ogee bit (Sears bit p/n 9-3202). A saw kerf along the inside edge completes the shape of the molding (see Detail D). Make this molding strip approximately 30" long and glue it to a piece of 1" (¾" actual) x 2" x 30" walnut. Both pieces should be fairly uniform in color and grain because when joined into an octagon, pieces from each end will have to match.

Next, set the miter gauge on your table saw to produce a 22½ degree angle. Cut the eight pieces of the octagon from the 30" strip. Number the pieces as you cut them and assemble them in numerical order; this way the grain and color will match. The angle of the joints must be extremely accurate because even a small error in each joint will add up to a large gap when you have eight joints to work with. To make sure your saw is cutting accurately, it's a good idea to first make a test octagon from scrap stock. Glue the octagon together and clamp it with a web clamp or several strong rubber bands. When the glue has set, cut out the circular hole in the center for the barometer with a jigsaw or coping saw.

Cut feathers in bold relief so they show up when viewed from a distance.

Cut the four transitional moldings with the molding-head cutters shown. Since the moldings are cut on three sides and are very small, it is easiest and safest to shape them before cutting them from larger boards or glue them to a long piece of scrap wood before shaping.

Next cut a square of 1" (¾" actual) walnut 3¼" x 3¼" for the hygrometer. Cut the hole for the hygrometer using a hole saw or a jigsaw. Use small carving tools to make the decorative recesses in the four corners (see Detail).

Before cutting the piece for the thermometer to size, cut out the recess for the thermometer to mount in. By cutting the recess first, you will have plenty of room to clamp the work down for the routing process. You could cut the recess by hand, however I used a router equipped with a guide bushing and a hardboard template. The template should be slightly larger than the actual size of the thermometer to allow for the thickness of the template guide bushing mounted on the router base. Make the template a little small at first and make a test cut in a piece of scrap, then file the template until you achieve the exact size and shape needed.

Although not shown in the drawing, the joints between each section are strengthened with dowels. After gluing and assembling all the joints (except for placing the eagle on top) position the unit with its back against a flat surface and clamp it down to prevent buckling; then use a bar clamp to clamp lengthwise. When the glue is dry, position the eagle and use a bar clamp to hold it in place.

I used three coats of Watco Danish Oil for the finish, sanding between each coat with 600 grit sandpaper. After the third coat is dry, apply a final coat and buff with a soft cloth. Don't sand the carving as this would remove the natural sheen left by the carving tools.

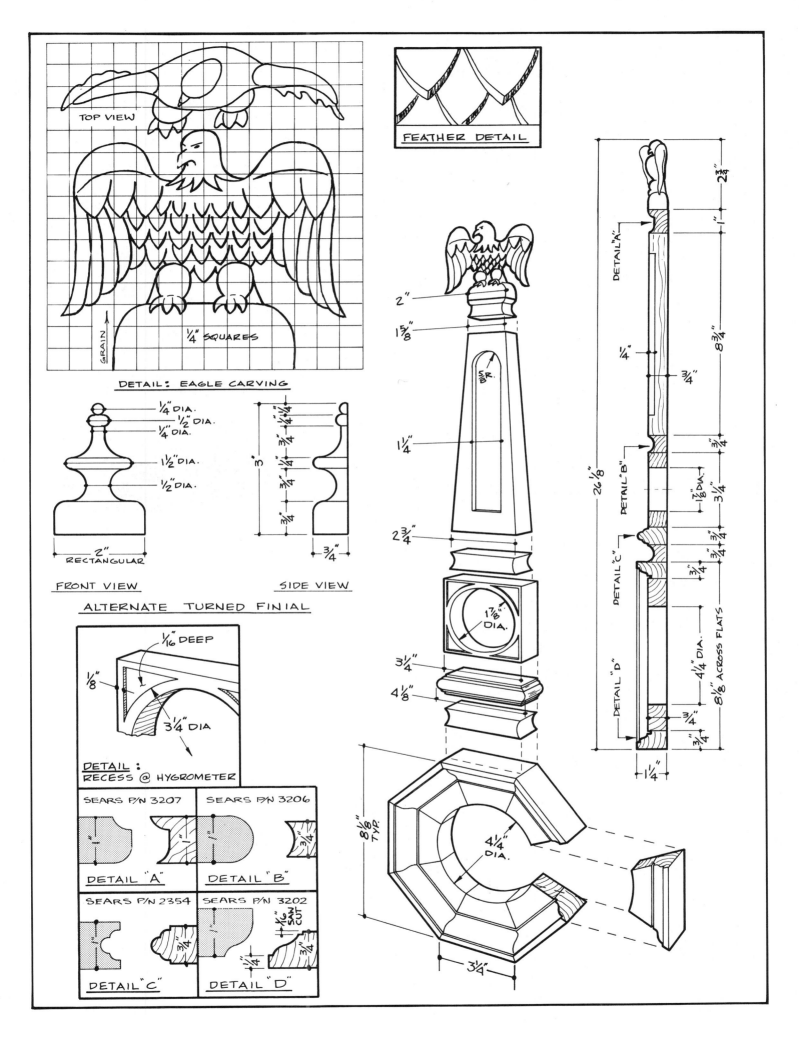

TOP VIEW

GRAIN

1/4" SQUARES

DETAIL: EAGLE CARVING

FEATHER DETAIL

1/4 DIA.
1/2 DIA.
1/4 DIA.
1/2 DIA.
1/2 DIA.

3"
3/4 1/4 1/4 3/4

2"
RECTANGULAR

3/4"

FRONT VIEW   SIDE VIEW

ALTERNATE TURNED FINIAL

1/16" DEEP
1/8"
3/4" DIA

DETAIL:
RECESS @ HYGROMETER

SEARS P/N 3207   SEARS P/N 3206

DETAIL "A"   DETAIL "B"

SEARS P/N 2354   SEARS P/N 3202

1/16" SAW CUT

DETAIL "C"   DETAIL "D"

2"
1 5/8"

5/8 R.

1 1/4"

2 3/4"

1 7/8" DIA.

3 1/4"
4 1/8"

8 1/8" TYP.

4 1/4" DIA.

3 1/4"

DETAIL "A"

1/4"
3/4"

2 3/4"
1"

8 3/4"

26 1/8"

DETAIL "B"

DETAIL "C"

DETAIL "D"

3/4"

1 1/8" DIA.

3/4"
3/4 1/4

3"
1/4 3/4 1/4

8 1/8 ACROSS FLATS

4 1/4 DIA.

3/4"
3/4"

1 1/4"

Mahogany Corner Shelf

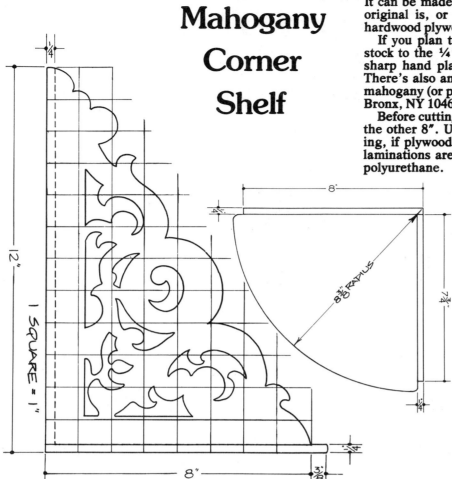

Those who like jigsaw work will find this an enjoyable project. It can be made from ¼" thick solid mahogany, as this antique original is, or from ¼" mahogany plywood. Most any other hardwood plywood is also suitable.

If you plan to use solid stock, you'll have to reduce thicker stock to the ¼" dimension. A power planer can do this, but a sharp hand plane, and a little patience, will do just as well. There's also another option; you can mail-order ¼" thick solid mahogany (or plywood) from Constantine, 2050 Eastchester Rd., Bronx, NY 10461.

Before cutting parts to size, note that one side measures 7¾", the other 8". Use glue and finishing nails to join. When finishing, if plywood is used, it's best to stain all edge grain so the laminations are less likely to show. Final finish with two coats polyurethane.

Sources of Supply

The following pages list companies that specialize in
mail-order sales of woodworking supplies.

United States

General Woodworking Suppliers

Constantine's
2050 Eastchester Rd.
Bronx, NY 10461

Craftsman Wood Service
1735 West Cortland Ct.
Addison, IL 60101

The Fine Tool Shops
170 West Road
Portsmouth, NH 03810

Frog Tool Co., Ltd.
700 W. Jackson Blvd.
Chicago, IL 60606

Garrett Wade
161 Avenue of the Americas
New York, NY 10013

Highland Hardware
1045 N. Highland Ave., N.E.
Atlanta, GA 30306

Seven Corners Ace Hardware
216 West 7th Street
St. Paul, MN 55102

Shopsmith, Inc.
6640 Poe Ave.
Dayton, OH 45414

Trend-Lines
375 Beacham St.
Chelsea, MA 02150-0999

Woodcraft Supply Corp.
41 Atlantic Ave.
Woburn, MA 01888

The Woodworkers' Store
21801 Industrial Blvd.
Rogers, MN 55374

Woodworker's Supply of New Mexico
5604 Alameda, N.E.
Albuquerque, NM 87113

W.S. Jenks and Son
1933 Montana Ave., N.E.
Washington, DC 20002

Hardware Suppliers

Allen Specialty Hardware
332 W. Bruceton Rd.
Pittsburgh, PA 15236

Anglo-American Brass Co.
Box 9487
4146 Mitzi Drive
San Jose, CA 95157

Horton Brasses
Nooks Hill Rd.
P.O. Box 120
Cromwell, CT 06416

Imported European Hardware
4320 W. Bell Dr.
Las Vegas, NV 89118

Meisel Hardware Specialties
P.O. Box 258
Mound, MN 55364

Paxton Hardware, Ltd.
7818 Bradshaw Rd.
Upper Falls, MD 21156

Period Furniture Hardware Co.
123 Charles St.
Box 314 Charles Street Station
Boston, MA 02114

Stanley Hardware
195 Lake Street
New Britain, CT 06050

The Wise Co.
6503 St. Claude
Arabi, LA 70032

Hardwood Suppliers

American Woodcrafters
905 S. Roosevelt Ave.
Piqua, OH 45356

Austin Hardwoods
2119 Goodrich
Austin, TX 78704

Bergers Hardwoods
Route 4, Box 195
Bedford, VA 24523

Berea Hardwoods Co.
125 Jacqueline Drive
Berea, OH 44017

Maurice L. Condon
250 Ferris Ave.
White Plains, NY 10603

Craftwoods
109 21 York Rd.
Cockeysville, MD 21030

Croy-Marietta Hardwoods, Inc.
121 Pike St., Box 643
Marietta, OH 45750

Dimension Hardwoods, Inc.
113 Canal Street
Shelton, CT 06484

Educational Lumber Co.
P.O. Box 5373
Asheville, NC 28813

General Woodcraft
531 Broad St.
New London, CT 06320

Hardwoods of Memphis
P.O. Box 12449
Memphis, TN 38182-0449

Kaymar Wood Products
4603 35th S.W.
Seattle, WA 98126

Kountry Kraft Hardwoods
R.R. No. 1
Lake City, IA 51449

Leonard Lumber Co.
P.O. Box 2396
Branford, CT 06405

McFeely's Hardwoods & Lumber
43 Cabell St.
Lynchburg, VA 24505

Native American Hardwoods
Route 1
West Valley, NY 14171

Sterling Hardwoods, Inc.
412 Pine St.
Burlington, VT 05401

(continued on next page)

Wood World
1719 Chestnut
Glenview, IL 60025

Woodworker's Dream
P.O. Box 329
Nazareth, PA 18064

Wood Finishing Supplies

Finishing Products and Supply Co.
4611 Macklind Ave.
St. Louis, MO 63109

Industrial Finishing Products
465 Logan St.
Brooklyn, NY 11208

The Wise Co.
P.O. Box 118
6503 St. Claude
Arabie, LA 70032

WoodFinishing Enterprises
Box 10017
Milwaukee, WI 53210

Watco-Dennis Corp.
1433 Santa Monica Blvd.
Santa Monica, CA 90401

Clock Parts

Craft Products Co.
2200 Dean St.
St. Charles, IL 60174

Klockit, Inc.
P.O. Box 542
Lake Geneva, WI 53147

S. LaRose
234 Commerce Place
Greensboro, NC 27420

Mason & Sullivan Co.
586 Higgins Crowell Rd.
West Yarmouth, MA 02655

Newport Enterprises
2313 West Burbank Blvd.
Burbank, CA 91506

Miscellaneous

DML, Inc. (Router Bits)
1350 S. 15th Street
Louisville, KY 40210

Formica Corporation (Plastic Laminate)
1 Stanford Road
Piscataway, NJ 08854

Freud (Saw Blades)
218 Feld Ave.
High Point, NC 27264

MLCS (Router Bits)
P.O. Box 53
Rydal, PA 19041

Homecraft Veneer (Veneer)
901 West Way
Latrobe, PA 15650

Sears, Roebuck and Co.
(Misc. Tools & Supplies)
925 S. Homan Ave.
Chicago, IL 60607

Wilson Art (Plastic Laminate)
600 General Bruce Drive
Temple, TX 76501

Canada

General Woodworking Suppliers

House of Tools Ltd.
131-12th Ave. S.E.
Calgary, Alberta T2G 0Z9

J. Philip Humfrey International
3241 Kennedy Rd., Unit 7
Scarborough, Ontario M1V 2J9

Lee Valley Tools
Unit 6, 5511 Steeles Ave. West
Weston, Ontario M9L 1S7

Stockade Woodworker's Supply
P.O. Box 1415
Salmon Arm, British Columbia V0E 2T0

Tool Trend Ltd.
3280 Steele's Ave. West
Concord, Ontario L4K 2Y2

Treen Heritage, Ltd.
P.O. Box 280
Merrickville, Ontario K0G 1N0

Hardware Suppliers

Home Workshop Supplies
RR 2
Arthur, Ontario N0G 1A0

Lee Valley Tools
Unit 6, 5511 Steeles Ave. West
Weston, Ontario M9L 1S7

Pacific Brass Hardware
1414 Monterey Ave.
Victoria, British Columbia V8S 4W1

Steve's Shop, Woodworking & Supplies
RR 3
Woodstock, Ontario M9V 5C3

Hardwood Suppliers

A & C Hutt Enterprises, Ltd.
15861 32nd Ave.
Surrey, British Columbia V4B 4Z5

Longstock Lumber & Veneer
440 Phillip St., Unit 21
Waterloo, Ontario N2L 5R9

Unicorn Universal Woods Ltd.
4190 Steeles Ave. West, Unit 4
Woodbridge, Ontario L4L 3S8

Clock Parts

Hurst Associates
151 Nashdene Rd., Unit 14
Scarborough, Ontario M1V 2T3

Kidder Klock
39 Glen Cameron Rd., Unit 3
Thornhill, Ontario L3T 1P1

Murray Clock Craft Ltd.
510 McNicoll Ave.
Willowdale, Ontario M2H 2E1

Miscellaneous

Freud (Saw Blades)
100 Westmore Dr., Unit 10
Rexdale, Ontario M9V 5C3

Index

Index

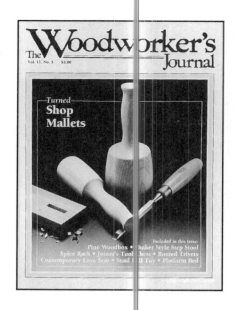
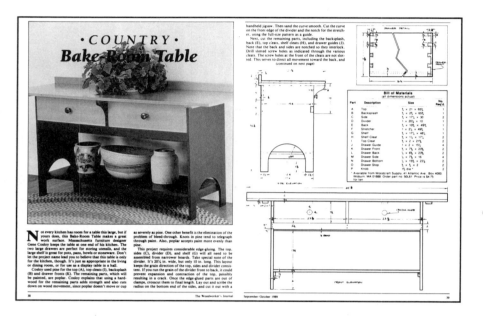